A Casebook on *Dylan Thomas*

A Casebook on
Dylan Thomas

EDITED BY

JOHN MALCOLM BRINNIN

University of Connecticut

THOMAS Y. CROWELL COMPANY

New York • Established 1834

First Printing, June, 1960
Second Printing, July, 1961
Third Printing, May, 1964
Fourth Printing, December, 1965
Fifth Printing, August, 1967
Sixth Printing, April, 1969

Library of Congress Catalog Card Number: 60-9937

Manufactured in the United States of America
by The Book Press, Brattleboro, Vermont

Designed by Laurel Wagner

OTHER BOOKS BY JOHN MALCOLM BRINNIN

The Garden Is Political
The Lincoln Lyrics
No Arch, No Triumph
The Sorrows of Cold Stone
Modern Poetry: American and British
edited with Kimon Friar
Dylan Thomas in America
The Third Rose: Gertrude Stein and Her World
The Poems of Emily Dickinson
edited, with an Introduction

Contents

Introduction

During his lifetime and ever since, Dylan Thomas has been regarded by many people as not only a significant new voice in English literature but by all odds the most exciting poet yet produced by the twentieth century. He was exciting because his language was brilliantly rich, gaudy, reverberant and lavishly spent, and he was exciting because, with less apology and more force than any of his contemporaries, he turned the power of his imagination upon the great primary issues of birth, death, sex, and eternity. His career was meteoric—a blaze quenched at the point of its whitest light. In its wake were left wonders and regrets: the echoes of a speaking voice that had enthralled audiences from public platforms in Great Britain and across the breadth of the United States; all the ingredients—comic anecdote, scandal, mystery, romance—of which legend is made; and the helpless anguish of scores of his friends who had to accede to the fact that genius chooses its own way of life and prepares its own death.

Dylan Thomas' work, from its first appearance in print, was the cause for reactions that ranged from blunt shock and angry consternation to sheer delight and unguarded rhapsody. His behavior as a private man, and soon as a public celebrity, was cause for something like despair among those who knew him. Just as often, it was the cause of hero-worship among those who did not. He broke through the boundaries that ordinarily contain literary figures and, once free, became subject to many varying attitudes. Young people, many of whom never had and never would read a line of his poems, were apt to place him in the company of other popular heroes of adolescence like the late James Dean and the late Charlie "Bird" Parker. In the devotional appraisals of Dame Edith Sitwell he became a kind of saint of literature. In the sober assessments of literary scholars he was a phenomenon to be accounted for by rule and analysis. In the eyes of many people who knew him mainly as a public reader of his poems or of the leading role in his verse-play, *Under Milk Wood,* he was a bardic clown with an angelic voice or perhaps a tragic actor trapped in the plot of his own existence.

Some people who fell under the spell of his personality seemed to forget that he was different from other great personalities in that he was, first and always, an artist with words. Others, dismissing the influence of his personality, sought the meanings of his poems as if they were not reflections of a man and an inseparable part of him, but propositions to be examined in verbal laboratories. In either case, the result was often uneasy simplification of an artist whose complexities resisted the frame of any single view.

The essays gathered into this volume are mainly concerned with his poems—the *fons et origo* of all the excitement and the only finally important thing about Dylan Thomas. Most of these essays are meant to be read as an accompaniment to thoughtful readings of his poems and may lack meaning and only set up confusion if they are read without knowledge of the poems. Some of the essays are nothing more than informal observations about the poet by people who knew him and, without exception, held him deeply in affection. Their observations serve to relate, in ways that his poems generally do not, the man to the world in which he lived. The value of these is secondary, and yet such observations are part of a record on which is written the living impact of an uncommon man who possessed, among many lesser gifts, poetic genius.

The challenging nature of that genius is the subject under consideration. Any reader of Dylan Thomas' poetry has the basic preparation, and may assume the right, to join in the symposium. Once a reader has entered the present company, he may find that his own observations are confirmed, denied, or otherwise qualified. In any event, he will find that he has entered into a great discussion, if not into a great debate, and that his own reactions and opinions will take on lesser or greater significance once they have been informed by the reactions and opinions of others.

As a man, Dylan Thomas was available to anyone on earth. He loved people and gathered them about him with a warmth which, as many of them testify, they do not expect to meet again. As a poet, Dylan Thomas was and is available only to those who regard language and the imagination as divine rights to be continually possessed and repossessed and who regard the art of poetry as a profound source of knowledge. He wanted readers, and though in his lifetime he too often gained merely companions and "ardents," as he termed his star-struck followers, his poems are still an open invitation to all men to share the world he made.

As W. H. Auden said in a poem written on the death of William Butler Yeats—and as one might say of Dylan Thomas and any other dead literary artist— "He became his admirers." These admirers make up a company upon whose number there is no limitation but intelligence and an open mind. In the following pages, Dylan Thomas lives in the particular terms in which his contemporaries saw him and judged him. For his friends, as well as for others who must know him only by their affectionate reports, Dylan Thomas is an experience. Submission to that experience may result in puzzlement, wonder, love, a widening of horizons, a quicker sense of life as it is lived, or any of a dozen other forms of participation and understanding. New readers, whatever the nature of their first impressions, have the opportunity to contribute to the reputation of a remarkable poet, and to the life of poetry he represents, their own new insights and fresh judgments.

JOHN MALCOLM BRINNIN

Ten Poems by *Dylan Thomas*

The following poems are reprinted by permission of New Directions from *The Collected Poems of Dylan Thomas*. Permission is also granted by J. M. Dent & Sons Ltd. and the Trustees of the Dylan Thomas Estate.

The force that through the green fuse drives the flower

The force that through the green fuse drives the flower
Drives my green age; that blasts the roots of trees
Is my destroyer.
And I am dumb to tell the crooked rose
My youth is bent by the same wintry fever.

The force that drives the water through the rocks
Drives my red blood; that dries the mouthing streams
Turns mine to wax.
And I am dumb to mouth unto my veins
How at the mountain spring the same mouth sucks.

The hand that whirls the water in the pool
Stirs the quicksand; that ropes the blowing wind
Hauls my shroud sail.
And I am dumb to tell the hanging man
How of my clay is made the hangman's lime.

The lips of time leech to the fountain head;
Love drips and gathers, but the fallen blood
Shall calm her sores.
And I am dumb to tell a weather's wind
How time has ticked a heaven round the stars.

And I am dumb to tell the lover's tomb
How at my sheet goes the same crooked worm.

I see the boys of summer

I

I see the boys of summer in their ruin
Lay the gold tithings barren,
Setting no store by harvest, freeze the soils;
There in their heat the winter floods
Of frozen loves they fetch their girls,
And drown the cargoed apples in their tides.

These boys of light are curdlers in their folly,
Sour the boiling honey;
The jacks of frost they finger in the hives;
There in the sun the frigid threads
Of doubt and dark they feed their nerves;
The signal moon is zero in their voids.

I see the summer children in their mothers
Split up the brawned womb's weathers,
Divide the night and day with fairy thumbs;
There in the deep with quartered shades
Of sun and moon they paint their dams
As sunlight paints the shelling of their heads.

I see that from these boys shall men of nothing
Stature by seedy shifting,
Or lame the air with leaping from its heats;
There from their hearts the dogdayed pulse
Of love and light bursts in their throats.
O see the pulse of summer in the ice.

II

But seasons must be challenged or they totter
Into a chiming quarter
Where, punctual as death, we ring the stars;
There, in his night, the black-tongued bells
The sleepy man of winter pulls,
Nor blows back moon-and-midnight as she blows.

We are the dark deniers, let us summon
Death from a summer woman,
A muscling life from lovers in their cramp,
From the fair dead who flush the sea
The bright-eyed worm on Davy's lamp,
And from the planted womb the man of straw.

We summer boys in this four-winded spinning,
Green of the seaweeds' iron,
Hold up the noisy sea and drop her birds,
Pick the world's ball of wave and froth
To choke the deserts with her tides,
And comb the country gardens for a wreath.

In spring we cross our foreheads with the holly,
Heigh ho the blood and berry,
And nail the merry squires to the trees;
Here love's damp muscle dries and dies,
Here break a kiss in no love's quarry.
O see the poles of promise in the boys.

III

I see you boys of summer in your ruin.
Man in his maggot's barren.
And boys are full and foreign in the pouch.
I am the man your father was.
We are the sons of flint and pitch.
O see the poles are kissing as they cross.

Light breaks where no sun shines

Light breaks where no sun shines;
Where no sea runs, the waters of the heart
Push in their tides;
And, broken ghosts with glow-worms in their heads,
The things of light
File through the flesh where no flesh decks the bones.

A candle in the thighs
Warms youth and seed and burns the seeds of age;
Where no seed stirs,
The fruit of man unwrinkles in the stars,
Bright as a fig;
Where no wax is, the candle shows its hairs.

Dawn breaks behind the eyes;
From poles of skull and toe the windy blood
Slides like a sea;
Nor fenced, nor staked, the gushers of the sky
Spout to the rod
Divining in a smile the oil of tears.

Night in the sockets rounds,
Like some pitch moon, the limit of the globes;
Day lights the bone;
Where no cold is, the skinning gales unpin
The winter's robes;
The film of spring is hanging from the lids.

Light breaks on secret lots,
On tips of thought where thoughts smell in the rain;
When logics die,
The secret of the soil grows through the eye,
And blood jumps in the sun;
Above the waste allotments the dawn halts.

The Hunchback in the Park

The hunchback in the park
A solitary mister
Propped between trees and water
From the opening of the garden lock
That lets the trees and water enter
Until the Sunday sombre bell at dark

Eating bread from a newspaper
Drinking water from the chained cup
That the children filled with gravel
In the fountain basin where I sailed my ship
Slept at night in a dog kennel
But nobody chained him up.

Like the park birds he came early
Like the water he sat down
And Mister they called Hey mister
The truant boys from the town
Running when he had heard them clearly
On out of sound

Past lake and rockery
Laughing when he shook his paper
Hunchbacked in mockery
Through the loud zoo of the willow groves
Dodging the park keeper
With his stick that picked up leaves.

And the old dog sleeper
Alone between nurses and swans
While the boys among willows
Made the tigers jump out of their eyes
To roar on the rockery stones
And the groves were blue with sailors

Made all day until bell time
A woman figure without fault
Straight as a young elm
Straight and tall from his crooked bones
That she might stand in the night
After the locks and chains

All night in the unmade park
After the railings and shrubberies
The birds the grass the trees the lake
And the wild boys innocent as strawberries
Had followed the hunchback
To his kennel in the dark.

After the funeral

(In memory of Ann Jones)

After the funeral, mule praises, brays,
Windshake of sailshaped ears, muffle-toed tap
Tap happily of one peg in the thick
Grave's foot, blinds down the lids, the teeth in black,
The spittled eyes, the salt ponds in the sleeves,
Morning smack of the spade that wakes up sleep,
Shakes a desolate boy who slits his throat
In the dark of the coffin and sheds dry leaves,
That breaks one bone to light with a judgment clout,
After the feast of tear-stuffed time and thistles
In a room with a stuffed fox and stale fern,
I stand, for this memorial's sake, alone
In the snivelling hours with dead, humped Ann
Whose hooded, fountain heart once fell in puddles
Round the parched worlds of Wales and drowned each sun
(Though this for her is a monstrous image blindly
Magnified out of praise; her death was a still drop;
She would not have me sinking in the holy
Flood of her heart's fame; she would lie dumb and deep
And need no druid of her broken body).
But I, Ann's bard on a raised hearth, call all
The seas to service that her wood-tongued virtue
Babble like a bellbuoy over the hymning heads,
Bow down the walls of the ferned and foxy woods
That her love sing and swing through a brown chapel,
Bless her bent spirit with four, crossing birds.
Her flesh was meek as milk, but this skyward statue
With the wild breast and blessed and giant skull
Is carved from her in a room with a wet window
In a fiercely mourning house in a crooked year.
I know her scrubbed and sour humble hands
Lie with religion in their cramp, her threadbare
Whisper in a damp word, her wits drilled hollow,
Her fist of a face died clenched on a round pain;
And sculptured Ann is seventy years of stone.

These cloud-sopped, marble hands, this monumental
Argument of the hewn voice, gesture and psalm,
Storm me forever over her grave until
The stuffed lung of the fox twitch and cry Love
And the strutting fern lay seeds on the black sill.

Poem in October

It was my thirtieth year to heaven
Woke to my hearing from harbour and neighbour wood
And the mussel pooled and the heron
Priested shore
The morning beckon
With water praying and call of seagull and rook
And the knock of sailing boats on the net webbed wall
Myself to set foot
That second
In the still sleeping town and set forth.

My birthday began with the water-
Birds and the birds of the winged trees flying my name
Above the farms and the white horses
And I rose
In rainy autumn
And walked abroad in a shower of all my days.
High tide and the heron dived when I took the road
Over the border
And the gates
Of the town closed as the town awoke.

A springful of larks in a rolling
Cloud and the roadside bushes brimming with whistling
Blackbirds and the sun of October
Summery
On the hill's shoulder,
Here were fond climates and sweet singers suddenly
Come in the morning where I wandered and listened
To the rain wringing

Wind blow cold
In the wood faraway under me.

Pale rain over the dwindling harbour
And over the sea wet church the size of a snail
With its horns through mist and the castle
Brown as owls
But all the gardens
Of spring and summer were blooming in the tall tales
Beyond the border and under the lark full cloud.
There could I marvel
My birthday
Away but the weather turned around.

It turned away from the blithe country
And down the other air and the blue altered sky
Streamed again a wonder of summer
With apples
Pears and red currants
And I saw in the turning so clearly a child's
Forgotten mornings when he walked with his mother
Through the parables
Of sun light
And the legends of the green chapels

And the twice told fields of infancy
That his tears burned my cheeks and his heart moved in mine.
These were the woods the river and sea
Where a boy
In the listening
Summertime of the dead whispered the truth of his joy
To the trees and the stones and the fish in the tide.
And the mystery
Sang alive
Still in the water and singingbirds.

And there could I marvel my birthday
Away but the weather turned around. And the true
Joy of the long dead child sang burning
In the sun.
It was my thirtieth
Year to heaven stood there then in the summer noon
Though the town below lay leaved with October blood.
O may my heart's truth
Still be sung
On this high hill in a year's turning.

Over Sir John's hill

Over Sir John's hill,
The hawk on fire hangs still;
In a hoisted cloud, at drop of dusk, he pulls to his claws
And gallows, up the rays of his eyes the small birds of the bay
And the shrill of child's play
Wars
Of the sparrows and such who swansing, dusk, in wrangling hedges.
And blithely they squawk
To fiery tyburn over the wrestle of elms until
The flash the noosed hawk
Crashes, and slowly the fishing holy stalking heron
In the river Towy below bows his tilted headstone.

Flash, and the plumes crack,
And a black cap of jack-
Daws Sir John's just hill dons, and again the gulled birds hare
To the hawk on fire, the halter height, over Towy's fins,
In a whack of wind.
There
Where the elegiac fisherbird stabs and paddles
In the pebbly dab-filled
Shallow and sedge, and 'dilly dilly,' calls the loft hawk,
'Come and be killed,'
I open the leaves of the water at a passage
Of psalms and shadows among the pincered sandcrabs prancing

And read, in a shell,
Death clear as a buoy's bell:
All praise of the hawk on fire in hawk-eyed dusk be sung,
When his viperish fuse hangs looped with flames under the brand
Wing, and blest shall
Young
Green chickens of the bay and bushes cluck, 'dilly dilly,
Come let us die.'
We grieve as the blithe birds, never again, leave shingle and elm,
The heron and I,

I young Aesop fabling to the near night by the dingle
Of eels, saint heron hymning in the shell-hung distant

Crystal harbour vale
Where the sea cobbles sail,
And wharves of water where the walls dance and the white cranes
stilt.
It is the heron and I, under judging Sir John's elmed
Hill, tell-tale the knelled
Guilt
Of the led-astray birds whom God, for their breast of whistles,
Have mercy on,
God in his whirlwind silence save, who marks the sparrows hail,
For their souls' song.
Now the heron grieves in the weeded verge. Through windows
Of dusk and water I see the tilting whispering

Heron, mirrored, go,
As the snapt feathers snow,
Fishing in the tear of the Towy. Only a hoot owl
Hollows, a grassblade blown in cupped hands, in the looted elms,
And no green cocks or hens
Shout
Now on Sir John's hill. The heron, ankling the scaly
Lowlands of the waves,
Makes all the music; and I who hear the tune of the slow,
Wear-willow river, grave,
Before the lunge of the night, the notes on this time-shaken
Stone for the sake of the souls of the slain birds sailing.

Poem on his birthday

In the mustardseed sun,
By full tilt river and switchback sea
Where the cormorants scud,
In his house on stilts high among beaks
And palavers of birds
This sandgrain day in the bent bay's grave
He celebrates and spurns

His driftwood thirty-fifth wind turned age;
  Herons spire and spear.

  Under and round him go
Flounders, gulls, on their cold, dying trails,
  Doing what they are told,
Curlews aloud in the congered waves
  Work at their ways to death,
And the rhymer in the long tongued room,
  Who tolls his birthday bell,
Toils towards the ambush of his wounds;
  Herons, steeple stemmed, bless.

  In the thistledown fall,
He sings towards anguish; finches fly
  In the claw tracks of hawks
On a seizing sky; small fishes glide
  Through wynds and shells of drowned
Ship towns to pastures of otters. He
  In his slant, racking house
And the hewn coils of his trade perceives
  Herons walk in their shroud,

  The livelong river's robe
Of minnows wreathing around their prayer,
  And far at sea he knows,
Who slaves to his crouched, eternal end
  Under a serpent cloud,
Dolphins dive in their turnturtle dust,
  The rippled seals streak down
To kill and their own tide daubing blood
  Slides good in the sleek mouth.

  In a cavernous, swung
Wave's silence, wept white angelus knells.
  Thirty-five bells sing struck
On skull and scar where his loves lie wrecked,
  Steered by the falling stars.
And to-morrow weeps in a blind cage
  Terror will rage apart
Before chains break to a hammer flame
  And love unbolts the dark

  And freely he goes lost
In the unknown, famous light of great
  And fabulous, dear God.

Dark is a way and light is a place,
  Heaven that never was
Nor will be ever is always true,
  And, in that brambled void,
Plenty as blackberries in the woods
  The dead grow for His joy.

  There he might wander bare
With the spirits of the horseshoe bay
  Or the stars' seashore dead,
Marrow of eagles, the roots of whales
  And wishbones of wild geese,
With blessed, unborn God and His Ghost,
  And every soul His priest,
Gulled and chanter in young Heaven's fold
  Be at cloud quaking peace,

  But dark is a long way.
He, on the earth of the night, alone
  With all the living, prays,
Who knows the rocketing wind will blow
  The bones out of the hills,
And the scythed boulders bleed, and the last
  Rage shattered waters kick
Masts and fishes to the still quick stars,
  Faithlessly unto Him

  Who is the light of old
And air shaped Heaven where souls grow wild
  As horses in the foam:
Oh, let me midlife mourn by the shrined
  And druid heron's vows
The voyage to ruin I must run,
  Dawn ships clouted aground,
Yet, though I cry with tumbledown tongue,
  Count my blessings aloud:

  Four elements and five
Senses, and man a spirit in love
  Tangling through this spun slime
To his nimbus bell cool kingdom come
  And the lost, moonshine domes,
And the sea that hides his secret selves
  Deep in its black, base bones,
Lulling of spheres in the seashell flesh,
  And this last blessing most,

That the closer I move
To death, one man through his sundered hulks,
The louder the sun blooms
And the tusked, ramshackling sea exults;
And every wave of the way
And gale I tackle, the whole world then,
With more triumphant faith
Than ever was since the world was said,
Spins its morning of praise,

I hear the bouncing hills
Grow larked and greener at berry brown
Fall and the dew larks sing
Taller this thunderclap spring, and how
More spanned with angels ride
The mansouled fiery islands! Oh,
Holier then their eyes,
And my shining men no more alone
As I sail out to die.

Fern Hill

Now as I was young and easy under the apple boughs
About the lilting house and happy as the grass was green,
The night above the dingle starry,
Time let me hail and climb
Golden in the heydays of his eyes,
And honoured among wagons I was prince of the apple towns
And once below a time I lordly had the trees and leaves
Trail with daisies and barley
Down the rivers of the windfall light.

And as I was green and carefree, famous among the barns
About the happy yard and singing as the farm was home,
In the sun that is young once only,
Time let me play and be
Golden in the mercy of his means,

And green and golden I was huntsman and herdsman, the calves
Sang to my horn, the foxes on the hills barked clear and cold,
And the sabbath rang slowly
In the pebbles of the holy streams.

All the sun long it was running, it was lovely, the hay
Fields high as the house, the tunes from the chimneys, it was air
And playing, lovely and watery
And fire green as grass.
And nightly under the simple stars
As I rode to sleep the owls were bearing the farm away,
All the moon long I heard, blessed among stables, the nightjars
Flying with the ricks, and the horses
Flashing into the dark.

And then to awake, and the farm, like a wanderer white
With the dew, come back, the cock on his shoulder: it was all
Shining, it was Adam and maiden,
The sky gathered again
And the sun grew round that very day.
So it must have been after the birth of the simple light
In the first, spinning place, the spellbound horses walking warm
Out of the whinnying green stable
On to the fields of praise.

And honoured among foxes and pheasants by the gay house
Under the new made clouds and happy as the heart was long,
In the sun born over and over,
I ran my heedless ways,
My wishes raced through the house high hay
And nothing I cared, at my sky blue trades, that time allows
In all his tuneful turning so few and such morning songs
Before the children green and golden
Follow him out of grace,

Nothing I cared, in the lamb white days, that time would take me
Up to the swallow thronged loft by the shadow of my hand,
In the moon that is always rising,
Nor that riding to sleep
I should hear him fly with the high fields
And wake to the farm forever fled from the childless land.
Oh as I was young and easy in the mercy of his means,
Time held me green and dying
Though I sang in my chains like the sea.

A Refusal to Mourn the Death, by Fire, of a Child in London

Never until the mankind making
Bird beast and flower
Fathering and all humbling darkness
Tells with silence the last light breaking
And the still hour
Is come of the sea tumbling in harness

And I must enter again the round
Zion of the water bead
And the synagogue of the ear of corn
Shall I let pray the shadow of a sound
Or sow my salt seed
In the least valley of sackcloth to mourn

The majesty and burning of the child's death.
I shall not murder
The mankind of her going with a grave truth
Nor blaspheme down the stations of the breath
With any further
Elegy of innocence and youth.

Deep with the first dead lies London's daughter,
Robed in the long friends,
The grains beyond age, the dark veins of her mother,
Secret by the unmourning water
Of the riding Thames.
After the first death, there is no other.

Dylan Thomas: Observations and Analyses

Dylan Thomas: A Pioneer

FRANCIS SCARFE

I. POINTS OF CONTACT

Dylan Thomas is one of the most promising of the poets under thirty, but he has suffered through catching the public eye a little too early, which resulted in unfounded criticism by both his supporters and detractors. He was promising in 1934 ('Eighteen Poems':Parton Press) and promising in 1936 ('Twenty-five Poems':Dent). To those who have followed his production since then he is still promising, and this premature estimate of him is being made to clarify the nature of that promise.

For many people his poems are puzzles, seeming to offer at first reading no more than a forbidding cliff, impenetrable to reason, from which there jut great crags of capricious imagery. Some people (notably Miss Sitwell) read him for his sound, but though the words peal fully and roundly, the rhythms are monotonous enough to make this pall. But many a good poet is monotonous. The only satisfactory approach seems to be to plumb these images and verbal din and see what lies beyond.

The poems, especially in the 1934 and 1935 volumes, seem to have three noticeable points of contact. Discussion of the Metaphysicals, Sitwellism and Surrealism are irrelevant. The dominant points of contact seem to be James Joyce, the Bible and Freud. The personal habits of language and mythology of Dylan Thomas can readily be identified through these three sources. The first is linguistic, the second mythological, the third psycho-pathological, the key to his interpretation of his world.

From *Auden and After* by Francis Scarfe (London: George Routledge & Sons Ltd., 1942), pp. 101–107. Reprinted by permission of Routledge and Kegan Paul Ltd.

II. LANGUAGE

It is agreed that James Joyce's language in 'Ulysses' is simple enough. It appears difficult only when sentences and parts of sentences do not appear logically related. 'Ulysses' is the masterpiece of the unexpected: the elements of surprise, so puffed by Poe and Baudelaire, and so unclassical, dominates every page. The words are not odd, they are merely at times oddly related. Later, when Joyce evolved a composite language, it appeared to some people (like myself) more satisfying and logical than the jargon of 'Ulysses', because this new language has a recognizable basis in philology. In 'Ulysses' there are such elementary experiments as 'A screaming bittern's harsh high whistle shrieks. Groangrousegurgling Toft's cumbersome whirligig turns slowly the room right round-about the room.' This is simple, it reveals meaning, is emotionally apprehended. 'Steel shark stone onehandled Nelson, two trickies Frauenzimmer plumstained from pram falling bawling.' Though the words are simple, this is not easy. It is not readily apprehended either emotionally or by analysis. It lives only in its context. Such writing reveals in miniature the linguistic habits of Dylan Thomas.

His basic device (which Joyce later systematized) is the invention of words. This device is fully in accord with Dylan Thomas's own statement, 'Poetry is the rhythmic, inevitably narrative, movement from an overclothed blindness to a naked vision', and his definition of poetic activity as '. . . the physical and mental task of constructing a formally watertight compartment of words, preferably with a main moving column' ('New Verse', October 1934). Dylan Thomas, in writing poetry, is not expressing so much as discovering his feelings. This is as it should be, for the reading and writing of poetry at any time are largely acts of discovery. The poet conventionally offers what he knows he has found, but Thomas offers the process of discovery itself. This unfinishedness is regarded by some as an insult to the reader, but in reality it is characteristic, honest, and one of the most attractive aspects of his work.

The invention of words, then, is inevitable in the expression of the half-perceived, incoherent sensations and ideas. And as his pen hovers between a host of choices, seeking some short-cut to expression as the Surrealists do by automatism, Dylan Thomas invents such terms as 'man-iron', 'bonerailed', 'seaspindle', 'seastruck', 'all-hollowed', 'pin-hilled', 'natron.' The presence of puns in these composites ('all-hollowed') indicates his pedantic dry humour. At other times, instead of fusing ideas together in this way, Thomas distorts their usual meanings, as in 'minstrel angle' (ministering angel?), 'triangle landscape' (here triangular + trinity, formed by the crosses of Christ and the robbers), 'ship-racked gospel', and the like. Real obscurity only starts when a false epithet is used, of which Joyce was rarely guilty. These are sometimes immensely expressive, as in 'dead nuisance' or 'iron mile', but the trick annoys when it hides rather than reveals meaning, as in 'colic season', 'cadaverous gravel', 'metal neptune.' This emotional epithet resembles fake-Surrealism. Real Surrealism is practically reached in his fourth trick: 'man of leaves', 'tree of nettles', 'wood of weathers', 'sixth of wind', 'house of bread.' This is very charming at first, but it bores by repetition. The final trick is the inaccurate use of verbs, which abounds in these poems in such lines as:

> Through the rampart of the sky
> Shall the star-flanked seed be riddled
>
> *'Poem 5'*

Most of these verbal tricks are from time to time completely successful and justified, as in the ten 'religious' sonnets in the 'Twenty-five Poems', where 'gallow grave', 'mountain minute', even 'glove of prints' and 'linen spirit' are impressive and logical in their context. At his best, Thomas reminds us of the Old Testament, James Joyce and Hopkins all at once. It matters little whether he reads them: his language partakes of all three.

In his later poems (since 1936) Thomas has diluted these verbal surprises. That his poems still startle our complacency is a proof that his first appeal was not due to mere bogus verbalism. It is well that he is losing some of these habits, which lead to preciousness of the most pompous kind. Not that it is to be despised, for preciousness itself can reveal a wealth of unsuspected fact. All poetry is precious.

III. BIBLICAL SYMBOLISM

I do not agree with a critic who said that there were two types of poems in the 1936 volume, 'sense' and 'nonsense' poems. The poems scarcely differ in method, and are made sensible by the pervading presence of the Bible and sexual symbolism.

Genesis, the Garden of Eden, the Fall, Adam, original sin, the presence of Cain, Job, Jacob, Abraham, Lazarus, the legends of Christ and Mary, form the bulk of the reference-matter, and even subject-matter of the 'Twenty-five Poems.' The fervency of these references is due to the fact that the Bible appears as a cruel and crazy legend, as seen through childish memories of hot-gospelling and the diabolical grimace of the Welsh Bethel. The Biblical element is further confused by a primitive metaphysics, related in the last analysis to a sexual interpretation of the universe:

> Dawn breaks behind the eyes;
> From poles of skull and toe the windy blood
> Slides like a sea;
> Nor fenced, nor staked, the gushers of the sky
> Spout to the rod
> Divining in a smile the oil of tears.
>
> *'Light breaks where no sun shines'*

The philosophy is simple: the universe is sexually dynamic; bird, beast and stone share the same (sexual) life with man (an advance on the pretty pantheism of Wordsworth), but, for-ever conscious of sin, Thomas conveys this as something terrible:

> The horizontal cross-bones of Abaddon,
> You by the cavern over the black stairs,
> Rung bone and blade, the verticals of Adam,
> And, manned by midnight, Jacob to the stars:
> Hairs of your head, then said the hollow agent,
> Are but the roots of nettles and of feathers
> Over these groundworks thrusting through a pavement,
> And hemlock-headed in the wood of weather.
>
> *'Poem 25' : II*

Why horizontals and verticals (genitals would do)? The same arbitrary association links Abaddon, Jacob and Adam. Hollow agent (joke) is Death. Only 'cross-bones', 'cavern' and 'hemlock' produce horror. These lines form part of a sonnet relating growth from childhood to manhood. Death is present from beginning to end.

The 'horreur de la vie et l'extase de la vie' of Baudelaire are evenly balanced in Dylan Thomas. His universe is dynamic, frighteningly active and alive:

> And now the horns of England, in the sound of shape,
> Summon your snowy horsemen, and the four-stringed hill,
> Over the sea-gut loudening, sets a rock alive;
> Hurdles and duns and railings, as the boulders heave,
> Crack like a spring in a vice, bone breaking April,
> Spill the lank folly's hunter and the hard-held hope . . .
>
> *'Poem 10'*

But, in consequence, death itself appears not as a negation, but as an equally dynamic force, as old as Adam:

> The wise men tell me that the garden gods
> Twined good and evil on an eastern tree;
> And when the moon rose windily it was
> Black as the beast and paler than the cross.
>
> *'Poem 3'*

Death, not life, is the measure of time:

> A worm tells summer better than the clock,
> The slug's a living calendar of days.
>
> *'Poem 7'*

So it is that the life-death problem in Dylan Thomas is as unresolved as the sex-sin problem. These dualisms are again related to a theological dualism, body-soul, as expressed in the first poem of the collection:

> I, in my intricate image, stride on two levels,
> Forged in man's minerals, the brassy orator
> Laying my ghost in metal,
> The scales of this twin world tread on the double,
> My half ghost in armour holds hard in death's corridor,
> To my man-iron sidle.
>
> *'Poem 1'*

This is more than lay philosophy, for it is implicit here that the triumph of the body is death of the spirit, since the 'man-iron' (flesh) and 'ghost in armour' (soul) are equally aggressive elements. It is only owing to this primitive interpretation that Thomas is able to confuse sexual and spiritual values in the ten 'religious' sonnets.

These so-called 'sonnets' (they are 14-line poems) cannot be considered separately, as together they form a unit ('Poem 25'). The technique is cumulative, impressionistic, though in one or two sonnets the subject is directly presented. Subjects, rather, for though the theme is the life-death antagonism, it is inextricably bound up with Old and New Testament mythology and sexual symbolism. It is rash to reduce such works to a formula, but for me they represent a double pattern of Biblical and sexual imagery, the recognizable characters being Satan (identified with death and sin), sex (i.e. life, represented by Adam and even Gabriel), Mary (the justification of sex through child-bearing and suffering, but none the less a worldly symbol), and Christ (victim and blood-offering rather than hero).

Sonnet II, quoted above, expresses the identification of sex with sin and nature through Biblical reference. The third sonnet is confused, and in it the Old Testament wait for the Messiah, the Paschal Lamb, the three-days' death of Christ and the Ram of the Zodiac are so related that only the author could give a satisfactory explanation, if there is one. Not that it matters, for even a few lines of that poem would show Dylan Thomas's capacity for 'montage', as he works together a sense of time, the foreshadowed conflict of life and death principles, against a scriptural and sexual background:

> First there was the lamb on knocking knees
> And three dead seasons in a climbing grave
> That Adam's wether in the flock of horns,
> But of the tree-tailed worm that mounted Eve,
> Horned down the skullfoot and the skull of toes
> On thunderous pavements in the garden time.

Such verse is not intellectually rich, but sensually and emotionally it is profound. The fourth sonnet is a passage of sexual mysticism, in which love and sex are identified as a prelude to the nativity (Sonnets V and VI). 'And from the windy West came two-gunned Gabriel' (V). The narrative begins moving with this first line, gangster-disguise of Gabriel (however naive) giving the sense of shock and incredible difficulty by the Annunciation. Again cabbalistic tricks come to the aid of the poet, who conjures us a miracle with a pack of cards and a mumbo-jumbo of literary and Biblical allusion. Sonnet VI continues in the same vein, being a gruesome conception and nativity in one, contrived once more by a cabbalistic formula:

> He in a book of water tallow-eyed
> By lava's light split through the oyster vowels
> And burned sea-silence on a wick of words . . .

But this time the difficulties are not shirked, and all the horrors of birth (as suggested by Genesis and Milton perhaps) are conveyed in a brutally effective language:

> And love plucked out the stinging siren's eye,
> Old cock from nowheres looped the minstrel tongue
> Till tallow I blew from the wax's tower
> The fats of midnight when the salt was singing;
> Adam, time's joker, on a witch of cardboard
> Spelt out the seven seas, an evil index,
> The bagpipe-breasted ladies in the deadweed
> Blew out the blood gauze through the wound of manwax.

The attending presence of the siren and cock (both symbolizing lust and sacrifice), Adam (the sinner), and the 'ladies in the deadweed' (again sirens, Fates, Furies, acting as midwives) heightens symbolically the horror of Christ's difficult, and indeed *unnatural*, birth. The next sonnet summarizes Christ's career: not the conventional tale so much as the bringing into focus of all Biblical legend, and a new identification of man with God and the universe. Its concentrated rhetoric—

> Now stamp the Lord's prayer on a grain of rice,
> A Bible-leaved of all the written woods,
> Strip to this tree: a rocking alphabet,
> Genesis in the root, the scarecrow word,
> And one light's language in the book of trees;
> Doom on deniers at the wind-turned statement—

brings together the literal fanatic, doubting Thomas and the twentieth-century modernist, while before them lies a world of living fact in which spiritual and physical realities meet.

The eighth sonnet, the Crucifixion, is the best.

> This was the crucifixion on the mountain,
> Time's nerve in vinegar, the gallow grave
> As tarred with blood as the bright thorns I wept;
> The world's my wound, God's Mary in her grief,
> Bent like three trees and bird-papped through her shift,
> With pins for teardrops in the long wound's woman.
> This was the sky, Jack Christ, each minstrel angle
> Drove in the heaven-driven of the nails
> Till the three-coloured rainbow from my nipples
> From pole to pole leapt round the snail-waked world.
> I by the tree of thieves, all glory's sawbones
> Unsex the skeleton this mountain minute,
> And by this blowclock witness of the sun
> Suffer the heaven's children through my heartbeat.

(To establish a hasty glossary, it seems evident that 'Time's nerve'= Christ, ie. most sensitive point in history; 'gallow'=shallow+gallows; line 3: 'I'=Christ (if it means Dylan Thomas the poem loses); line 5, 'three trees'=crosses; 'bird-papped'=association of dove, also undeveloped, virginal; 'pins for teardrops'—compare Picasso's imagery, the very tears wound; 'Jack Christ'—Hopkinese, Christ is Everyman; 'minstrel angle'=ministering angel, also literally minstrel angle, that is each corner of the singing sky; 'heaven-drive'—the responsibility of the 'crime' rests with God, not man; 'three-coloured rainbow'—a new covenant made by the Trinity (see Milton); 'snail-waked'—snail symbol of destruction, sloth and lust; 'sawbones'—doctor; 'mountain' —gigantic, important; 'blowclock'—literally so, or the lifeless Christ's body become a symbol.)

In a sense this poem seems to symbolize the birth of love through the death of sex. Mary suffers the true punishment of Eve—not merely the pangs of child-birth, but the death of her offspring. The full symbolism only appears towards the end of the poem, with the words 'Unsex the skeleton this mountain minute.' A similar instance of sexual frustration occurs in 'I in my intricate image', in the words

> a cock on the dunghill
> Crying to Lazarus the morning is vanity.

The conclusion to be drawn from this fine crucifixion poem is disturbing. After presenting in all his poems a brilliant sexual interpretation of life, Dylan Thomas has here presented a sexual interpretation of death. The secret of death, and its horror, is that it is sexless. (Note: this may seem a farfetched interpretation of a straightforward poem. The answer is that all interpreting is dangerous, and never quite in focus. The poet is rarely entirely responsible for his implications, they rest with the reader.)

These poems owe their success to their density rather than to their outlook, though the outlook is original and stimulating. One or two of them are too exclusively montage, but as a whole they concentrate admirably in a final synthesis the tentative self-exploration of the rest of the volume.

In Dylan Thomas's later poems this Biblical background narrows (some would say broadens) considerably. The 'Poem in October' ('The Year's Poetry', 1935) is a variation on the theme 'In the beginning was the Word', for in it all living things and natural objects are defined in terms of letters, vowels, syllables, etc. This poem could well have appeared nauseatingly literary, were it not for the fact that the subject is sustained by a strong sense of universal analogy, the oneness of life, and justified by the poet's presence in the poem. This is a good instance of Thomas's pseudo-cabbalistic mystery, an effect which is readily obtained with few properties, but for a full development of which Thomas has not the necessary background. Let us remember (as a warning to schoolgirls who regard Dylan Thomas as a magician) that Professour Saurat once affirmed that Rimbaud's 'Les Voyelles' was based on the mysteries of the Cabbala. At seventeen, Rimbaud could easily obtain a smattering (about five lines) of knowledge of those mysteries from a Larousse dictionary. . . .

Towards 1937 Thomas broke slightly away from Biblical background, only to err consciously and unconsciously towards church ritual. This may have been due to Eliot or George Barker. That it was not successful can be seen in the poem 'It is the sinners' dust-tongued Bell claps me to churches' ('The Year's Poetry', 1937). Though there are some fine movements in the poem, in spite of the clarifying of the images the theme is less clear than in his earlier poems, and it leaves a sense of frustration. 'In Memory of Ann Jones' ('The Year's Poetry', 1938), which is perhaps his best poem since then, is fundamentally religious, and is Biblical rather than church-going. Even the poem 'There was a Saviour' ('Horizon', May 1940) is only a new outlet for the Messianic legend, and the typical imagery is ritualistic.

It would be ridiculous to claim Thomas for any church. It is sufficient to note to what entirely different uses T. S. Eliot and Dylan Thomas have put the Bible for purposes of poetry. Thomas is much nearer Blake, one might even say nearer Donne, but also perilously near Rimbaud's 'Les Premières Communions.'

IV. SEXUAL SYMBOLISM

'Poetry must drag further into the clear nakedness of light more even of the hidden causes than Freud could realize' (Dylan Thomas, 'New Verse', October 1934).

So wrote Dylan Thomas in his admission that he had been influenced by Freud. The influence is first of all general, understandable in a poet whose chief preoccupation is to explore childhood and adolescence. Only a reader of Freud can receive the full impact, which is enormous, of Dylan Thomas's predominantly sexual imagery. The influence of Freud would seem to go even farther in view of the poet's acknowledgment that his activity as a poet is one of self-discovery rather than self-expression or even self-analysis. In their finished state the poems suggest that self-analysis could be undertaken by such a poet only by analysing what he had written. That is to say, they are not the product of analysis, but the very raw material for it. They are in the fullest sense documents: they are not intellectual or cerebral, but so spontaneous that the poet himself might well be amazed and bewildered in face of them.

The sexual symbolism in the poems seems to work largely as an assertion of sexuality, of the sexual basis of all thought and action. Secondly, the poems also contain some implied defences of this sexuality, justifications offered by the poet to society and to his own conscience. A little probing reveals not a liberated body but an obsessed mind (as in D. H. Lawrence):

> And I am dumb to tell the crooked rose
> My youth is bent by the same wintry fever.
> *'The force that through the green fuse'*

Dylan Thomas's imagery is predominantly masculine, to the point of onanism and homosexuality. And although the male sexual images are bold, harsh and triumphant, there is a sense of impending tragedy and frustration.

> I see that from these boys shall men of nothing
> Stature by seedy shifting
> Or lame the air with leaping of its heats.
> I am the man your father was.
> We are the sons of flint and pitch.
> Oh see the poles are kissing as they cross.
> *'Two'* in *'New Verse'*, June 1934

The male is constantly expressed, naturally, in heroic images, such as the tower, turret, tree, monster, crocodile, knight in armour, ghost, sailor, Jacob's ladder, skyscraper. But side by side with these are other equally male sex-images which carry also the idea of death and disgrace, such as the snake, the slug, the snail and the maggot:

> In old man's shank one-marrowed with my bone,
> And all the herrings smelling in the sea,
> I sit and watch the worm beneath my nail
> Wearing the quick away.
> *'New Verse'*, August 1934

It seems evident that Thomas's allegiance to Freud has not resulted, in his poems, in the cleansing of sexuality from the Old Testament sense of sin. Even the 'Paradise Regained' poem (as one might call the last of the sonnet-sequence) ends on a combined note of creation and destruction:

> Green as beginning, let the garden diving
> Soar, with its two bark towers, to that Day
> When the worm builds with the gold straws of venom
> My nest of mercies in the rude, red tree.

For the vision of the worm creating is only gained after the sexual immolation of the male (Christ):

> I by the tree of thieves, all glory's sawbones
> Unsex the skeleton this mountain minute,
> And by this blowclock witness of the sun
> Suffer the heaven's children through my heartbeat.

The words 'unsex the skeleton' are a good indication of Thomas's problem, the reconciling of the creative and destructive elements of sex. In view of the prevailing sense of sin, this suspicion that sex is not an end in itself, and that the ultimate objective is irremediably obscure, it must be concluded that the poet's interpretation of sex is still as close to the Old Testament as to the psychology of Freud. The Bible provides the mythology by which the problem can be raised to a high and universal plane, while Freud gives the impetus to what is perhaps the most overwhelming and poignant sexual imagery in modern poetry.

V. SHAPE

'The more subjective a poem, the clearer the narrative line' (Dylan Thomas, 'New Verse', October 1934). This is eminently satisfying if considered only in reference to Dylan Thomas himself. His poems are admittedly subjective, and their structure is remarkably simple. Not only is the 'main moving column' of words present; there is in consequence a strong core of subject round which the imagery is grouped. For this reason, although many people are dismayed by the accumulation of imagery and pseudo-imagery in the poems (for he is a spendthrift poet), the poems are far from being chaotic. Thomas's fundamental simplicity is shown in two of his finest poems, 'The hand that signed the paper felled a city' and 'The force that through the green fuse drives the flower.' These two poems reveal a classical ability to develop fully a simple subject. They alone would prove him a considerable poet. (After painting his complex portrait of Gertrude Stein, Picasso needed all his genius to draw like a child.)

In many poems the overlaying of images seems to go too far. That this is not a sign of weakness, however, and that Thomas still has (or had until recently) this basis of simplicity, is shown in what appears to me his best poem, 'In Memory of Ann Jones' (1938). The poem is planned in a manner worthy of Valéry himself, and a wealth of imagery subdued to the subject. There are four phases: the burial, the feast, the character and the homage. Tied images unite these phases, all of them relating to death, her home, her character. The poem is, in the poet's words, 'a monstrous thing blindly magnified out of praise.' Here Thomas achieves a concentration which is to be found in glimpses in his earlier poems:

> I know her scrubbed and sour simple hands
> Lie with religion in their cramp, her threadbare
> Whisper in a damp word, her wits drilled hollow,
> Her fist of a face died clenched on a round pain;
> And sculptured Ann is seventy years of stone. . . .

The typical furniture of her room, which appears early in the poem ('In a room with a stuffed fox and a stale fern'), serves as a dominant tied image, reappearing brilliantly at the end to drive home the idea that her love might even bring the dead to life:

> . . . until
> The stuffed lung of the fox twitch and cry Love
> And the strutting fern lay seeds on the black sill.

Dylan Thomas's poems are somewhat coarse-grained because of the profusion of imagery, most of it in overtones, grouped round the centre. But in the best poems, as in 'In Memory of Ann Jones', the magnifying habit scores heavily. In more recent poems there is less over-laying, and in 'There was a Saviour' there is evidence of a more refining process of selection.

VI.

Technically, Dylan Thomas has achieved nothing new. His alliterative and inventive tricks are as old as poetry. His personal rhythms are not unusual when compared with those of Hopkins. He writes with equal ease in fixed and loose forms. His outstanding merit, when compared with the other young poets, is his rich vocabulary, his sensual appreciation of words, his intense persuasive idiom which reveals him as one who is reaching towards all that is most living in our language. In that respect he is an anachronism, for he has not abandoned the wealth of the past for the somewhat thin idiom of Hollywood and the Middlesex suburbs as many poets are doing.

Thomas is lacking in genuine humour, though he is humourous enough in everyday life. He displays in his writings, surely enough, the traditional Welsh easy flow of speech. But most of his jokes are either purely verbal, or sad and a little sinister. The characteristic tone of his poems is grave and depressing. There is sorrow in his wit, which is grim. This grimness is to be found also in his stories, such as 'The Burning Baby' and 'The School of Witches', where it reaches cruelty.

Dylan Thomas is fundamentally a poet of the feelings, and is not a visual poet. He does not see clearly, and consequently is a cuckoo in the nest of the 'New Verse' observation poets. His main object is to feel clearly, which he has not yet achieved:

> I have been told to reason by the heart,
> But heart, like head, leads helplessly.
>
> *'Poem 19'*

He seeks the world in himself, and consequently his work is entirely autobiographical.

His future depends on an enlarging of his simple vision of the sexual basis of life, and it is to be hoped that he will not abandon his essential subject. That problem itself, and his evident conflict as to its solution, should provide him with an inexhaustible and vital theme. He is potentially the most modern of the young poets now writing, because of his assimilation of Joyce, Freud and the Bible, and because so far he has rejected the influence of the generation immediately preceding his own. He, like no young poet save perhaps George Barker and Ruthven Todd, is his own poet. Thomas is the most old-fashioned of his generation in his apparent separation of his poetry from his politics. This might yet prove valuable. Technically he has little to do save to give his verbal inventions a better grounding in reality and in philology, to concentrate even more on that 'main moving column', and to concede less to that delight in a grimace by which every poet is tempted.

August 1940

Dylan Thomas

G. S. FRASER

I

When Dylan Thomas died in New York in his thirty-ninth year at the end of 1953, he had been a poet of considerable reputation for twenty years and, with the recent publication of his *Collected Poems*, was at the height of his fame. The collected volume was known to have sold, even before his death, more than ten thousand copies, an enormous figure by contemporary English or American standards. He was one of the two or three poets of this time whose name, like that of Mr. Eliot or Mr. Auden, was familiar to the man in the street. Shortly after his death, the success over the air and on the stage of his dramatic prose fantasy for radio, *Under Milk Wood,* introduced his work to an even wider audience than that which appreciated his poetry. It was not only, however, as a writer that Thomas was known to a wide public. He had a remarkable gift as an entertainer, and was a first-rate broadcaster, particularly of his own short stories based on his childhood in Wales. He was an extremely gregarious man, and had a very warm and lovable personality. His death produced a spate of tributes in prose and verse from scores of friends and acquaintances. And for those who did not know him personally, Thomas had become, as few poets of our age have become, a kind of legend. He corresponded, as most poets do not, to some popular ideal, vision, or fiction of what a poet, in real life, should be. He was the pattern of the poet as a bohemian, and this was in many ways a misfortune for him. Had he been a more aloof, a less gregarious, a more prudent man; had he been less ready to expend himself in casual sociability; had he had less of a knack, in his later years, for earning money

From *Vision and Rhetoric* by G. S. Fraser (London: Faber and Faber Limited, 1959), pp. 211–241.

quickly and spending it even more quickly: in any of these cases, he might have lived longer and produced more; but he would not have been, in any of these cases, the writer that he is.

Thomas has achieved, and has retained, a popular fame as a poet in spite of the fact that many of his poems are, at least on an intellectual level, extremely hard to comprehend. The design of at least many of his earlier poems is notably obscure; many of his later poems are much clearer in outline than his earlier work, but they are still full of puzzling details. Yet he is one of the few modern poets who can be read aloud to a large, mixed audience, with a confidence in his 'going down.' There is a massive emotional directness in his poems that at once comes across. And the more critical reader, who may be suspicious of what seems a direct attack on his feelings below the level of the intellect, soon becomes aware that Thomas's obscurity is not that of a loose and vague but of an extremely packed writer. In one of the best short studies that has been written of Thomas since his death, Dr. David Daiches quotes what is certainly, at a first glance, an almost totally opaque passage.

> Altarwise by owl-light in the halfway house
> The gentleman lay graveward with his furies
> Abaddon in the hangnail cracked from Adam,
> And, from his fork, a dog among the fairies,
> Bit out the mandrake with tomorrow's scream. . . .

Dr. Daiches comments:

> The careful explicator will be able to produce informative glosses on each of these phrases, but the fact remains that the poem is congested with its metaphors, and the reader is left with a feeling of oppression. . . . But it must be emphasized that this is not the fault of a bad romantic poetry, too loose and exclamatory, but comes from what can perhaps be called the classical vice of attempting to press too much into too little space.

In spite of this excessive congestion of much of his poetry, Thomas obviously did succeed in communicating in verse, to a very large public by modern standards, something which that public felt to be important. What was that something, and how did Thomas get it across? It was certainly something very different from the public personality, the personality of an entertainer, which Thomas conveyed in a prose book, *Portrait of the Artist as a Young Dog*. Thomas was not, like Byron or Yeats, for instance, the poet as actor; he did not dramatize his personal life in his poetry, or build himself up as a 'character.' He did these things in conversation, and in the sketches and short stories, brilliant improvisations, which were fundamentally an extension of his genius for conversation. His poems are exceedingly individual, but they are also impersonal; when he writes about his childhood he is not so much recalling particular experiences as transforming them into a vision of innocence before the Fall. Yet at the same time, he is a concrete rather than a generalizing poet; he does not, like Mr. Auden, take a more or less abstract theme and proceed to relate it, in a detached way, to particularized observations about man and society. Both the appeal and the difficulty of his poetry come from the fact that it is a poetry of unitary response. Many of the best modern writers have been concerned with a kind of split in the consciousness of our time between what men think and what they feel or would like to feel, between what men suppose to be true and what they would like to believe, between what men feel is a proper course of action and what they feel is an attractive one. These urgent contemporary themes of stress, doubt, division in the self, tragic irony and tragic choice, do not enter into Dylan Thomas's poetic world. It is a world quite at one with itself. At the heart of his poetic response to experience there is a baffling simplicity.

II

It is Thomas's poetry that makes him important and, because of this baffling simplicity at the heart of it, his personal history, outside the history of the poems, can perhaps throw very little direct light on his achievement as a poet. His prose works, with the exception of *Under Milk Wood,* also throw little light on his poetry. They are second-level achievements, representing Thomas as the brilliant entertainer rather than the dedicated poet; they stand also, as so much of Thomas's personal life did, for that search for distraction which the concentrated nature of his dedication to poetry made necessary. Thomas's poetry is the main theme of this essay, but I shall precede my consideration of it by a few brief remarks on Thomas's life, his personality, and his achievements in prose.

Thomas was the son of a Swansea schoolmaster, a teacher of English in a grammar school, who had himself poetic ambitions; Thomas's father must have had remarkable gifts as a teacher, for many of the leading figures today in Welsh literary life were, at one time or another, his pupils. The Welsh, like the Scots, have a very strong family sense, and in his later years memories of holidays with farmer uncles meant a great deal to Thomas. He was not a particularly brilliant schoolboy, but he did very well at English, took an enthusiastic part in amateur dramatics, and wrote neat and very conventional poems for his school magazine. His father would have liked him to work hard to gain a scholarship to a university, but he did not do so. On leaving school, he became for a short time a reporter on a Swansea newspaper, a job which must have combined for him the appeal of bohemianism with that of the outer verges of literature.

Thomas's Welshness is an important part of his make-up. He never spoke or understood the Welsh language, and he very early taught himself to speak English not with the slight Welsh sing-song but with what he himself described mockingly as a 'cut-glass accent'. He disliked Welsh nationalism, and, indeed, all types of nationalism, but Wales remained to him home. His knowledge of the Bible, and his fundamentally religious—emotionally rather than intellectually religious—attitude to life were typically Welsh; his bohemianism was partly a reaction against the severe puritanism of much of middle-class Welsh life. His sense of verbal music, his feeling for the intricate interplay of vowel and consonant, and also, in prose and conversation, his love of the extravagant phrase and the witty exaggeration were Welsh. He was un-English also in his universal gregariousness, his unwillingness to make social discriminations, his complete lack of class-consciousness.

He first became known as a poet through contributing poems to and winning prizes from, the poetry page of *The Sunday Referee*, edited by Victor Neuberg. *The Sunday Referee* finally financed the publication of his first volume, *Eighteen Poems*. Thomas was thus flung on the London literary world, particularly its bohemian side, as a boy of twenty, and in his early years in London he depended a great deal on the generosity and hospitality of friends. In his later years, however, his wide range of secondary gifts, as a broadcaster, a writer of sketches and short stories and film scripts, even as a comic journalist, were bringing him in a considerable yearly income; this tended, however, to be spent as soon as it was earned, and his payment of income tax was perpetually overdue. He lost, in later years, his taste for London life, and spent as much time as he could with his wife and children at Laugharne. It was monetary need that drove him to undertake the American poetry reading tours, which both he and those who organized them found a considerable strain as well as a stimulus, and on the last of which he died. Mr. John Malcolm Brinnin's book about these tours is obviously almost antagonizingly accurate in its descriptions of many embarrassing episodes, but it is a portrait of a sick man under the strain of financial and moral worry, and of being perpetually on public show, and it should not be taken as giving a fair idea of the character or personality of Dylan Thomas as his English friends knew him. In particular it conveys a vivid impression of the element of stress, but no impression at all of the element of fulfilment, in Thomas's married life; Mr. Brinnin's remarks about this should be corrected by Roy Campbell's that Thomas and his wife were 'always in love, even years after marriage to the day of his death. They would quarrel like newly-weds on the slightest pretext with never a dull moment and make it up in two minutes.'

In America, Thomas tended to drink whisky rather than beer, though he knew spirits were bad for him. In England and Wales, he stuck on the whole to beer, not for its own sake, but as what his friend Mr. Vernon Watkins calls 'a necessary adjunct to conversation'. The tempo of his English life was slower, more genial, and less harassed than that of his tours in America. The charm of his rambling, vivid, extravagantly anecdotal conversation comes out in *Portrait of the Artist as a Young Dog* and in many of his broadcast sketches. The warmth of his personality, his zest in every kind of human oddity, his love for his fellow men, come out in his last completed work, *Under Milk Wood.* Here, more than in any other prose work of his, he managed to combine his prose gift for humorous fantasy based on realistic observation with his poetic gift for a piled-up richness of evocative language. *Under Milk Wood* is also, purely formally, notable as an invention. It derives not from any literary model, but from the radio form of the 'feature', in narrative and dialogue, evoking the spirit of a place; it turns that form into literature. It also makes more broadly and obviously apprehensible than, perhaps, any of Thomas's poems do that 'love of Man and . . . praise of God' which, in the introduction to the *Collected Poems,* Thomas wrote of as underlying all his work. *Under Milk Wood* is not, in the ordinary sense, dramatic. The characters are not confronted with choices; they behave according to their natures, mean, thriftless, or generous, and are to be accepted, like natural objects, for being what they are; and the movement is not dramatic, but cyclical, from early morning through day to night.

There are perhaps two moral centres in *Under Milk Wood:* the Reverend Eli Jenkins, with his touching 'good-bad' poems and his gentle appeals to a gentle God to look kindly on human failings; and the old blind sea-captain, the fire of whose lust and love—it is typical of Thomas's unitary response to refuse to distinguish between these

—is not quenched even by the waters of death and utter forgetfulness. Thomas was as a man, like the Reverend Eli Jenkins, utterly without malice. Reading *Under Milk Wood* it is possible to understand what a famous newspaper, in a remarkable obituary notice of Thomas, meant by asserting that he had the courage to lead the Christian life in public. 'The harlots and the publicans shall go into heaven before you'.

III

In an early statement about his poems, published in Mr. Geoffrey Grigson's poetry periodical of the 1930s, *New Verse,* Thomas spoke of the process of writing a poem as one of stripping away darkness, of struggling up to light; and also of that struggle as taking place through a dialectic of images. In his preface to his *Collected Poems,* on the other hand, he spoke, as we have seen, of his poems being written 'for the love of Man and in praise of God.' These two statements help us to measure a certain progress, or development, in a poetic achievement which is too often thought of as having been one of more or less stationary self-repetition. In many of his early poems, Thomas does, in fact, seem immersed, in a way that is bewildering to the reader and may have been bewildering to himself, in an attempt to grasp the whole of life, human and natural, as an apparently confused but ultimately single process. In his later poems, he more often seems to be, quite consciously and much less bewilderingly, *celebrating* that process—celebrating it, as Dr. Daiches says, religiously, and with sacramental imagery.

Perhaps also it is wrong to speak of him as celebrating some particular process; an American critic has suggested that what Thomas can be thought of as celebrating is the fact, or notion, of process in general, Mr. Eliot's 'three things', 'birth, and copulation, and death', seeing them as cyclical, seeing every birth as involving death, every death as involving birth, seeing also human life and natural process as exactly equated.

Such a set of clues certainly helps us a good deal in Thomas's earlier poems:

> The force that through the green fuse drives the flower
> Drives my green age; that blasts the roots of trees
> Is my destroyer.
> And I am dumb to tell the crooked rose
> My youth is bent by the same wintry fever. . . .

Thomas, there, is massively identifying the body of man with the body of the world. The forces, he is saying, that control the growth and decay, the beauty and terror of human life are not merely similar to, but are the very same forces as we see at work in outer nature. But how is Thomas able to hold and move us by saying this? In a way, it is a platitude: it is a statement, at least, which most of us would accept without too much excitement or perturbation up to a point, or with qualifications. Man, as an animal, is part of nature; is that a new or startling idea? My own answer, when many years ago I first considered the puzzle of the extremely powerful impact of this passage, was this. The man-nature equation here gains strength from an inter-transference of qualities between—or, more strictly, of our emotional attitudes towards—man and nature. We feel a human pity for Thomas's 'crooked rose', and, on the other hand, the 'wintry fever' of an adolescent's unsatisfied sexual desires acquires something of the impersonal dignity of a natural process.

It is still, I think, the best clue that we have at least to Thomas's earliest volume, *Eighteen Poems,* to think of him as engaged in this way in bestowing on something humanly undignified, adolescent frustration, natural dignity:

> I see you boys of summer in your ruin.
> Man in his maggot's barren.
> And boys are full and foreign in the pouch.
> I am the man your father was.
> We are the sons of flint and pitch.
> O see the poles are kissing as they cross.

The American critic, Mr. Elder Olson, interprets the whole poem from which this stanza comes—the first poem in Dylan Thomas's first book—as a dialogue between perverse youth and crabbed age, with the poet occasionally intervening as an impersonal commentator. Mr. Olson's ingenuity leaves out, however, the most obvious thing. The poem is not only *about* the boys of summer in their ruin, but *by* one of them. It seeks to give oratorical emphasis and nobility of gesture to a subject which literature can usually touch on only furtively or with condescending pity—the subjects of the sexual frustrations suffered by, and also the agonizing intense erotic imaginings that obsess, in an advanced and therefore in many ways repressive civilization like our own, the middle-class adolescent male. Thomas began to write his poems in his late 'teens. It is in his late 'teens that the sexual desires of the male are at their most urgent, and that his sexual potency is at its greatest; it is in his late 'teens also, in our society, that he has least chance of satisfying or exercising one or the other in a normal fashion. What Thomas is doing in many of his earliest poems is finding poetic symbols adequate to this experience, which is centrally important in most masculine life-histories, but which it is difficult to treat not only with literary, but even with ordinary, decency. He also expresses the wider sense of traumatic shock, a shock at once of awe and horror, which is likely to accompany, for any young male in our civilization, the full imaginative realization of 'the facts of life'. He went on to do things more broadly significant than this; but this, in itself, was a significant achievement.

IV

Thomas's second volume, *Twenty-five Poems*, brought him on the whole more praise and more fame than his first. Dame Edith Sitwell, in particular, saluted it with enthusiasm in a memorable short review in *The Observer*. Yet like many second volumes of verse—and like all second novels!—*Twenty-five Poems* is in many ways unsatisfactory. It shows Thomas experimenting with new themes, new images, new styles. Two poems in the book have, indeed, been much praised, but to me it seems undeservedly. One is 'And Death Shall Have No Dominion', which strikes me as a set of large but rather empty rhetorical gestures, a poem in which the poet faced by the harsh fact of death is not properly confronting it but 'cheering himself up'. The other is Thomas's one political poem, 'The Hand That Signed the Paper'. That ends with this stanza:

> The five kings count the dead but do not soften
> The crusted wound nor stroke the brow;
> A hand rules pity as a hand rules heaven;
> Hands have no tears to flow.

That stanza has been praised as an example of a poet splendidly and successfully mixing metaphors; may not some, with all respect, find it rather an example of bathos?

There are other poems in *Twenty-five Poems* like 'Should Lanterns Shine', which show us that Thomas had been reading both Rilke, probably in translation, and Yeats:

> And from her lips the faded pigments fall,
> The mummy clothes expose an ancient breast. . .

I have heard many years of telling,
And many years should see some change.

The ball I threw while playing in the park
Has not yet reached the ground.

Such lines show a minor good taste in a composite manner which is essentially *not* Thomas's. He had become, in his second volume, much more uncertain about the way he was going than in his first, and there is one poem which expresses his doubts admirably. Was, perhaps, his poetic method a method of self-deception?

I have longed to move away
From the hissing of the spent lie
And the old terror's continual cry
Growing more terrible as the day
Goes over the hill into the deep sea;
I have longed to move away
From the repetition of salutes,
For there are ghosts in the air
And ghostly echoes on paper,
And the thunder of calls and notes.

I have longed to move away but am afraid;
Some life, yet unspent, might explode
Out of the old lie burning on the ground,
And, crackling into the air, leave me half-blind.
Neither by night's ancient fear,
The parting of hat from hair,
Pursed lips at the receiver,
Shall I fall to death's feather.
By these I would not care to die,
Half convention and half lie.

Thomas rarely uses in his poetry the wit and humor of his personal conversation and his narrative prose. But here he manages to evade deep fears by mocking at shallow fears: '. . . night's ancient fear,/ The parting of hat from hair' is simply a grotesque image of a man's being so frightened that his hair stands on end and pushes his hat off: as in a comic drawing by such a cartoonist as H. M. Bateman. The 'receiver' is simply a telephone receiver, and poet's lips are 'pursed', as in a melodrama, because he is receiving a horrifying message. 'Death's feather' has no deep, obscure symbolic meaning but is simply an allusion to the humorous Cockney phrase: 'You could 'ave knocked me down with a feather!' (That, I think, is its use here; but it is quite a favourite phrase of Thomas's, and what he has often in mind is the custom of holding a feather to a dead man's lips to make sure he is no longer breathing.) These thrillerish fears, or self-induced, half-pleasant shudders, are 'half convention and half lie'. Neither the poetic imagination, nor sane, practical common sense, can afford to pay much attention to them. But the spent lie, from which some life, yet unspent, might explode as it lay burning on the ground, is another matter; so are the ghosts, the ghostly echoes on paper, the repetition of salutes.

This, in fact, is the one poem of Thomas's whose subject-matter is poetical self-criticism. The poet is pondering whether he ought to make a bonfire—accompanied by small fireworks, perhaps dangerous ones—of childish fears, obsessions, and superstitions; a bonfire, also, in his writing of poetry of 'given' phrases, lines, and images—'ghostly echoes on paper'—about whose source and meaning he is not clear. He is wondering whether he ought to become, like so many of his contemporaries of the 1930s, an 'adult' and 'socially concious' poet. He decides that he cannot afford to make this bonfire for the reason that the poetic lie, the undue fearsomeness and rhetoric—the 'ghosts' and the 'repetition of salutes'—are somehow bound up with the possibility of the full, life-giving poetic vision. The old lie, exploding, might leave him half-blind; the terrors from which he wants to move away are somehow inextricably linked with an image full of peace, dignity and beauty:

> . . . as the day
> Goes over the hill into the deep sea.

I have been trying here to follow Mr. Robert Graves' ideal technique of making a poem's drift clear by expounding it, at greater length, mainly in its own words. If the reader agrees with me about the poem's drift, he will admire the insight into his own poetic scope which Thomas shows in this poem. He was right to take the risk of regressiveness, rather than cut the tangle of links that bound him with his childhood; the obsession with childhood, even with its fictions and fantasies, was to lead him in the end to a rediscovery of innocence.

The most important and most obscure poems in *Twenty-five Poems* are, however, the ten sonnets beginning 'Altarwise by owl-light.' Mr. Elder Olson has argued very persuasively that these sonnets evoke in succession pagan despair, the new hope consequent upon the birth of Christ, the Christian despair consequent upon the Crucifixion, and the renewed Christian hope consequent upon the Resurrection; very ingeniously, but perhaps a little less persuasively, he has suggested that these ideas are expressed through an almost pedantically exact symbolism drawn from the movements of the constellation Hercules, standing both for man, and for the sainthood of Christ. For other readers, the sonnets had always seemed the most baffling of Dylan Thomas's works, though to a sympathetic reader the Christian overtones and the occasional presence of 'the grand style' were obvious from the start. There are fragments in these sonnets—which as wholes remain, in Dr. Daiches' phrases, oppressive and congested even after one has grasped and accepted the main lines of Mr. Olson's exposition —more nobly eloquent than anything Dylan Thomas ever wrote:

> This was the crucifixion on the mountain,
> Time's nerve in vinegar, the gallow grave
> As tarred with blood as the bright thorns I wept . . .
>
> Green as beginning, let the garden diving
> Soar, with its two black towers, to that Day
> When the worm builds with the gold straws of venom
> My nest of mercies in the rude, red tree.

The sonnets, a failure as a whole, splendid in parts such as these, are important because they announce the current of orthodox Christian feeling—feeling rather than thought—which was henceforth increasingly to dominate Thomas's work in poetry.

V

Thomas's third volume, *The Map of Love,* which contained prose pieces as well as poems, appeared in 1939, on the verge of the Second World War. It had a great and in many ways unfortunate influence on some of the younger English writers of that time, in particular on the movement called at first the New Apocalypse, and later, when it became a wider and even more shapeless stream of tendency, the New Romanticism. The prose pieces in *The Map of Love* were not at all like the straightforwardly descriptive and narrative, funny and pathetic pieces of *Portrait of the Artist as a Young Dog,* which came out in the following year, 1940. They were much influenced by the belated English interest in the French Surrealist and Dadaist movements. Mr. David Gascoyne's excellent short book on Surrealism had appeared two or three years before *The Map of Love,* and more recently there had been Herbert Read's anthology of Surrealist texts and paintings published by Faber. The prose pieces in *The Map of*

Love are not strictly Surrealist—they are too carefully worked over, as to their prose rhythms, and so on—but they have a semi-Surrealist flavour in their superficial incoherence, their reliance on shock tactics, and the cruelty or obscenity, or both, of much of their imagery. They are failures on the whole, artistically, but they have a real interest in relation to the total pattern of Thomas's work. They are his *pièces noires,* the pieces in which he accepts evil: they are one side of a medal of which the other side is Thomas's later celebration of innocence, and the benignity of the Reverend Eli Jenkins. In writing these pieces, Thomas was grappling with, and apparently succeeded in absorbing and overcoming, what Jungians call the Shadow.

Perhaps because of the comparative failure of these prose pieces, *The Map of Love* was the least popular of Thomas's volumes. It cannot have been printed in large numbers, or have gone into many impressions, for it is almost impossible—where with the other volumes it is fairly easy—to procure a second-hand copy of it. Yet it contains some of Thomas's most memorable poems, chief among them the elegy 'After the Funeral' for his elderly cousin, Ann Jones. This is a piece of baroque eloquence; in the poet's own words,

> . . . this for her is a monstrous image blindly
> Magnified out of praise. . . .

There are, however, three or four lines towards the end which transcend the baroque manner and which rank with the passages already quoted from the sonnets as among Thomas's finest isolated fragments. Their appeal is simple, human and direct:

> I know her scrubbed and sour humble hands
> Lie with religion in their cramp, her threadbare
> Whisper in a damp word, her wits drilled hollow,
> Her fist of a face died clenched on a round pain;
> And sculptured Ann is seventy years of stone.

Other, slighter poems in *The Map of Love* have interest as explorations of new aptitudes. A slight but charming poem, 'Once it was the colour of saying', gives a foretaste of one of Thomas's main later themes, the reminiscent celebration, through the evoking of a landscape that the perspective of time has made legendary, of childish innocence:

> Once it was the colour of saying
> Soaked my table the uglier side of a hill
> With a capsized field where a school sat still

And a black and white patch of girls grew playing . . .
The gentle seasides of saying I must undo
That all the charmingly drowned arise to cockcrow and kill.
When I whistled with mitching boys through a reservoir park
Where at night we stoned the cold and cuckoo
Lovers in the dirt of their leafy beds,
The shade of their trees was a word of many shades
And a lamp of lightning for the poor in the dark;
Now my saying shall be my undoing,
And every stone I wind off like a reel.

The 'capsized field' there—looking as if it had been upset or overturned on the hillside, and also, from the distance, just the size of a schoolboy's cap—is a delightful example of the subdued punning which a careful reader of Thomas soon learns to look for everywhere. Yet even as late as 1939, Thomas's voice was still not always quite his own. Or rather, he had his own voice, but he would still from time to time try on other people's to see how they fitted. Asked, for instance, who was the author of the following stanza from *The Map of Love* an intelligent reader might well name Mr. C. Day Lewis or Mr. W. H. Auden. The turn and the mood of the last two lines, in particular, suggests that preoccupation of most of the poets of the 1930s with harsh historical necessity, which Dylan Thomas on the whole did not share:

Bound by a sovereign strip, we lie,
Watch yellow, wish for wind to blow away
The strata of the shore and drown red rock;
But wishes breed not, neither
Can we fend off rock arrival. . . .

It was biological necessity, rather, that preoccupied Thomas. That comes out in the last poem in this volume, flatly melancholy in its tone, but displaying a gift, new and unexpected in Thomas, for the forceful gnomic statement:

Twenty-four years remind the tears of my eyes.
(Bury the dead for fear that they walk to the grave in labour.)
In the groin of the natural doorway I crouched like a tailor
Sewing a shroud for a journey
By the light of the meat-eating sun.
Dressed to die, the sensual strut begun,
With my red veins full of money,
In the final direction of the elementary town
I advance for as long as forever is.

VI

Among many critics of Thomas, there has been a tendency to attempt to enclose him within a formula; that of the man-nature equation used here to throw light on *Eighteen Poems:* that of adolescent sexual excitement used here for the same purpose; that of the religious celebrator of natural process; that of the disorderly breeder of images, struggling from sleep to wakefulness, and so on. There has been no general agreement about which formula is right, but there has been a general agreement that some formula would be, and also that there is a remarkable similarity about all Thomas's poems. I have been trying, in this sketch, to deal with each volume of Thomas's in turn, almost as if I had been reviewing it when it first came out. I hope I have conveyed my impression—an impression which, when it first came solidly home, very much surprised me—that in tone, in style, in subject-matter Thomas is a much more various, a much less narrowly consistent poet, than people make him out to be. In *Eighteen Poems*, for instance, there is, in the ordinary senses of these words, no human or religious interest; the sonnets, at least, in *Twenty-five Poems* have a remarkable religious interest; and 'After the Funeral' and some other poems in *The Map of Love* have a human interest that is new.

Thomas was found unfit for military service and spent most of the years of the Second World War in Wales, coming up to London from time to time to see his friends, do broadcasting work, or meet publishers. He never tackled the war directly as a subject, but at least two of his poems, the obscure but powerful title poem of *Deaths and Entrances* and the famous 'A Refusal to Mourn' have, for background, the bombing raids on London. I have been told that some work he did on a documentary film on the bombing raids, which in the end was found too grim for public release, had a profound effect on his imagination; an effect that may partly explain the retreat, in many of his later poems, to the themes of childhood innocence and country peace. Certainly, in these years, Thomas did more and more tend to turn, for the central themes of his poetry, to his Welsh childhood. The same episodes which, in *Portrait of the Artist as a Young Dog*, had provided material for comedy, now, more deeply explored, brought forth a transformation of memory into vision; a vision of a lost paradise regained.

Thomas's last English volume of new poems, *Deaths and Entrances*, came out in 1946. It increases the impression of variety, and of steady development, which the earlier volumes, read in the order of their appearance, give. It contains a remarkable number of successful poems of notably different kinds. One kind, in particular, at once caught the fancy of a wide public. It is a kind which, very roughly throwing out words at a venture, one might call the recaptured-childish-landscape, semi-fairy-tale, semi-ode kind: more concisely, the long poem of formal celebration. Such, for instance, are seven late poems by Thomas: 'Poem in October', 'A Winter's Tale', 'Fern Hill', 'In Country Sleep', 'Over Sir John's Hill', 'Poem on His Birthday', 'In the White Giant's Thigh'. All these poems have a larger and looser, a more immediately apprehensible rhythmical movement than most of Thomas's earlier work. They do not aim at dark, packed, and concentrated, but at bright, expansive effects. Their landscapes are always partly magical landscapes. Their common flavour can, however, perhaps be better conveyed by a series of quotations than by such remarks:

Bird, he was brought low,
Burning in the bride bed of love, in the whirl-
Pool at the wanting centre, in the folds
Of paradise, in the spun bud of the world.
And she rose with him flowering in her melting snow . . .

'A Winter's Tale'

It was my thirtieth year to heaven
Woke to my hearing from harbour and neighbour wood
And the mussel pooled and heron
Priested shore
The morning beckon
With water praying and call of seagull and rook
And the knock of sailing boats on the net webbed wall
Myself to set foot
That second
In the still sleeping town and set forth. . . .

'Poem in October'

I hear the bouncing hills
Grow larked and greener at berry brown
Fall and the dew larks sing
Taller this thunderclap spring, and how
More spanned with angels rise
The mansouled fiery islands! Oh,
Holier than their eyes,

And my shining men no more alone
As I sail out to die . . .
'Poem on His Birthday'

Now as I was young and easy under the apple boughs
About the lilting house and happy as the grass was green,
The night above the dingle starry,
Time let me hail and climb
Golden in the heydays of his eyes,
And honoured among wagons I was prince of the apple towns
And once below a time I lordly had the trees and leaves
Trail with daisies and barley
Down the rivers of the windfall light.
'Fern Hill'

The dust of their kettles and clocks swings to and fro
Where the hay rides now or the bracken kitchens rust
As the arc of the billhooks that flashed the hedges low
And cut the birds' boughs that the minstrel sap ran red.
They from the houses where the harvest kneels, hold me hard,
Who heard from the tall bell said down the Sundays of the dead
And the rain wring out its tongues on the faded years,
Teach me the love that is evergreen after the fall leaved
Grave, after the Belovéd on the grass gulfed cross is scrubbed
Off by the sun and Daughters no longer grieved
Save by their long desires in the fox cubbed
Streets or hungering in the crumbled wood: to these
Hale dead and deathless do the women of the hill
Love for ever meridian through the courters' trees
And the daughters of darkness flame like Fawkes fires still.
'In the White Giant's Thigh'

Neither the style nor the mood of these passages would have been easily predictable even by an exceptionally acute critic of Dylan Thomas's earlier verse. The mood is close to some of the verse of Vaughan and some of the prose of Traherne, or to take a closer and more contemporary comparison from another art, there is something in this glowing transformation of everyday things—a boy in an apple tree, a young man going out for an early walk in a seaside town on his birthday—that recalls some drawings by David Jones or some paintings by Stanley Spencer. One would not, with the same confidence, mention Wordsworth or Blake; there is a kind of massiveness and sobriety in Wordsworth's explorations of childish memory, there is a naked directness in Blake's *Song of Innocence,* that we do not find here, Thomas, like Vaughan, Traherne, Spencer, or Jones, could be described affectionately as 'quaint', his vision of paradise as a 'touching' one; such epithets would be out of place if one were discussing Blake or Wordsworth.

The style, also, has changed. Its main mark is no longer an obscure concision, a dense packing of images, but a rapid and muscular fluency that puts one in mind sometimes of a more relaxed Hopkins, sometimes of a more concentrated Swinburne. The tone of voice is a deliberately exalted one. The seven poems I have mentioned, and some of which I have quoted, are likely to remain Thomas's most popular pieces. But for the special effect he is aiming at in them he has eliminated that quality of cloudy pregnancy which, rightly or wrongly, was for many readers one of the main fascinations of his earlier poems. It is not that these eloquent, sincere, and moving long poems are in any sense shallow; they make us gloriously free of a visionary world; yet there does remain a sense, if the Irishism is permissible, in which the depths are all on the surface. The poems give what they have to give, grandly, at once. One does not go back to them to probe and question. A passion for probing and questioning can, of course, vitiate taste. Yet there will always remain critics (by his own confession, Professor William Empson is one) to whom these lucid late successes are less 'interesting' than other late poems, more dense and obscure, much less certainly successful but carrying the suggestion that, if they *were* successful, their success might be something higher still.

The quality that Thomas jettisoned in these late, long poems, rightly for his purposes, was a quality of dramatic compression. The title poem of *Deaths and Entrances* is, for instance, almost certainly on the whole a failure: if only for the reason that Thomas does not provide us with clues enough to find out what exactly is happening in the poem, and yet does provide us with clues enough to make us bother about what is happening. The setting is certainly the bombing raids on London:

> On almost the incendiary eve
>   Of several near deaths,
> When one at the great least of your best loved
>   And always known must leave
> Lions and fires of his flying breath,
>   Of your immortal friends
> Who'd raise the organs of the counted dust
>   To shoot and sing your praise,
> One who called deepest down shall hold his peace

That cannot sink or cease
Endlessly to his wound
In many married London's estranging grief.

To read that stanza is like seeing a man make a set of noble gestures on a tragic stage and not quite catching, because of some failure of acoustics, what he is saying. Yet the gestures *are* noble, and I would claim that the last line in particular,

In many married London's estranging grief,

is a fragmentary achievement of a kind of poetry higher in itself than the dingles and the apple boughs and the vale mist riding through the haygold stalls and even than the very lovely heron-priested shore; a kind of poetry which grasps and drastically unifies an unimaginably complex set of interrelated pains. Such a line suggests the immanence in Thomas, in his last years, of a poetry of mature human awareness.

There are some shorter poems in *Deaths and Entrances* that seem similarly to reach out for, and sometimes to grasp, a mature human awareness. Among them are the beautifully constructed 'The Conversation of Prayer', 'A Refusal to Mourn the Death, by Fire, of a Child in London' (of which Mr. William Empson has given a masterly exposition); the two very short, which are also among Thomas's few very personal, poems, 'To Others than You' and 'In My Craft and Sullen Art'; the plangent *villanelle*, with its Yeatsian overtones, addressed by Thomas to his dying father, 'Do Not Go Gentle into That Good Night', of which the intended sequel, recently reassembled by Mr. Vernon Watkins from Thomas's working notes, would have been an even more striking poem: and with less certainty 'There Was a Saviour'.

One of these poems, 'The Conversation of Prayer', is worth looking at on the page as an example of Thomas's extraordinary virtuosity as a creator of textures. I have marked, in italics, the hidden rhymes:

The conversation of *prayers* about to be *said*
By the child going to *bed* and the man on the *stairs*
Who climbs to his dying *love* in her high *room*,
The one not caring to *whom* in his sleep he will *move*,
And the other full of *tears* that she will be *dead*,

Turns in the dark on the *sound* they know will *arise*
Into the answering *skies* from the green *ground*,
From the man on the *stairs* and the child by his *bed*.
The sound about to be *said* in the two *prayers*
For sleep in a safe *land* and the love who *dies*

Will be the same grief *flying*. Whom shall they *calm*?
Shall the child sleep *unharmed* or the man be *crying*?
The conversation of *prayers* about to be *said*
Turns on the quick and the *dead*, and the man on the *stairs*
Tonight shall find no *dying* but alive and *warm*

In the fire of his *care* his love in the high *room*.
And the child not caring to *whom* he climbs his *prayer*
Shall drown in a grief as *deep* as his true *grave*,
And mark the dark eyed *wave*, through the eyes of *sleep*,
Dragging him up the *stairs* to one who lies *dead*.

Apart from the extraordinary complexity of this rhyme scheme, the reader should notice that the vast majority of the words in the poem, most of the exceptions being participles, are monosyllables. The only word that is more than a disyllable is 'conversation' and it is also the most abstract word in the poem and the word that, as it were, states the poet's theme. No doubt any skilful craftsman might invent and carry through a form like this as a metrical exercise. But Thomas's poem does not read at all like an exercise; most readers, in fact, do not notice the rhyme-scheme till it is pointed out to them. Again, most poets would find it hard to construct a series of stanzas mainly in monosyllables without giving the effect of monotony. Thomas's line is so subtly varied as to defy an attempt at rule-of-thumb scansion. It is a four-stress line, with feet very freely substituted, and in one case the four feet are four anapaests but with a dragging effect, because of their setting, that anapaests do not usually have:

For the *man*/ on the *stairs*/ and the *child*/ by his *bed*.

Usually, however, the effect is far more subtle:

Who *climbs*/ to his *dy*/ing *love*/ in her/ *high room*.

There we have an iambus, an anapest, an iambus and an unstressed two-syllable foot followed, according to English custom, by a two-stress foot. And that, to be sure, seems to make *five* stresses; but because 'high' chimes loudly with the first syllable of 'dying', earlier in the line, the word 'room' has actually only a secondary stress. Such minutiae are dry reading except for the teacher of metrics, but since Thomas has been accused by some critics, such as Mr. Geoffrey Grigson, of careless and slapdash writing it is worth providing an almost mechanical demonstration of his mastery of his craft.

Yet the craft exists only for the sake of the art. 'The Conversation of Prayer', perhaps one of the most perfect of Thomas's short poems, may have been neglected because the idea around which it moves is, at least in Protestant countries, becoming marginal to our culture. It is the idea of the reversibility of grace; the idea that all prayers and all good acts co-operate for the benefit of all men, and that God, in His inscrutable mercy, can give the innocent the privilege of suffering some of the tribulations which have been incurred by redeemable sinners. The man in this poem might be the father of the boy, or he might have no connection with him; or the man and the boy might be the same person at different stages of their life histories. Both pray, and there is a sense in which prayer is eternally heard. The boy prays for 'sleep unharmed', for a night undisturbed by bad dreams, and the man whose wife or lover is dying prays that she may be better. The prayers, as it were, cross in the air, the man is granted his wish, for one night at least the sick woman is happy and well again, but the sleeping boy has to endure all the man's nightmare of climbing up the stairs to discover the loved one dead. Only this idea makes sense of the poem. How, it may be asked, could Thomas, bred a Bible Protestant, and never interested in abstruse notions, have come across it, or worked it out for himself? Perhaps it is an idea that all men who really struggle with prayer do, at least implicitly, work out for themselves. For, though Thomas's attitude to life was, as he grew older, an increasingly religious, and in a broad sense an increasingly Christian one, he was certainly not a poet, like Mr. Eliot for instance, to whom dry theological and metaphysical speculations were, in themselves, poetically exciting. His world was not a conceptual world and his coherency is not a conceptual coherency. Across the page in the *Collected Poems* from 'The Conversation of Prayer' there is the famous 'A Refusal to Mourn', whose drift Professor Empson has summed up as a 'pantheistic pessimism'. Thomas's longest personal religious poem, 'Vision and Prayer' offers us a naked confrontation of the desire for utter extinction with the hope of personal salvation. The last line of 'A Refusal to Mourn',

After the first death, there is no other,

has a resonance and authority both for unbelievers and believers. At one level, the meaning may be, as Professor Empson suggests, that life is a cruel thing and that the utter finality of physical death is welcome; but the logically contradictory Christian overtones—'Do not let us fear death, since, once the body is dead, the soul lives for ever'—cannot possibly be excluded. We must respect the baffling simplicity of Thomas's unitary response and not impose abstract categories on him.

One poem in *Deaths and Entrances,* 'The Hunchback in the Park', a more descriptive and 'realistic' poem than Thomas was in the habit of writing, may help us, perhaps, to grasp this simplicity by watching it operate at a less profound level. This begins with a long but not obscure two-stanza sentence:

> The hunchback in the park
> A solitary mister
> Propped between trees and water
> From the opening of the garden lock
> That lets the trees and water enter
> Until the Sunday sombre bell at dark
>
> Eating bread from a newspaper
> Drinking water from the chained cup
> That the children filled with gravel
> In the fountain basin where I sailed my ship
> Slept at night in a dog kennel
> But nobody chained him up. . . .

The boys in the park, of whom Thomas is one, mock and torment the solitary hunchback who, ignoring them, seeks happiness in a dream in which the park stands for all the richness of life from which he is locked out; and the boys are locked out from the poetic understanding of that richness which the hunchback has attained to through deprivation and pain. They are part of the richness, and how should they understand it (that may be part of the implication of the phrase, 'the wild boys innocent as strawberries', which several critics have found sentimental)? Hunter and hunted; mocked and mocker; boys and hunchback; growth and decay; life and death; dream and reality: all sets of polar opposites are, for Thomas, at some level equally holy and necessary, holy is the hawk, holy is the dove. . . . This theme, the coincidence of opposites, runs through all Thomas's work and the end of this poem states it clearly: how the hunchback, the 'old dog sleeper'

> Made all day until bell time
> A woman figure without fault
> Straight as a young elm
> Straight and tall from his crooked bones
> That she might stand in the night
> After the lock and chains

All night in the unmade park
After the railings and shrubberies
The birds the grass the trees the lake
And the wild boys innocent as strawberries
Had followed the hunchback
To his kennel in the dark.

Other poems in *Deaths and Entrances* show Thomas experimenting along still other lines. 'Ballad of the Long-Legged Bait' in his only poem, with the partial exception of 'A Winter's Tale', of which the movement is primarily a narrative one. It is a phantasmagoric narrative like Rimbaud's *Bateau Ivre*. Its immediate impact is extremely confusing. Mr. Elder Olson has worked out a logical structure for it. The poet goes fishing in a magic boat, using a naked woman for a bait, and all the sea creatures eat her up, and then as in the Book of Revelation, 'there is no more sea'. She is a woman, and she is also his heart, and he has been sacrificing the desires of his heart to restore a lost Eden. In the end, Eden is restored, and so is the woman, and the heart in its lost innocence; the poet steps out of the boat, now on dry land and

stands alone at the door of his home
With his long-legged heart in his hand.

The poem, thus, for Mr. Olson is a kind of small allegory about the struggle inside Thomas, a typically Welsh struggle, between natural sensuality and a puritan mysticism. Thomas himself, more modestly, over a bar in New York, said that the poem is about how a young man goes out fishing for fun and games, for all the excitements of the wild free life, and finds in the end that he has caught a wife, some children, and a little house. The poem, even with the help of these clues, remains unsatisfactory—it leaves one feeling a little sea-sick—but it is yet another example of Thomas's eagerness, throughout his poetic career, to go on extending his range. And as a whole *Deaths and Entrances* does remain one of the two or three most impressive single volumes of poetry published in English over the last ten years.

VII

Let us now try to sum up. In the few years since his death, Dylan Thomas's reputation as a poet has undoubtedly suffered at least a mild slump. He was always far too directly and massively an emotional poet, and in the detail of his language often too confusing and sometimes apparently confused a poet, to be acceptable to the analytical critics of the *Scrutiny* school who today exercise a far wider influence on general English taste than they did four or five years ago. Quite apart from that, there is quite generally in literary history a time lag, sometimes of as long as twenty or thirty years, between a notable writer's death and the attempt to reach a balanced judgment on him. The difficulty, also, at least at the level of attempting to explain in prose what the poet is doing, of Dylan Thomas's work has meant that the three short books so far published about him, by Mr. Henry Treece in his life-time (a revised edition has been published since Thomas's death), and since his death by Mr. Elder Olson and Mr. Derek Stanford, have been much more concerned with exposition of his sense than with attempts to 'place' him or even to illustrate in detail his strictly poetic art. Mr. Stanford thinks he may rank in English literary history rather as Gray ranks; this may be too high an estimate, for where is Thomas's long poem of mature moral interest, where is his 'Elegy Written in a Country Churchyard'? But he might well rank as Collins ranks; he has written some perfect poems, his poetic personality is a completely individual one, he brings in a new note. One might call Gray a minor major poet; one might call Collins a major minor poet. That, possibly, is also Thomas's rank, but at the same time we should be profoundly suspicious of this class-room, or examination-school, attitude to poets. There is a very real and profound sense in which poets do not compete with each other. No true poet offers us something for which anything else, by any other true poet, is really a substitute. It is enough, for the purposes here, to insist that Thomas was a good poet and worth our attention; and to attempt to define, and make vivid, his specific quality.

The reaction against Thomas, since his death, has, in fact, really been concerned to deny that Thomas was a good poet; or to assert that he might have been a good poet, but cheated poetically, in a way that disqualifies him. Thus, Mr. John Wain has remarked that a meaning, or a set of meanings, can nearly always be got out of Thomas's poems but that the critic's worry is whether Thomas ever cared much what the meanings were so long as the thing sounded all right. Even more sharply, in his witty and provocative Clark Lectures, *The Crowning Privilege*, Mr. Robert Graves condemns Thomas as a poet who takes care of the sound and lets the sense take care of itself: Mr. Graves compares Thomas to a soldier firing off a rifle at random while a confederate in the butts—the confederate being the gullible reviewer of contemporary poetry—keeps on signalling bulls and inners, whether or not the bullet has come anywhere near the target.

How much justice is there in such strictures? There are certainly poems by Dylan Thomas of which many readers must find even the main drift, as sense, hard to grasp; there is hardly any poem of Thomas's of which some details, at least, are not likely to puzzle most readers. But I hope I have shown two things: that in Thomas's best poems there is a coherent meaning, and that it is not always mechanically the same meaning. It is simply not true that he went on writing, with variations of form and imagery, the same archetypal poem over and over again; he grew and changed and at his death was still developing, in the direction of a wider and more genial human scope. The importance of *Under Milk Wood* is that it shows him, at the very end of his life, transforming into a kind of poetry that humorous apprehension of life which, in *Portrait of the Artist as a Young Dog*, is still something quite separate from poetry. Had he lived, he might have worked into his poetry the shrewdness and the gaiety that make him a first-rate entertainer. His feeling for life, at the end, was growing, not shrinking; and the separate elements of it, the outer and the inner being, the legendary sweet funny man and the fine solemn poet, were growing together.

Let me end this sketch by quoting a short, a very personal poem of Thomas's, which warns us wholesomely against the kind of undue familiarity to which his public legend, the memory of his personality, the critic's dangerous passion for summary judgments, might all invite us:

To Others Than You

Friend by enemy I call you out.

You with a bad coin in your socket,
You my friend there with a winning air
Who palmed the lie on me when you looked
Brassily at my shyest secret,
Enticed with twinkling bits of the eye
Til the sweet tooth of my love bit dry,
Rasped at last, and I stumbled and sucked,
Whom I now conjure to stand as a thief
In the memory worked by mirrors,
With unforgettably smiling act,
Quickness of hand in the velvet glove
And my whole heart under your hammer,

Were once such a creature, so gay and frank
A desireless familiar
I never thought to utter and think
While you displaced a truth in the air,

That though I loved them for their faults
As much as for their good,
My friends were enemies on stilts,
With their heads in a cunning cloud.

I hope that the truths displaced in the air in these pages have been displaced towards their proper locations; I hope that in all I have been saying my head, too, has not been in a cunning cloud. I remember Dylan Thomas's own head, benignly calm, as it looked in a photograph of his death-mask which a close friend of his, the poet Ruthven Todd, brought to show to Thomas's friends in London: it should have made me think of two lines of Thomas's, not well known:

And when blind sleep drops on the spying senses,
The heart is sensual, though five eyes break.

The Religious Poet

W. S. MERWIN

Apart from the verse prologue to his *Collected Poems* (1934–1952, J. M. Dent, 12 s. 6 d.), and the poem 'In My Craft or Sullen Art', both of which I mean to discuss later, the two salient remarks that I have known Dylan Thomas to make about his own poetry were one in a letter to Henry Treece where he described the manner in which he wrote poetry, and the prose statement at the beginning of the *Collected Poems* concerning the purpose of his poetry: 'These poems', he says, 'are written for the love of Man and in praise of God.' It is not because I am taking Dylan Thomas at his prose—a poet may be the last person to be able to speak accurately, in prose, about his own poetry—but because I am trying to take his poems at their word, that I wish to consider Dylan Thomas as a religious poet, and notice some of the means, the craft and language with which he has made his themes.

I think it is safer at this point not to set up a pair of artificial antinomies: as it were, the religious artist and whatever we may call his opposite, but to start by saying that the religious artist is primarily a celebrator. A celebrator in the ritual sense: a maker and performer of a rite. And also a celebrator in the sense of one who participates in the rite, and whom the rite makes joyful. That which he celebrates is Creation, and more particularly the human condition. For he will see himself, man, as a metaphor or analogy of the world. The human imagination will be for him the image of the divine imagination; the work of art and the artist will be analogous with the world and its Creator. In both man and the world he will perceive a force of love or creation which is more divine than either man or the world, and a force of death or destruction which is more terrible than man or the world. Although his ultimate vision is the tragic one of creation

From *Adam International Review*, 1953.

through suffering, his ultimate sense will be of joy. For in the act of love, the central act of Creation, he will see the force of love, in man and the world, merge inextricably and mysteriously with the force of death, and yet from this union new creation born through suffering. And his vocation as an individual artist will be to remake in terms of celebration the details of life, to save that which is individual and thereby mortal, by imagining it, making it, in terms of what he conceives to be the eternal. The emotion which drives him to this making will be compassion, or better, love of Life and the particulars of life.

The poems of Dylan Thomas are peculiarly consistent: as I understand them, they are the work of a religious poet trying, at times desperately, to find and come to grips with his subject, finding it, and making it into a poetry of celebration—into some of the greatest poetry that has been written in our time. How much of this was consciously aimed at, and how much was at least half-dark necessity, I suspect but do not know; but I think the religious theme as I have described it is the main vein of Dylan Thomas's poetry. He has written a number of genuine personal poems in which the 'I' is overtly the individual poet, but these for the most part are well along in his work, and many of them deal with the religious theme from their particular vantage. In most of the earlier poems the 'I' is 'man' trying to find a means of imagining and thereby redeeming his condition; much of the seemingly baroque and motiveless 'agony' of the earlier poems stems from the desperateness of this need.

The brilliant and powerful first poem in the book, 'I see the boys of summer', presents doom as the final reality in the very moments of man's euphory, and insofar as man ignores or is truly ignorant of this fact about his condition, the poet describes him with contempt. He recommends that the passage of time, and death, be challenged and embraced, but he can give no reason why they should be—birth and death are an endless loveless dull round—and the poem ends in ironic despair. But by the third poem, 'A process in the weather of the heart', which describes the growing of death in life, the natural world and the human body are consistently metaphoric of each other; the heart at the end of the poem is the sea, which 'gives up its dead', though it does so through its own death. In the fourth poem, 'Before I knocked', man is seen as Christ his divine image, and there is an attempt at presenting human life as a continuity by describing the prenatal growth of the consciousness of death, and in the fifth, 'The force that through the green fuse drives the flower', the doom within life is described again, but described because of compassion for things mortal, and the compassion makes the poet at once wish to be able to communicate with all other things that are doomed, to tell them he understands their plight because his own is similar, and makes him feel the depth to which he is inarticulate and painfully unable to do so.

But dumb compassion for mortality, though relieved by this remarkable poem and by the beautiful but hardly more than putative sea-faiths of 'Where once the waters of your face', could not rest content. In the poem, 'If I were tickled by the rub of love', the poet states that if love were real to him he would have the means of facing the fear of death; the poem's remarkable and hopeful conclusion, since the reality of love does not seem attainable, is 'I would be tickled by the rub that is:/Man by my metaphor'. And in the next poem, 'Our Eunuch Dreams', he examines 'reality' and its simulacra in terms of each other, concluding that the world is real, and is an image of man, and the poem ends in faith and joy. The poem, 'Especially when the October wind', takes this development a stage further: here the poet first fully assumes his Orphic role, celebrating a particular day, a particular place, in autumn, offering to make it, or aspects of it, and as he names and celebrates them, doing so.

This is moving forward a bit too fast and smooth; (if the poems are not arranged chronologically, then as far as I can see Dylan Thomas has put them in an order admirably suited to present his theme). For a day in autumn, or even man's condition may to some extent be named and remade and redeemed without love, but personal particular death remains real to the poet. And without the reality of love, the 'Have faith . . . And who remain shall flower as they love', of 'Our Eunuch Dreams', comes to ring hollow to him. The perception of death as the very urge and joy in the act of love, in the poem, 'When like a running grave', makes both sexual love and the love of the world impossible: the poet advocates despair of either and, instead, love of death himself for his devilish iniquity. And in 'From love's first fever to her plague' Dylan Thomas vainly tried, as a way out, to make a myth of his own physical growth, but concludes that even the creations of the imagination are futile: 'The root of tongues ends in a spent-out cancer'. This poem, reasonably enough if what I am saying makes sense, is one of the few poems of Dylan Thomas's which seems uncompleted, less as if he had not bothered to write it out to an end than as if he had known no end to write it out to.

In the next poem, 'In the beginning', he found what he needed: the poem is about creation, and sees the creation of the world as the metaphor of the creation of man. It sees the individual man through his divine image Christ; (it is worth comparing this poem with 'Before I knocked' to see how much more sure of his subject Dylan Thomas has become); and it sees imaginative creation and natural creation as one: 'In the beginning was the word, the word/That from the solid bases of the light/Abstracted all the letters of the void'. 'Light breaks where no sun shines' is a further elaboration of the vision of man as a metaphor of the world.

I can see several reasons why the next two poems, 'I fellowed sleep', and 'I dreamed my genesis' should have been written as about dreams. 'I fellowed sleep' is a visionary poem about uncreated ghosts, the dreams of the world which the world climbs always to create. A dream can be a kind of metaphor—as in 'Our Eunuch Dreams'—once the imagination has harnessed it; but the *sense* of the subject is not always certain in this poem, which I take to mean that it would have been almost impossible for Dylan Thomas to have approached it more directly—and even St. Augustine admitted that our responsibility to dreams is different from our responsibility to the rest of Creation. (What it comes down to, of course, is that Dylan Thomas wrote his poems as he could, and the use of dream-subjects helped him to get a step *closer* to what he was trying to say.) 'I dreamed my genesis' describes man's birth through his death, his knowledge of death in his birth, and his passage into the world.

In these earlier poems, as in Dylan Thomas's poetry generally, the language is what is most immediately striking. A language for a poet is always raw even if vitiated; Dylan Thomas's most characteristic twistings of the expected idiom have been mentioned often enough; the puns, the using of one part of speech for another, the manipulation of colloquialisms. He has done violence to the language when it was necessary to his theme—and at times when it was not: even in his later poems he can be vulgar, precious, meretriciously clever. And the style of these earlier poems is often egregious and turgid—a thing is said with devious novelty merely to avoid saying it any other way; as though the words came first and the subject as it could. (And the kind of poetry which he once described himself as writing in a letter to Henry Treece sounded as though it might very well be more a poetry of warring conclusions than of imaginative wholes.) But I think all this is a further indication of the intensity with which Dylan Thomas, with all the means at his disposal, was trying to find and make his subject—but the fact that a poet however gifted may find his subject only with difficulty does not necessarily indicate that he has no subject: it may merely indicate that he has a subject which is difficult to find. It is interesting how many of Dylan Thomas's 'private' recurring words, many of which he uses already in these poems, bear directly on the theme I have been talking about: the constant use of the word 'die' in the sense both of physical death and of sexual climax; 'grain' which is also the dust of the dead; 'grief' to designate the experience of 'death' in the sexual act; 'lock' and 'key' as sexual symbols. Also in these poems one finds already Dylan Thomas's characteristic development of a poem by repetition. There is peculiar to this manner of a live poem's progression of a kind of chaste passion and anonymity whatever the subject; at the same time it gives the language and/or emotion of the subject an exceptional range for improvization. And it presents strikingly, as might a ritual, the difference between the movement of the subject and the movement of the poem.

I have tried to indicate the direction which I think Dylan Thomas's earlier poetry was following, the theme it was trying to make and serve. It would be possible to follow the uses and developments of this theme through many of the succeeding poems, but often less directly, for as his knowledge of the theme deepened and became more comprehensive, the range of experience he was able to handle increased; his skill in his craft at the same time was growing more varied; and in particular he began writing more overtly occasional and personal poems; 'Out of the sighs' is to my reading the first genuinely personal poem in the *Collected Poems*. After 'I dreamed my genesis', there are a group of poems which explore the relationship of love and death, the world as duality, the subject of the continual creation of the world and of the individual. I think the culmination of these particular poems, though it is not the last in the group, is 'I in my intricate image' where the exultant conclusion already has the ring and vision of much of Dylan Thomas's later poetry: 'This was the god of beginning in the intricate seawhirl,/ And my images roared and rose on heaven's hill.'

Such a poem as 'Do you not father me' carries both the subject of the individual's continuity in man's continuing creation, which Dylan Thomas had first developed in 'Before I Knocked', and the subject of 'The force that through the green fuse drives the flower' a stage further by identifying man the creator-creature with all other mortal creatures. 'A grief ago' explores the theme in terms of the act of love itself, and for the sake of the loved one. The sonnet sequence, 'Altarwise by owl-light' is a glorification of the act of creation, identifying man with that which he conceives as divine. The power and compassion of the personal poems increase; the occasions become more genuinely intense as they become more direct: 'I have longed to move away', 'I make this in a warring absence', 'After the funeral', especially the deeply moving 'A Refusal to Mourn the Death, by Fire, of a Child in London'.

True personal poetry, where the poet speaks in his own voice directly about his particular experience, is rarer than might seem, particularly among modern poets, and, of course, especially so if it be personal poetry of any stature. Some of Dylan Thomas's personal poems are among the most moving and powerful he has written. And in these poems as well, both the fear, and still more important, the joy, have as their reference the religious artist's vision of the world. The theme of 'Hold hard, these ancient minutes in the cuckoo's mouth' (where we already have the hawk and birds of 'Over Sir John's Hill') becomes more intimate in 'When all my five and country senses see', in 'We lying by seasand', and 'Twenty-four years'; enormously amplified, it is still the background, with the personal fate foremost, in the poem which for me is, until now, the culmination of Dylan Thomas's personal poetry: 'In the White Giant's Thigh'. In this poem it is ancient, desperate barren love which haunts the speaker and lures his creative powers themselves down to death. The poems which bid that death be defied become more actual, more direct with mastery: in the earliest poems the motive for defiance seemed no better than desperation, but in the recent villanelle, 'Do not go gentle into that good night' (which, with Empson's 'Missing Dates' seems to me one of the great poems in this form in English) it is quite clearly love —love at such a pass as to be otherwise helpless against death. And the exultation of such marvellous poems as 'Poem in October', 'Fern Hill', 'Poem on his Birthday', and 'Author's Prologue' is not an exultation proper to the liberal humanist: it is the exuberance of a man drunk with the holiness and wonder of creation, with the reality and terror and ubiquity of death, but with love as God, as more powerful than death.

I think that in general it is the later poems of Dylan Thomas which represent his most important achievement. As love and compassion both have become more sure and comprehensive, so his poetry has become, among other things, increasingly dramatic. I do not find this surprising; I think the work of a religious artist, as his scope and mastery increased, would naturally tend to become more dramatic. For an art which is dramatic cannot burgeon if existence is seen as pointless and fragmentary; but a sense of the reality of love and a sense of the reality of the imagination would seem to me to be two of the most potent means of seeing creation as capable of order (the imagination makes order) and as significantly varied (love embraces details rather than generalities). And as the act of celebration—the metaphor—became more real it would tend to gain a dimension, gain independence of the individual 'lyric' moment (become less 'subjective') and become ritual or dramatic. One can see how a love poem would probably be more dramatic than a generalized statement of private anguish: a case in point, I think, is 'Especially when the October wind' where the *audience*, more explicit than in the earlier poems, may be the reader, but might very well be the beloved; and where the works of the imagination are mentioned 'made' as things with a 'life of their own'. (I should have thought, nevertheless, that his peculiar pitch of language would have precluded his writing poetry that was explicitly dramatic. It would be of immense interest to see what he has done with his hitherto unpublished choral fragment 'The Town That Was Mad' [an early version of *Under Milk Wood*].) As his poetry has grown more dramatic, Dylan Thomas's tragic vision of Creation has deepened and grown richer, and with it his power of joy. The faith, sure of itself but not sure why, of 'A grief ago', is a tragic faith; the sense of death is more real and terrible in so magnificent and tender a recent poem as 'In Country Sleep', but the faith is the same, and certain why it is there, and joyful.

'A Winter's Tale' is one of the few narrative poems Dylan Thomas has attempted, and I think it is one of the great poems he has written. Its achievement is if anything still more remarkable: for in 'A Winter's Tale' the fact has made myth. I say this without knowing whether or not Dylan Thomas used a known legend for the 'story' of his poem—for several reasons I suspect that he did. It might have run something like this: "Once in the dead of winter, in the middle of the night, a man who lived alone in a house in the woods saw outside a beautiful she-bird, and all around her it was spring. He ran from the house to find her; she flew ahead of him, and all night he ran and at last she came down and he came to where she was; she put her wings over him and the spring faded back to winter; then she rose and vanished, and when spring came and the snow melted they found his body lying on a hill-top". (I know of a similar legend among the American Indians.) The main reasons why I suspect that the poem comes from some such legend is that it contains most of the essential elements of a mid-winter ceremony of the re-birth of the year (of the earth, of man). In Wales until the Christian era, and among parts of the population for a long time afterwards, the presiding deity was a goddess;

the mid-winter rite was in her praise; she was often represented as a bird; the all-night running of the bride-groom corresponds with the marriage labours in many legends. Also the illusory vision of spring, coming from the land of the dead in Dylan Thomas's poem, and then the reality of winter coming back, might very possibly have come from a confusion of time-sequence such as often happens in legends when their ritual decays—that is, if the poem was based on some such legend, then we might suppose that in the original ritual the real spring came, and that the one-night version was later. But my point is that what I have persistently called Dylan Thomas's 'religious' vision of Creation is completely congruous with the vision of life which made the re-birth ritual in the first place. And as poetry comes to be in a manner similar to that in which legend does, Dylan Thomas might very possibly have invented a story whose mythical ramifications were thus comprehensive and deep. He has 'made' the myth whether or not he invented the skeletal story, for it is his own imagination which has given it its immediacy and power, which has seen love-in-death, the 'she-bird', with such certainty as heavenly and all-powerful, which has made articulate within the metaphor itself the triumph of the rite which is life.

In two other major later poems, 'Vision and Prayer' and 'Over Sir John's Hill' the mythology and vision are developed in a different, and dramatic, direction. In these poems the poet, while presenting the condition of Creation, intercedes on behalf of mortality. This is a different kind of standing-apart from that of the earlier poems, for there it was the failure to conceive of Creation as ordered, and at the same time the overweening preoccupation with personal doom (however generalized) which kept the poet separate. In these poems he bespeaks the tragic order as he sees it, and it is in his very capacity of witness and tongue and celebrator that he stands-without as intercessor. In 'Vision and Prayer', because of the vision of man as divine, as love (Christ), of Creation as divine and therefore of resurrection as real, he prays that death may die indeed. In 'Over Sir John's Hill' he would redeem mortality itself:

> . . . and I who hear the tune of the slow,
> Wear-willow river, grave,
> Before the lunge of the night, the notes on this time-shaken
> Stone for the sake of the souls of the slain birds sailing.

Dylan Thomas's own sense of his poetic vocation has been stated more clearly than anywhere else in two poems, 'In My Craft or Sullen

Art' and the "Author's Prologue' to the *Collected Poems.* In the former he states that he writes his poems 'Not for ambition or bread', nor for public acclaim nor for the edification of the self-righteous, nor for the dead, but for the lovers 'With all their griefs in their arms'. If the act of love is conceived as the central holy act of Creation, where love, in joy and then in pain and then in joy, overcomes death, it is clear why he should have felt that his poems were so directed. In 'Author's Prologue' as in 'In My Craft or Sullen Art', where he has written 'I labour by singing light', the creative act, in this case the creation of the imagination, is seen as holy:

> . . . song
> Is a burning and crested act,
> The fire of birds in
> The world's turning wood. . . .

It is seen as triumphant over death:

> I build my bellowing ark
> To the best of my love
> As the flood begins. . . .

and moreover as perpetual, present always, making anew, now: 'And the flood flowers now'. This is the office of celebration, it is the reason for the faith and the joy, it is the statement of vocation of a great religious poet. As for the 'craft', Dylan Thomas remains the most skillful maker of verse writing English; the stanzaic forms which he often fashioned for his rhythms are as complex and, for him, unhampering and informative as they seem to have been among the Welsh ollaves. He has 'made' what seems to me to be the major theme to a point of masterful authority, and in the range and intensity of passion which he controlled he surpassed any of his contemporaries. He seems to have assimilated most of his primary influences (though the 'debt' to Joyce in particular was more than verbal—Joyce was prodigiously an artist of celebration—and the 'debt' to Hopkin's 'The Windhover' bore recent fruit in 'Over Sir John's Hill'). He has survived the fads of the thirties, the first wave of fashion and notoriety. He has 'arrived'. How the future will judge him, we cannot tell. We only know that Thomas is a major poet of our century and nobody will be able to ignore him.

Dylan Thomas: A Review of His Collected Poems

JOHN WAIN

Reviewing this volume is not, in the ordinary sense, reviewing at all. Here are the poems we have been familiar with for years, which have been explored, acclaimed, damned, rejected and worshiped throughout the entire adult life of anyone aged less than thirty-five; and 'reviewing' them is merely a matter of passing them around and giving each critic an opportunity to say where he, personally, stands with regard to Mr. Thomas's work.

Most people have said their say by now; this would be, if one could be bothered, a good opportunity to survey the kind of thing that has been said. But I doubt if any such summary could, at this stage, be useful or entertaining: most kinds of critical mistakes have been made in dealing with these poems and will no doubt go on being made, and that is about all there is to it. The wild overpraise of Thomas's original backers was answered by the savage onslaught of those who felt that the whole thing had gone too far, and by about 1946 one felt that the critics were quite simply talking to each other rather than to the public, and certainly not bothering overmuch about the poems. The small-arms fire has now grown so hot that anyone who shows his head is sure to be riddled from some quarter; for instance, Mr. Read's famous 'these poems cannot be reviewed: they can only be acclaimed' (of *Twenty-Five Poems*) drew such furious abuse and raillery that nowadays no one dare be so outspoken, even if they feel really strongly impelled to praise Thomas; and so one finds, for instance, a Sunday reviewer saying that 'it need no longer be eccentric'

From *Preliminary Essays* by John Wain (London: Macmillan & Company Ltd. and New York: St. Martin's Press, 1957), pp. 180–185. Reprinted by permission of Macmillan & Company Ltd. and St. Martin's Press.

to say that Thomas is the greatest living writer of English poetry. What he meant was that he thought so himself, but did not dare say so outright in case some anti-Thomas bully came round to thrash him, so had to dress it up with a meaningless qualification. In that particular case, of course, it is unnecessary to do more than say No; it is, clearly, eccentric, not to say imperceptive, to call Thomas the greatest living writer of English verse as long as Eliot is still writing, to say nothing of Auden, Graves and several others. At the other extreme we have the disgraceful treatment of Thomas in *Scrutiny*, which is, I am afraid, only typical of that magazine's bad record over contemporary poetry in general. It is rather significant that the best review of this collection should have appeared in the *New Statesman*—a paper for whose criticism *Scrutiny* can never say a good word.

But I must get on with the job, which is to say briefly (for what it is worth) where I stand on the Thomas question. I think, then, that he is a fine, bold, original and strong poet whose work is marred by two great drawbacks. First, a disastrously limited subject-matter. There are really only three subjects treated: (i) childhood, and the associated topic of what it is like to remember one's childhood; (ii) the viscera; (iii) religion. The first is very well handled, but really nobody could improve on the *Portrait of the Artist as a Young Dog* as saying all that can be said about growing up, and if you add the related group of verse pieces, chiefly the quasi-Wordsworthian *Poem in October*, you really find that there is nothing left to do. The second, the viscera, is of course an important subject, and the early poems with their obsessive concern with anatomy and crude physical sensation are fine and valuable poems, but here again you can say the last word, and say it pretty quickly. Thomas has added almost no good love poetry to the language, because he always seems to treat sexual love as an affair of glandular secretions and the mingling of fluids, which is only true as far as it goes. The third subject, religion, seems to me Thomas's worst pitch; he never succeeds in making me feel that he is doing more than thumbing a lift from it. Indeed it is only a helpful subject to him in those poems which are content to leave every important matter to be settled by the reader: the line 'After the first death, there is no other', has been praised as an example of significant ambiguity (either 'when you are dead there's an end of it' or 'after this mortal life comes the eternal one'), and no doubt that is very valuable, but if a poet is going to be a religious poet there has (one would think) to be a little more definition about it.

This leads on to the second great flaw which keeps Thomas's poetry at a remove from greatness: the suspicion (which has, goodness knows, been voiced often enough) that his writing, in the more 'difficult' poems, is quasi-automatic. It is perfectly possible to furnish even his wildest pieces with a 'meaning' (i.e. a paraphrasable content or set of alternative paraphrasable contents), but the gnawing doubt remains as to whether the writer really *cared* whether it meant anything precise or not. This, of course, is the great point that has to be settled; not until every one of the more obscure poems has been thoroughly thrashed out (as, in time, they will be) can we feel confident of reaching an answer. Meanwhile we want a little less gas about Thomas, and some criticism that really talks turkey and gets down to particular instances. The thing is meanwhile, very worrying to the honest reader. Take, for instance, the line,

And I am struck as lonely as a holy maker by the sun.

Why does the sun strike a holy maker lonely? Or rather, to put first things first, does it just strike the poet lonely, as lonely as a holy maker? Of course a holy maker is lonely, whether the expression means (i) a specifically religious poet, (ii) just any poet ('all makers are holy'), (iii) God. This third suggestion comes from a friend who said it was 'obvious' that the line referred to God creating the sun, and feeling lonely because for the first time there existed in the universe something with which it was possible to have a relationship, and therefore the concept of loneliness appeared. But if so, why 'a' holy maker and not 'the'? At this point, does one plunge ahead, hoping to reach the further shore, or does one simply go back in despair and say that the effect is of a latter-day Swinburne who just wants to make a nice noise? Answers to these and all the other questions of interpretation are easy to supply; but (and this is the point) they are not easy to cleanse, when supplied, of a certain *voulu* or facticious quality.

This, by the way, would be the place for a few remarks in contradiction of one of the most obstinate absurdities that bedevil discussion of this poet: the idea, brought up on occasion by his supporters and opponents alike, that he is a divinely inspired simpleton; what Mr. Eliot, speaking of Blake, called 'a wild pet for the super-cultivated'. His association in the public mind with Miss Sitwell, who is simply not interested in the ordinary processes of being intelligent, has helped to put this nonsense about, but it is obvious to anyone who reads the poems carefully that Thomas put into them a good deal of ordinary common-or-garden cleverness and capability of the breadwinning, examination-passing type, not a fanciful fourth-dimensional 'poetic' afflatus. This is clear from the very great skill with which he has assimilated his literary influences, the chief of which are, of course, Hopkins and Yeats, though there is a noticeable streak of William Empson (cleverly combined with the Yeats influence in one of the new poems here, the villanelle). Thomas is also a brilliant parodist, another sure test of acuteness of the ordinary day-to-day type (no fool ever wrote a successful parody even if, which I doubt, a fool ever wrote a successful poem).

To turn definitely to the credit side, there is, of course, all the obvious—magnificently and overwhelmingly obvious—grandeur, generosity and harmony of these poems. The superb balance of rhymes in *The Conversation of Prayer,* for instance, is something to be grateful for; doubly so when one thinks that Thomas came of literary age at a time when the typical successful poet was getting away with lines like these:

> You who go out alone, on tandem or on pillion,
> Down arterial roads riding in April,
> Or sad beside lakes where hill-slopes are reflected
> Making fires of leaves, your high hopes fallen:
> Cyclists and hikers in company, day excursionists,
> Refugees from cursed towns and devastated areas;
> Know you seek a new world, a saviour to establish
> Long-lost kinship and restore the blood's fulfillment.

Compare:

> Once it was the colour of saying
> Soaked my table the uglier side of a hill
> With a capsized field where a school sat still
> And a black and white patch of girls grew playing;
> The gentle seasides of saying I must undo
> That all the charmingly drowned arise to cockcrow and kill.

If the Thomas passage shows the tendency towards over-richness and artfulness (the field is 'capsized' because there is a school sitting still in it, and schoolboys wear caps, as well as because it is tilted on the side of a hill), one forgives it at once by comparison with the utter nullity of the other extract, which incidentally I chose from an anthology and did not ferret out from among the author's early and buried work. In the criticism of contemporary literature, one's standards are bound to be, essentially, comparative; we cannot know what will interest posterity, but that Thomas's poems will continue to interest the men of his own time cannot be questioned and need not, certainly, be grudged.

The Nature of the Poet

ELDER OLSON

Thomas remarked, famously, that his poetry was the record of his individual struggle from darkness to light. The universe of these early symbols is the universe of his darkness; he builds new worlds as he advances in that struggle toward light. It is notable that after the "Altarwise by owl-light" sonnets, he discards nearly all of this particular body of symbols, transforms the remainder, and gradually develops new symbols and new diction to correspond with his changing view of life. In the early poems, Adam is a symbol of sin and of the perishing flesh; in the later, Adam is "upright Adam/[who] Sang upon origin." Eden is at first thought of as the garden where the Apple was eaten; it later becomes associated with the pristine innocence of the earth; the earth is seen as recapturing that innocence at times, in token of the Redemption. The Flood is a terror in the early work; in the later, there is refuge from it in the Ark.

There is always a danger, when a poet's work exhibits some kind of rounding-out and development, that we may tend to treat his poems merely as parts of one long poem. I should like to avoid that danger, but it must be said that Thomas did, after all, achieve some portion of light. If the poetry of the dark period is concerned almost wholly with personal problems, the poetry of the middle phase is charged with powerful and poignant feeling for others—for his wife, his children, his aunt, and the victims of air raids—and the poems of the later volumes are for the most part, exultant expressions of his faith and love. There are even touches of humor in "Once below a time," the "Author's Prologue," and particularly in "Lament." "Over Sir John's hill" and "Poem on his birthday" contemplate death with calm accept-

Reprinted from *The Poetry of Dylan Thomas* (pp. 19–29) by Elder Olson, by permission of The University of Chicago Press.

ance; the universe of darkness, with its swarming horrors out of Hieronymous Bosch, has disappeared. He does not move from that Inferno to a Paradiso, but he has recaptured, in the charming natural world of Wales, something of the lost Eden and something of a foretoken of Heaven. There is undoubtedly a development from doubt and fear to faith and hope, and the moving cause is love; he comes to love of God by learning to love man and the world of nature.

If the three periods in his work are distinct in their subject matter, they are even more sharply distinct in their diction and prosody. The language of the first period is so very limited, its vocabulary so very small, that it reminds one of Basic English. Repetition of certain words is so frequent as to suggest obsession with them; indeed, at least one critic, Henry Treece, has thought their frequent use an instance of verbal compulsion. "Fork," "fellow," "half," "vein," "suck," "worm" seem to dot every page; the phrase "death's feather," among others, recurs in poem after poem. When a limited vocabulary is used to designate a multiplicity of things, ambiguity is bound to result, and we find Thomas using, or rather exploiting, his key-words in a whole variety of senses. "Fork," for instance, is used in nearly all of its senses as noun or verb. The sentences of this period are generally very short or consist, however prolonged, of short members; the verse itself is short-breathed, very much based on the line-length, and its pulsations are irregular in beat and uneven in strength, as if a heart were to beat violently for a moment, flag, stop altogether, and suddenly resume.

The poems following the "Altarwise by owl-light" sonnets are, generally speaking, characterized by a marked increase in vocabulary and a discarding of some of the old—"fork," I think, is never used again after the first sonnet—as well as by extension of breath through longer and longer grammatical units. In the sonnets the iambic pentameter line, although now used as a unit of construction rather than as a limit, is still very much in evidence; in "A Refusal to Mourn" a single sentence extends into the third stanza; in "Poem in October" most of the very long and complex stanzas consist of a single sentence. As the old symbolism is rejected or transformed, symbols also diminish and in frequency of use, and there is increasing employment of metaphor and image.

In the last period terseness is supplanted by verbosity; sentences, clauses, phrases even, become not merely long but tremendously so. Adjective is piled on adjective, masses of words are jammed together to make one compound epithet, until the ordinary reader can scarcely stretch his breath over the long reaches of language. Despite the enchanting imagery, one has the feeling that eloquence is sometimes strained. The early work had presented a multiplicity of ideas and emotions in very small compass; the last poems stretch a single thought or emotion to its utmost limits, and perhaps beyond. Curiously enough he never achieves lucidity; the obscurity wrought by his early terseness slips into the obscurity wrought by his final verbosity. I must confess, too, that I find him often very noisy; that charming poem, the "Author's Prologue," makes a racket quite beyond any demand of its emotion or thought. The early poems depend upon a technique of isolation, of singling out the essential factors of an experience; the very last depend upon a technique of accumulation. Perhaps he becomes a bit too consciously the bard, overwhelming us with his copiousness of language, his eloquence, booming at us, working upon us too obviously, even exciting himself unnecessarily. I do not think him melodramatic in his early poems; but I confess there is some foundation for supposing him sentimental in his last. It is not that one would rather not have had these poems; one would rather have had them better.

All of this goes back to the kind of poet he essentially is. That can best be seen, I think, by comparing Thomas the poet with Thomas the prose-writer. The poet is great; the prose-writer, despite many evident marks of genius, merely highly competent; but the prose-writer is far more versatile than the poet. The prose-writer assumes many characters, devises many characters, plays upon emotions which range from the serious to the comic. The poet assumes a single character; and, strictly speaking, he is a poet only of the most exalted emotions, the most exalted grief or joy. Call him what you will, tragic poet, bard, poet of sublimity; the point is that his proper character is a lofty, a heroic one. You will look in vain in his poetry for wit, elegance, polish, and all the graces which makes us preserve many a lesser poet—graces which, indeed, can be found in his own prose. You will find anger, but it will be no common anger, but the wrath of Achilles. You will find despair, but it is the despair of Philoctetes. So with everything he feels. Compare "A Refusal to Mourn" or "Ceremony After a Fire Raid" or "After the funeral" with John Crowe Ransom's "Bells for John Whiteside's Daughter" or Walter de la Mare's "Sunk Lyonesse," and it will be manifest to you that Thomas never achieves, indeed never attempts, certain ranges of emotion.

Although he comes through love to his faith, we never see him, in the poems, really thinking how others think or feel; they exist simply as objects of his own emotion. In his poetry he is capable of immense emotion for another; but he cannot stand in another's skin. As we read him, we are shaken by what he feels for another, not by the sufferings and the feelings of that other. Moved by grief for a burned child, nobly and powerfully moved as he is, he does not suffer imaginatively the experience of the child, does not share in it in the least; he sees the pain and the horror from without, and the resolution he reaches is a resolution for him, not for the child. This curiously external view is revealed in one of his least successful poems: the death of a hundred-year-old man provides him matter for a string of fantastic conceits, and the poem is really unintelligible, not because it is particularly obscure, but because the emotion he exhibits is impossible to relate to any emotion that the event, however conceived, conceived if you will from the point of view of a man from Mars, could have aroused in us. I have remarked, indeed argued, that Thomas' imagination could transport him anywhere, through all space and all time; but it is also true that, wherever it takes him, he sees nothing but himself. He can enter into worm and animal, but he will look out through his own eyes. He can create worlds; but he creates his worlds in his own image, and remains the center of his own thought and feeling. He is not a Dante, a Chaucer, a Shakespeare, or a Browning, who stood inside the men they made; he is a Keats, a Byron, a Yeats, or an Eliot.

These two limitations—his restriction to certain ranges of emotion and his restriction to one character—must not be taken too seriously, for they amount to this: that he was a lyric poet of the lofty kind. But also they cannot be disregarded; a poet so restricted must either aim at and achieve the sublime, or he fails. When the conception underlying his poem is a powerful and lofty one, and controls all the devices of his poem, Thomas is magnificent; when the conception is trivial, or when his treatment of it does not sufficiently manifest it, he is utterly disappointing. His art demands great energy of thought and passion and all the accoutrements of the grand style; when the high conception is wanting, energy becomes violence and noise, the tragic passions become the melodramatic or the morbid, ecstasy becomes hysteria, and the high style becomes obscure bombast. When the bard is not the bard, the bardic robes may easily be put off; not so the habitual paraphernalia of his art. When Thomas is not master of his tricks, his tricks master him. Within a given period, his good work and his bad involve the same devices; it is their employment, what they are employed on and what they are employed for, that differs; and it makes all the difference.

Let me explain a little what I mean by the "high conception." How it differs from the bare theme, an example or two may make clear. The "Ballad of the Long-legged Bait," one of his best poems, has as its bare theme the notion that salvation must be won through mortification of the flesh. A common enough notion; but in the fiery imagination of Thomas the process of purification becomes the strange voyage of a lone fisherman; the bait is "A girl alive with his hooks through her lips"; she is "all the wanting flesh his enemy," "Sin who had a woman's shape"; and the quarry sought is no less than all that Time and Death have taken; for, since Sin brought Time and Death into the world, the destruction of Sin will restore all that has been lost. With the death of the girl, the sea gives up its dead; Eden returns, "A garden holding to her hand/With birds and animals"; and the sea disappears, accomplishing the prophecy "And there was no more sea." In the terrible actuality of the voyage we never guess its essential fantasy; "the whole/Of the sea is hilly with whales," "All the fishes were rayed in blood," and most beautifully:

> He saw the storm smoke out to kill
> With fuming bows and ram of ice,
> Fire on starlight, rake Jesu's stream;
> And nothing shone on the water's face
>
> But the oil and bubble of the moon. . . .

Just as in these last lines the storm is given the menace, the fury and power of a kind of supernatural warship, firing "on starlight" and on "Jesu's stream" (the Milky Way) until nothing shines on the water's face "but the oil and bubble of the moon," so the theme of the whole poem is given the emotional power of its legend: the subjugation of sensual desire becomes mysterious and cruel as the sacrifice of the girl, the salvation takes on the beauty and mystery of the resurrection of the dead and of the past from the sea. There is no hyperbole, no exaggeration here; when we comprehend what Thomas has in mind, we see that his conception is merely accurate; that is to say, as accurate as human conception can be.

Similarly, "Fern Hill" and "Poem in October," both luminous with all the weathers of childhood; "A Refusal to Mourn the Death, by Fire, of a Child in London," apprehending the child's death in its relation to the whole universe (all creation is spanned, awesomely, from beginning to end, in the first stanza, and the last carries us back to the "first dead"); the "Altarwise by owl-light" sonnets (surely among the greatest poems of our century)—all of these are founded upon conceptions possible, we feel, only to a man of great imagination and feeling. Sometimes the conception is of the very essence of passion and feeling such as only a towering character could support. Look at these stark and terrible lines from a poem which I think has gone unnoticed:

> Out of the sighs a little comes,
> But not of grief, for I have knocked down that
> Before the agony; the spirit grows,
> Forgets, and cries;
> A little comes, is tasted and found good;
> All could not disappoint;
> There must, be praised, some certainty,
> If not of loving well, then not,
> And that is true after perpetual defeat.

This is the shape and stamp of a despair as deep as falls on Macbeth after the death of his wife.

Compare such magnificent triumphs with this:

> Tell his street on its back he stopped a sun
> And the craters of his eyes grew springshoots and fire
> When all the keys shot from the locks, and rang.

This, it seems to me, is pure trifling. There is no difficulty here, but there is also no imagination. "He stopped a sun"; that is, he stopped a sun-like bomb, and the sun of the dawn also stopped for him. "The craters of his eyes grew springshoots and fire"; that is, the bomb infused all its fires into him so that they came out of his eyes as out of the craters of volcanoes. Perfectly impossible, I should say, and of no importance. We are told later that a "heavenly ambulance drawn by a wound" awaits him and that "a hundred storks" (symbolic of his hundred years) "perch on the sun's right hand." The poet seems to be trying to be triumphant about this death; he fails so utterly that he is almost derisive. The emotion is unclear; the grounds of it are uncertain; there is not a single detail which could not have been imagined by almost anyone in a fanciful mood. We cannot be much moved by the ambulance and the storks, symbolic or otherwise. In fact, we should be much more moved by a newspaper headline; we are more moved by the title of the poem, which sounds like a line from a newspaper ("Among those killed in the dawn raid was a man aged a hundred"), than we are by the poem. The solitary right touch seems to be "all the keys shot from their locks, and rang," for that suggests the power of the blast; but on second thought that doesn't seem right either: suppose the keys were blown from their locks, a blast in which their ringing would be audible wouldn't be much of a blast. Take the keys symbolically, even; they still make no difference.

I am not, I hope the reader will understand, concerned with Thomas' faults; but the very principles which exhibit his genius when he *is* a genius also exhibit his failures when he fails. I am also not trying to legislate; I will merely point out that the principles by which we judge success or failure are the same.

Put it this way. There are no "rules" or "laws" of art. The only necessity by which the artist, as artist, is bound is that imposed upon him by the particular work he seeks to execute. But if he is executing it, as he must, in a particular medium—language, let us say—he can only make it do what language can do. He can discover new possibilities of language and realize them; but they must be possibilities and not impossibilities. If he is representing something dramatically (i.e., on the stage), his work will have to be something that can possibly be represented on the stage. And if he proposes to affect us, his audience, in any way, he will have to invent something that *will* affect us. All this means that through his single commitment the artist has involved himself in a good many more. Bound to one thing, he is at once bound to many; he suffers the restrictions of his medium, of the way in which he proposes to use it, and of the laws of human nature.

Now this last is particularly stringent. Any artist who proposes to produce an effect in a human audience—whatever effect you will, in whatever audience you will—must incorporate in his work causes which will produce that effect. If he wishes to evoke fear or pity, he must set before us objects which are really objects of fear or pity. He may make us pity or fear things that we never did before; but he will first have to persuade us that they are really pitiable or fearful. He may make us cease to fear or pity that which we previously did; but only, however, by first persuading us that it is not really fearful or pitiable. As a matter of fact it does not even matter whether he proposes to affect us or not: if the work incorporates certain causes, it will produce a certain effect, even though the artist did not intend it; if the work does not incorporate certain causes, it will not produce their effect, though the artist desired that effect with all his soul.

Moreover, if the artist offers his work for our approval, or even proposes to execute a work in some way good, he involves himself in questions of value. We need not worry about theories of aesthetic value here; we have only to consider how we *do* evaluate. We value the arts in terms of their effects on us. If we have any sense of art at all, we tend to value entertainment less highly than art, because entertainment produces only a passing pleasure and because, all things being equal, a passing pleasure is less valuable than an enduring one. We evaluate art itself on principles which are really quite simple; that is to say, the system of values by which we measure and evaluate everything else, and the importance of the effect of art in terms of that system of values. Our reflection on the value of the work, so measured, leads to an evaluation of it as a human performance, and our reflection on the value of the human performance leads to an evaluation of the artist.

Thus we respect the poet who observes no more than we do and conceives it no more profoundly than we should, if only he formulates it better than we could; we respect him still more if he does this better than most poets have. We respect still more the poet who observes more than we do, and still more the poet who feels or conceives more than we; and in proportion as the performance surpasses such standards, our respect increases. We range from the slightest esteem to the greatest awe and wonder according as he does surpass such standards; let him fall below them, and our feelings descend as far as utter contempt. We measure performance as against what it seems impossible anyone should have done; against what only the fine artist could have done; against what most artists could do, what most people could do, what anyone could have done, what only a fool would have done.

Particular judgments arrived at through these principles may be incorrect, because the particular work may somehow be misapprehended; the artist may complain of the particular judgment, but he has no appeal against the principles. Not that they are necessarily right; they may very well be wrong; the point is that they are the ground on which we inevitably judge. The subject and the crudest judgments proceed from them.

In "Dawn Raid" Thomas sees and feels less than we should have, perhaps less than anyone should have seen and felt, and so his verbal skill goes for naught. When he *is* Thomas, when he rises to his true stature, he towers indeed. To see that, you have only to ask yourself whether you think much of a birthday as a poetic theme; and then read "Twenty-four years," "Poem in October," and "Poem on his birthday."

Gerard Manley Hopkins and Dylan Thomas

HENRY TREECE

"We can find in this poet's work the two elements which have been mentioned: (a) a passionate emotion which seems to try to utter all its words in one, (b) a passionate intellect which is striving at once to recognize and explain both the singleness and division of the accepted Universe. But to these must be added a passionate sense of the details of the world without and the world within, a passionate consciousness of all kinds of experience."

CHARLES WILLIAMS: Introduction to Hopkins's Poems

O then if in my lagging lines you miss
The roll, the rise, the carol, the creation . . .

G. M. HOPKINS

I

Gerard Manley Hopkins, Jesuit priest and a contemporary of Swinburne, has exercised a profound influence over a large number of our contemporary poets, and particularly over the younger ones.[1] In fact,

From *How I See Apocalypse* by Henry Treece (London: Lindsay Drummond, Ltd., 1946), pp. 129–139.

1 "Lapwing"

Leaves, summer's coinage spent, golden are all together whirled,
Sent spinning, dipping, slipping, shuffled by heavy handed wind,
Shifted sideways, sifted, lifted, and in swarms made to fly,
Spent sun-flies, gorgeous tatters, airdrift, pinions of trees.

REX WARNER

he may be classed as a prime technical influence, for no other poet, not excluding T. S. Eliot, has been responsible for such a show of technical assimilation.

This, on consideration of Hopkins's dates, might seem surprising. Why, if we must go back to the last century for our models, do we not choose one of the "successful" poets, Meredith, Rossetti, or Swinburne? Why do we bow to the ghost of an obscure Jesuit priest, whose work was read by few in his own lifetime, and fewer in ours until the sponsorship of his poems by the late Laureate, Dr. Robert Bridges?

One answer to these questions is not hard to find, and it is this: Gerard Manley Hopkins was a poet of conflict, of intensity and rebellion in a way, and to a degree, unapproached by any other poet of his period. His work shows a tension, a dissatisfaction with accepted formulae, yet a hope for the future, which our young poets, nurtured on *The Wasteland*, and already becoming reactionary to it, could most easily and most sincerely take as a model. The Depression, once stated, is barren and sterile; later comes a reaction, a renewed hope, and the tremendously vital work of Hopkins points the way to consummation.

Technically, he is the most surprising poet of his generation.[2] His alliterations and inversions were perhaps not startling (only in so far as he employed them as a means of elucidating his content: whereas, with his contemporaries, Meredith, and particularly Swinburne, music was the *avant toute chose*, so that in their work the matter runs parallel with the manner and not together with it); but the violence of his syntax, his "accumulated masses of nouns, verbs, adjectives and adverbs, unleavened by prepositions or conjunctions"[3] impress the reader immediately and forcefully as the work of an outstanding individual mind: "A passionate intellect which is striving at once to recognize and explain both the singleness and division of the accepted Universe."

I am soft sift
In an hourglass—at the wall
Fast, but mined with a motion, a drift,
And it crowds and it combs to the fall;

XXII

Head-gears gaunt on grass-grown pitbanks, seams abandoned years ago;
Drop a stone and listen for its splash in flooded dark below. . . .

W. H. AUDEN

Lilian Bowes Lyon, Rayner Heppenstall and R. P. Hewett are also derivative in manner from Gerard Manley Hopkins.

[2] Some supporters of Doughty have questioned this. No serious critic will.
[3] Michael Roberts: *The Faber Book of Modern Verse.*

> I steady as water in a well, to a poise, to a pane,
> But roped with, always, all the way down from the tall
> Fells of flanks of the voel, a vein
> Of the Gospel proffer, a principle, Christ's gift.[4]

Quite as revolutionary and as startling are Hopkins's advanced metrical schemes, his "outrides," and the complicated internal harmonies of his rhythmic counterpoint. His changing rhythms and his shifting stresses mirror the man: they are his conflicts, even when reconciled in an apparent contentment:

> Our evening is over us, óur night / whélms, whélms, ánd will end us.
> Only the beakleaved boughs dragonish / damask the tool smooth bleak light; black,
> Ever so black on it. Óur tale, O oúr oracle! / Lét life, wáned, ah lét life wind
> Off hér once skéined, stained, véined variéty / upon, áll on twó spools; párt, pen, páck.
> Now her áll in twó flocks—black, white; / right wrong; reckon but, reck but, mind
> But thése two; wáre of a wórld where bút these / twó tell, each off the óther; of a rack
> Where, self-wrung, self-strung, sheathe—and shelterless, / thóughts agáinst thoughts ín groans grínd.[5]

The metrical signs themselves hint at that complexity which the poet recognized within himself, and show his wish to unravel and to explain.

His use of half-rhyme is not as strange to our ears as it must have been to those of his contemporaries; we have, in the meantime, become accustomed to the poetry of Wilfred Owen.

Important as Hopkins is, however, to our younger poets, it is to his manner rather than his fundamental matter that their derivation mainly belongs. They recognize the conflict in his way of writing, but cannot reconcile the conflict in his mind with that in their own.[6]

Hopkins's search for God and his contentions with God are disregarded as being irrelevant. So Rex Warner, in *Lapwing* gives us a fine picture of a bird (and perhaps something of the poet); but his model,

[4] Stanza four: "The Wreck of the Deutschland." Hopkins.
[5] "Spelt from Sibyl's Leaves."
[6] Those poets most frequently indebted to Hopkins (L. Bowes Lyon, Rex Warner and R. P. Hewett) seem to employ his stylisms decoratively, and not as a means to elucidation.

The Windhover: To Christ our Lord, is more than a visual description: at the least, it is the glory of God in a bird.

Dylan Thomas is the only poet I have yet read who has learnt in any mentionable degree, both from the manner and the matter of Gerard Manley Hopkins, how to tackle his own independent technical and spiritual problems. But those who look for "the roll, the rise, the carol, the creation" in the work of this Welsh poet will be disappointed: it is not there. Where there is a lyricism at all in Thomas, it is in the contemplation of his own dark processes, and not in the sight of a bird. And, whereas Hopkins might cry aloud in ecstasy for all to hear, in Thomas there is only "the midnight of a chuckle."

In other respects there is, however, a deal of resemblance between the two poets. Most particularly there is the similarity in origin of their sources of poetic energy: both look within, to find tension and disorder; both experience that "important moral conflict, related to an outer . . . intellectual conflict."[7] Their methods of combating this disorder are individual: while Hopkins calls out to God, throwing the light of Heaven upon his anguish, Thomas again looks inwards, and as a God unto himself, analyses and diagnoses his own disorder:

> God, lover of souls, swaying considerate scales,
> Complete thy creature dear O where it fails,
> Being mighty a mastery, being a father and fond.[8]

So pleads the one, almost sure of the success of his prayers.

> Am I not father, too, and the ascending boy,
> The boy of woman and the wanton starer
> Marking the flesh and summer in the bay?
> Am I not sister, too, who is my saviour?
> Am I not all of you by the directed sea
> Where bird and shell are babbling in my tower?
> Am I not you who front the tidy shore;
> Nor roof of sand, nor yet the towering tiler?[9]

shouts the modern poet, proud in his apparent self-sufficiency. But the uncertainty is there, and the inner conflict is never fully resolved, in God or in the poet's self.

II

Perhaps the most convincing method of emphasizing the similarities between these two poets is that of quoting certain major comments

[7] Michael Roberts: *The Faber Book of Modern Verse.*
[8] "In the Valley of the Elwy." Hopkins.
[9] *25 Poems* (Dent), p. 15.

on the one, and observing how closely and how appropriately the same criticisms might have been used in reference to the other:

> The very race of the words and the lines hurries on our emotion; our minds are left behind, not, as in Swinburne, because they have to suspend their labour until it is wanted, but because they cannot work at a quick enough rate.[10]

Nowhere may we find, in so few words, a criticism so explanatory, of the work of Dylan Thomas. The aptness of this comment is obvious in almost all of his work, and particularly in *Eighteen Poems* and the last few pages of *Twenty-five Poems:*

> All all and all the dry worlds couple,[11]
> Ghost with her ghost, contagious man
> With the womb of his shapeless people.
> All that shapes from the caul and suckle,
> Stroke of mechanical flesh on mine,
> Square in these worlds the mortal circle.

> And then from the windy West came two-gunned Gabriel
> From Jesu's sleeve trumped up the king of spots,
> The sheath-decked jacks, queen with a shuffled heart;
> Said the fake gentleman in a suit of spades,
> Black-tongued and tipsy from salvation's bottle,
> Rose my Byzantine Adam in the night;[12]

There is an energy here, "a passionate emotion which seems to try to utter all its words in one," which is equalled only by:

> Cloud-puff-ball, turn-tufts, tossed pillows / flaunt forth, then chevy on an air-
> built thoroughfare: heaven roysterers, in gay gangs / they throng: they glitter in marches.
> Down roughcast, down dazzling whitewash, / wherever an elm arches,
> Shivelights and shadow tackle in long / lashes lace, lance and pair[13]

The breathless race is the same; the goal is possibly the same, though the gait of the runners is different.

[10] Charles Williams: Intro. to Poems of G. M. Hopkins. (O.U.P.)
[11] 18 *Poems.* [12] 25 *Poems.*
[13] "That Nature is a Heracleitan Fire."

"The single pursuit of even the most subordinate artistic intention gives unity, significance, mass to a poet's work."[14]

The most vehement critic of the poetry of Dylan Thomas will be unable to deny its force and singleness of purpose. There is a compelling quality inherent in all his work which draws the reader, if only to leave him gasping, and, perhaps at times, sickened. This drive, this quality, is the result of a "single pursuit of . . . an artistic intention," and whether or not this "artistic intention" is a subordinate one is a matter of little importance here. To my way of thinking it is not. In all of Dylan Thomas's books of verse there is a pursuit which never swerves from its intention. The reader may open either book, wherever he wishes, and in every case will he be conscious of this intention: he will recognize that "struggle from darkness towards some measure of light," that "casting of light upon what has been hidden for too long," that "naked exposure":[15]

> I see the summer children in their mothers
> Split up the brawned womb's weathers,
> Divide the night and day with fairy thumbs;
> There in the deed with quartered shades
> Of sun and moon they paint their dams
> As sunlight paints the shelling of their heads.[16]
>
> This world is half the devil's and my own,
> Daft with the drug that's smoking in a girl
> And curling round the bud that forks her eye.
> An old man's shank one-marrowed with my bone,
> And all the herrings smelling in the sea,
> I sit and watch the worm beneath my nail,
> Wearing the quick away.[17]

Here is a searching, a seeing and a discovery. It is the result of an individual struggle, a highly personal conflict, and therefore its general intelligibility is a matter for speculation: but nevertheless it is a manifestation of that singleness of intention, the recurrence and obvious sincerity of which gives a unity to some of Dylan Thomas's best work, and a significance to most of it:

[14] Middleton Murry, *Gerard Manley Hopkins* (Aspects of Literature). Here the critic is explaining Hopkins's striving towards "The roll, the rise, the carol, the creation."

[15] See *Answers to an Enquiry—New Verse.*

[16] 18 *Poems.*

[17] 18 *Poems.*

> His intellect, startled at a sight, breaks now into joy, now into inquiry, now into a terror of fearful expectation—but always into song.[18]

In all the poetry of Dylan Thomas one may find two of these elements: inquiry, and a terror of fearful expectation. And, if the first seems a slighter, or a more exotic inquiry than that of the God-seeking Hopkins, the latter is intensified to a degree which the secluded Jesuit priest was never conscious of. If there is little joy in the poems of Dylan Thomas, it is because his inquiring, clinical intellect has prohibited it. His probings have laid bare the tumour: his labours "towards some measure of light" have unearthed those things which are antithetical to a joyous lyricism. Momentarily, he has glimpsed his own origin and end, and, through himself, the origin and end of all men. His problems are theirs; their world his:

> I have longed to move away
> From the hissing of the spent lie . . .
> From the repetition of salutes.

> I dreamed my genesis in a sweat of sleep, breaking
> Through the rotating shell, strong
> As motor muscle on the drill, driving
> Through vision and the girdered nerve.

> I see the boys of summer in their ruin
> Lay the gold tithings barren,
> Setting no store by harvest, freeze the soils;

Here can be no lyricism, no ringing laughter. When such a poet chuckles, children will halt in their play.

Of the two factors, inquiry and a terror of fearful expectation, there are abundant examples in both books. Indeed, it is obvious that without some capacity for inquiry few of these poems could have been written at all. The poet's consistent and constant desire to uncover what has been too long hidden is itself the proof of his curious nature: and where might such a man more commendably start than by inquiring into his own processes, reactions and origins? But the poet does not stop there: his inquiry expands outwards until it embraces the whole system in which man moves; and with this inquiry, again comes criticism:

[18] Charles Williams: Intro. to the Poems of G. M. Hopkins (O.U.P.)

Once in this wind the summer blood
Knocked in the flesh that decked the vine,
Once in this bread
The oat was merry in the wind;
Man broke the sun, pulled the wind down.

This flesh you break this blood you let
Make desolation in the vein,

and the whole of the poem in 25 *Poems* about The Hand.

"Terror of fearful expectation" broods over most of the poems. It is a terror of the darkness, and a fear of hidden things. In bringing these fears into an antiseptic daylight, dragging them into sight and parading them, the poet is teaching himself, and some of us, to grapple with them, and to overcome them.

Often it is the terror of the body,[19] the fear of the self, the powerful black-magic of the subconscious that inspires the poet and disturbs the reader:

I dreamed my genesis and died again, shrapnel
Rammed in the marching heart, hole
In the stitched wound and clotted wind, muzzled
Death on the mouth that ate the gas.

Sharp in my second death I marked the hills, harvest
Of hemlock and the blades, rust
My blood upon the tempered dead, forcing
My second struggling from the grass.

Again, as we have observed previously, it is the terror of man and society:

I have longed to move away
From the repetition of salutes,

[19] Another young poet, David Gascoyne, in "The Supposed Being," has expressed something of this dread:

Supposing the sex
a cruelty and dread in the thighs
a gaping and blackness—a charred
trace of feverish flames
the sex like an X
as the sign and the imprint of all that has gone before
as a torch
to enlighten the forests of gloom and the
mountains of unattained night.

For there are ghosts in the air
And ghostly echoes on paper . . .

I have longed to move away but am afraid . . .

Whether this is the desire of the sensitive mind to avoid the torments to which it is subjected by an insensitive society, the desire of the hermit; or whether it is the longing for death as a release from painful life, the terror is the same, and fear is always there.

I have longed to move away
From the hissing of the spent lie
And the old terror's continual cry
Growing more terrible as the day
Goes over the hill into the deep sea;

III

Apart from such obvious similarities as the foregoing quotations have indicated, there are also other factors common to both poets which not only indicate an identity of outlook, but also a strong technical influence from Hopkins to Dylan Thomas.

The first, an identity of outlook, is most apparent in such extracts as the following, where each poet is attempting, by the use of an individual "clinical" vocabulary, to illuminate some aspect of man. Here is the model:

Lord of the living and dead;
Thou hast bound bones and veins in me, fashioned me flesh,
And after it almost unmade, what with drear,
Thy doing . . .[20]

This is what Thomas makes of it:

I sent my creature scouting on the globe,
That globe itself of hair and bone
That, *sewn to me by nerve and brain*
Had stringed my flask of matter to his rib.

and:

He holds *the wire from this box of nerves.*

There is an objective treatment in both poets; it is the physical

[20] "The Wreck of the Deutschland." Hopkins.

vision elevated into poetry; it is man described as a working model, as a machine; it is the legacy of John Donne.

The emotional rush of words, common to both writers, and the assonantal and alliterative form which such a rush takes even exposes them to similar faults, and betrays the blind spot in them both. In Hopkins, this blind spot gives rise to:

Stirred for a bird.

and, "Piecemeal peace is poor peace. What pure peace." and in Thomas, the lesser faults:

Chaste and the chaser . . .

Grief thief of time . . .

But conclusive proof of Thomas's derivation from Hopkins lies, I think, in the similarity, and very frequently the coincidence of their compound words. There is, in both poets, an abundance of such compounds: the early Hopkins poems seem to owe much to Keats in this respect, but the later ones show an individuality which is nowhere else apparent, save in the poetry of Dylan Thomas.[21]

Frequently the compound words used by the two poets fall into the same fundamental groupings; by which I mean those groupings which are the common heritage of all writers, and which are consequently never original and hence never derivative. Such alliterative-and triple-compounds as "May-mess," "bell-bright," "day-labouring-out," (Hopkins), and "sky-scraping," "fair-formed," "hero-in-tomorrow" (Thomas), are cases in point.

But when it is found that two poets employ compounds, in which the verbal elements coincide and fall into identical groupings, the deduction is an obvious one. Here, as examples, are: "moon mark," "star-eyed," "sea-corpse," "bone house" (Hopkins), and "moonturned," "star-gestured," "sea-faiths," "bone-rail" (Thomas), where the moon-, star-, sea-, and bone-elements are held in common.

This, to my mind, is a major point in the consideration of influences on the work of Dylan Thomas; yet, since it is one which, after the initial statement, may gain little advantage by discussion, I have added an Appendix on the point, in which are gathered together, under certain arbitrary groupings, those compounds which I consider as showing most effectively the commerce between the writers.

21 See Appendix on Compounds.

APPENDIX

Compound Words Of Hopkins And Thomas

Class	*Hopkins*	*Thomas*
1. Alliterative	May-mess	Sky-scraping, fair-formed
2. Triple-compounds	Day-labouring-out	Hero-in-tomorrow
3. MAN-	Manshape, man-wolf	Manshape, man-iron
4. Number-compound	Fire-leaved	One-sided, three-pointed
5. WOMB	Womb-life	Womb-eyed
6. HEART-	Heartsore, heart-forsook	Heartbone, heart-shaped
7. CHRIST	Christ-done-deed	Christward
8. RE-	Rewinded	Resuffered
9. BONE-	Bonehouse	Bonerail
10. UN-(Negative prefix)	Uncumbered	Unsucked
11. SEA-	Sea-corpse	Sea-faiths
12. WATER-	Waterworld	Water-clock
13. STAR-	Star-eyed	Star-gestured
14. JACK-	Jackself	Jackchrist
15. MOON-	Moon mark	Moon turned
16. -LIGHT	Hornlight	Owl-light
17. -EYES	Star-eyed	Red-eyed, womb-eyed
18. -TALE(s)	Tell tales	Tell-tale
19. -FATHOMED	No-man-fathomed	Five-fathomed

Critics, Style and Value

DEREK STANFORD

I

Thomas, as a poet, seems to me an extraordinarily difficult figure to summarise. Part of this difficulty arises, I think, from the non-intellectual nature of his work (Henry Treece[1] considers him the least intellectual poet of his generation), which cannot easily be reduced to a formula without distorting its intention or meaning. It is true that there is a consistency discoverable in his work, but it is one that derives from a certain prevailing atmosphere rather than from a number of recurrent concepts. The continuity in Thomas' work is not the continuity of rational argument, but of something like biological growth. His poems evolve by a mode of transformation rather than by a step-by-step advance.

Because of this, it would appear that the intuitive critical approach to Thomas' verse as a whole is uncalled-for. What seems required is a sympathetic word-for-word unravelling of the separate poems; and in the attention which certain of his pieces received from Francis Scarfe, William Empson, Henry Treece, and Marshall W. Stearns, fortunate precedents were established.

This is not in any way to belittle the early statements which Sir Herbert Read and Dr. Edith Sitwell made about his poems; for when the former wrote that "these poems cannot be reviewed; they can only be acclaimed", describing them as constituting "the most absolute poetry that has been written in our time", the purpose of the words was not to define but to draw attention to a new phenomenon. And that attention once secured (largely through the commendation

From *Dylan Thomas* by Derek Stanford (London: Neville Spearman Limited, 1954), pp. 144–154. Reprinted by permission of Neville Spearman Limited.

[1] *Dylan Thomas* (1949).

of these writers), the next task for criticism was to undertake an examination of these strange poems one by one; and only then to pronounce upon the generality of Thomas' muse.

Ironically, the very school one would have expected most fitted for this business—the textual analysts[2] associated with Dr. Leavis of Downing College, Cambridge, and the magazines *Scrutiny* and *The Critic*—failed lamentably to interpret or evaluate the poet. Both these magazines which came out against the work of Thomas have since ceased publication, and were it not for one factor, the inability of their contributors to recognise the positive achievement of the poet could conveniently be forgotten. The factor that precludes such happy oblivion as the most sensible comment, is that *Scrutiny*, in particular, played an important role in forming the taste of teachers of English in many of the higher schools in this country for something between ten and fifteen years. This being so, a few short remarks on the spirit of these critics may be spared.

Writing in *Scrutiny* (Summer, 1946), Mr. Wolf Mankowitz concluded that "Mr. Thomas does not offer very much to the literary critic for analysis. He is responsible for a great deal which transcends analysis in the work of other young writers. He offers at best an appeal to the sophisticated eye on the look-out for the cheap *frisson* of recognising a trick which some other competitive poetry-lover lost." Apart from the severity of judgment and the acerbity of tone, which certain of Dr. Leavis' followers appear to have inherited from him, there is nothing in this statement which might make the reader suspicious of the critic's credentials. It has the authoritative pitch, and that—with many—passes for wisdom. But when we turn to Mr. Mankowitz's responses to the poet's actual lines and phrases, the shortcomings of his sensibility are obviously apparent.

Speaking of what he calls Thomas' "false analogies", Mr. Mankowitz remarks that "a variety of 'striking' images such as 'the children innocent as strawberries' . . . fall down as soon as analysed." That Mr. Mankowitz is unable to sense the likeness between the unreflecting rosy-cheeked children and the fresh, red, unspoiled fruit ("innocent" because uncorrupted, uncorrupted because they are not rotten),

[2] Although affiliated to this group, a critic of the stature of William Empson, in his excellent exposition of Thomas' poem *A Refusal to Mourn* (*Strand*, March, 1947), proved conclusively that fine natural sensibility must always transcend group prejudice and fashion. It is amusing and instructive to compare Empson's masterly exegesis of this poem with the carking "superior" bafflement which Mr. Henry Gibson proudly displays, as his only critical trophy from the poem, when he came to examine the same piece in *The Critic* (Autumn, 1947).

shows that his own notion of analogy is narrowly, pedantically, inadequate. The same inflexibility of mind is present when he complains of such a "poetic pseudo-statement" as the phrase "happy as the grass was green". What Thomas is referring to here is surely common knowledge to all who remember their childhood (which is the context of the poet's phrase). When one was younger the grass seemed greener; and this intenser hue of the grass is used as a measure of the poet's happiness when he speaks about his boyhood.

The critic who cannot see the justification for running counter to accepted speech-forms in such phrases as this would seem to reveal a too niggardly awareness for us to trust in his conclusions.

II

I have already indicated my hesitation in summarising Thomas' poetry as a whole. For what it is worth, one can easily talk of how his early 'body' poetry, with its centre in subjective sensation, has tended to evolve towards a more traditional descriptive poetry, with its centre in the object depicted. But this—though helping to determine the direction of the poet's writing—presents no general image of it, and does not suggest its over-all nature.

The difficulty of arriving at such a formulation is especially seen when we attempt to frame a general definition of the poet's style.

To by-pass this difficulty by maintaining, with Geoffrey Grigson, that there is no style there at all—only a discrete formlessness "with the meaningless hot sprawl of mud"[3]—does not seem a particularly felicitous solution.

One of the best attempts to locate a characteristic method of Thomas is made by Cecil Day Lewis in his book *The Poetic Image*. Commenting on the poet's own account[4] of how he wrote his verse,

[3] In the essay *How much me now your acrobatics amaze* in his book *The Harp of Aeolus* (1947).

[4] In a letter to Henry Treece, Thomas wrote "a poem by me needs a host of images. I make one image—though 'make' is not the word; I let, perhaps, an image be 'made' emotionally in me and then apply to it what intellectual and critical forces I possess; let it breed another, let that image contradict the first; make of the third image, bred out of the two together, a fourth contradictory image, and let them all, within my imposed formal limits, conflict. Each image holds within it the seed of its own destruction, and my dialectical method, as I understand it, is a constant building up and breaking down of the images that come out of the central seed, which is itself destructive and constructive at the same time. . . . The life in any poem of mine cannot move concentrically round a central image, the life must come out of the centre; an image must be born and

the critic observes, that "At the centre of Mr. Thomas' poems there is not a single image, but 'a host of images'. For the reader the impression may be of escape of gas under water—I do not intend this with any disrespect—and bubbles breaking out apparently at random all over the surface: for the poet, the bubbles are the heart of the poem. Secondly, the process by which this host of images creates a poem is one of conflict—the second image will 'contradict the first', and so on. Now, in what sense can one image be said to contradict another? Logic is obviously not in question. Nor, I think, are we chiefly concerned with that kind of physical antagonism between image and idea which produces conceit, although such conceit can sometimes be found in Mr. Thomas' verse, as for example the Crashaw-like second line of

> A hand rules pity as a hand rules heaven;
> Hands have no tears to flow.

Nor, again, is it a matter of the poet letting one image follow another into the poem automatically just as they race through his mind, for Mr. Thomas speaks of applying 'intellectual and critical forces' to his images, and of 'imposed formal limits'. By 'contradiction' I think we must understand the bringing together, in images, of objects that have no natural affinity; or perhaps it might be more accurate to say objects which would not on the face of it seem to make for consistency of impression."[5]

This tells us much about Thomas' style, but in terms of cause rather than effect. Is there any simple way by which we can suggest the predominant quality of Thomas' finished poetic speech?

One American critic has summed-up his impression of Thomas' verse by referring to the poet's "style of sound". This term, which implies a recognition both of the rhetorical and incantatory elements in Thomas' work, applies extremely well to the early poems, but does not characterise the high proportion of visual and factual imagery in the verse from *Deaths and Entrances* onwards. In these later poems, what

---

die in another; and any sequence of my images must be a sequence of creations, recreations, destructions, contradictions. . . . Out of the inevitable conflict of images—inevitable, because of the creative, recreative, destructive and contradictory nature of the motivating centre, the womb of war—I try to make that momentary peace which is a poem."

[5] For a most fruitful application of this principle of composition to Thomas' poem *After the Funeral,* the reader is referred to pp. 123–125 of Mr. Day Lewis' book.

Thomas appears to be striving after is not an interpretation of experience, but a sensuous verbal equivalent for it—for a body of words which should have the density, the logic-proof nature of sensation itself.

But between the style of these later poems and his early 'auditory' pieces, can there be said to be any likeness? I think there can; and find the clue given in an excellent essay on the poet by M. Roger Asselineau.[6] M. Asselineau speaks of how from the first line of a poem by Thomas, one is precipitated in *media res*. "The openings of his poems," he observes, "possess a surprising brutality: 'I see the boys of summer [in their ruin]', 'My hero bares his nerves along my wrist', 'If I were tickled by the rub of love'. Titles are never employed by him. A title is already the start of an explanation, and to make any concession to the reader is something repugnant to him."

In remarking how a poem by Thomas precipitates us into the thick of the situation which it expresses, M. Asselineau leads us to consider the autotelic method of this poet's composition. By severing the ropes of intellectual relativity, which tether most poems to a set of circumstances not immediately poetic, Thomas has largely fashioned a style intended as impenetrable to the 'prose' mind. In the early poems, this resistance to reason is embodied in a style whose suasions are rhetorical and incantatory: in the latter poems, the chief device against the inroads of rational thought is a close-packed sensuous imagery—a sealed column of verbalised sensation.

So far, then, as Thomas' poetry repudiates all intercourse with non-poetic thought, his style may be said to reach out after a verbal ideal of glorious isolation. But this should not lead us to think of his verse as the latest bloom of 'pure poetry'; since by that epithet is often understood a poetry whose content, as well as form, is verbal—a poetry whose subject itself is words. Unlike the work of the exponents of this school, the poetry of Thomas is not *about* words. It is about memory and sensation—and all the ingredients of experience, in fact—but always about experience from within: about sensation, by one engaged in it; about memory, by one remembering. The abstracts of these states—which is what the rational reflective mind usually deals in when it comes to them—was anathema to the poet. What he wrote from was the act of experience—the condition of fashioning it or enduring it; and what he wrote with was rhetoric and imagery—the warm simulacra of experience in words.

[6] *Etudes Anglaises* (Janvier, 1954).

III

To locate Thomas' position in English poetry at the present time would be premature. His death has stirred most of us to a greater degree of willing sympathy than probably makes for the justest criticism; and this is as it should be. Certainly we need, at the moment, to approach his work with the most voluntary feelings of identification possible. We need to submit ourselves to the enchantments of his verse, and shall come away with our sensibility the richer. But before we can be sure how much the richer we are for this contact, the clarification of time is necessary. To-day we stand too close to our subject: perspective is demanded, and the years will provide it. What I have to say, then, in this postscript, concerning the place and status of the poet, can only be advanced as conjectural and tentative in the extreme. In offering the substance of my critical hazard, I hope that the avoidance of two extremes will be conducive to moderation in future and more definite assessment of the poet.

In regarding the poetry of Thomas, and the interest attached to it of late years, we must allow for the working of three factors: literary fashion, literary history, and intrinsic literary merit. The first of these is of course a powerful but ephemeral force. The fashion for Thomas was doubtlessly created by the very violence of the poet's shock-tactics (quite outside a consideration of their real poetic efficacy); and such renown as Thomas owes to the agency of this force will essentially diminish with the years. But likewise, too, the counter-fashion—current among the disciples of Dr. Leavis, and the admirers of Lord Gorell—will wane, perhaps even more rapidly.

Of more durable consideration, in the assessment of Thomas, is his achievement in extending literary technique. To instance but one of the devices by which he had enriched poetic usage—his adaption of colloquialisms to a lyrical end and purpose. Already, in the 'Twenties, T. S. Eliot had caused an appreciable stir by inserting phrases from common speech, bare and unworked, into his verse. But with the alien presence of such 'prose' words, Thomas was not content. And so, in his verse, we get such figures as "a grief ago" (for 'a while ago'), "happy as the heart was long" (for 'happy as the day is long'), and "the man in the wind and the west moon" (for 'the man in the moon and the west wind'). Certain of these poetic variations have been spoken of aversely by critics; but whether or not examples of this device in Thomas' poems can be considered successful, the fact remains that the method has added to the sum of poetic equipment.

Another aspect to be observed in Thomas' contribution to literary history is the revival which his work occasioned of a more lyrical manner of writing. The naturalisation of the poetic idiom, which the Imagists began, had—by the middle of the 'Thirties—gone so far that an unnatural flatness resulted. Instead of the varying speech-rhythms which Eliot's generation had wished to assimilate, we were offered, too often, the rhythms of prose, along with 'prose' thoughts and sentiments. From this level of melodic dullness, Thomas' work helped to awaken us; and without evaluing over-highly the neo-romantic movement which followed, we must allow a number of good poems which Thomas' verse helped to incept.

To decide what proportion of the poet's present fame derives from his intrinsic literary merit is a much harder issue. Stating the matter without too much fine point, I should say that about one-third of the poems in his *Collected Poems* (which contains ninety-nine pieces) represents good or near-successful work. The remaining two-thirds seems to me sadly marred by a variety of faults: strained and wilful mannerisms, mystifications, and needless obscurities. That it will continue to be studied for the light it throws on the better pieces, and that such study will increasingly reveal isolated triumphs of language, appears to me also certain. Yet Thomas' status will, I think, be determined by the smaller body of his poems; and the size of this body will necessarily limit his lasting renown. At the same time, we might well remember that the ages of great out-put in verse seem over, and not place too much stress on bulk as a criterion.

But neither in the number of his worth-while pieces nor in the length of his individual poems was Thomas remarkable. One of his (by common consent) finest compositions, *Fern Hill* is some ten lines shorter than Shelley's *Ode to the West Wind* and over half as short as Gray's *Elegy in a Country Churchyard.* Of his other poems, there are not more than a dozen of equal or greater length than *Fern Hill*, and probably not one quite as good.[7]

These comparisons are not intended to provide a more than quantitative perspective; but they are not without some bearings on the status that Thomas will come to assume. If T. S. Eliot had not written *The Waste Land* nor any of the *Four Quartets*, he would be—as far

[7] I am aware of the strongly personal, and perhaps unshared, nature of this statement. There are some critics, I believe, who consider *A Winter's Tale* or *Vision and Prayer* as Thomas' best piece; and they are certainly striking poems. Then, too, the claims of such later poems as *In country sleep, Poem on his birthday,* and *In the white giant's thigh* will doubtlessly find strong defenders.

as out-put is concerned—a poet of the same calibre as we have to assess in Thomas.

Among Thomas' shorter pieces are some half a dozen which I would rank with the very best 'short-lyric' poetry written during the last fifty years: *The force that through the green fuse drives the flower, Especially when the October wind, Why east wind chills, And death shall have no dominion, The Hunchback in the Park,* and *In my Craft or Sullen Art.* Over and above which there remains something like another twenty pieces of good, original and largely lucid poetry. Upon such rough approximate accounting, can one arrive at any conclusion?

In his *New Bearings in English Poetry*, Dr. Leavis argues for the acceptance of Gerard Manley Hopkins as a major English poet. Without fully assenting to this evaluation, we cannot deny the key-position which Hopkins occupies in the history of modern verse. Now many critics have remarked Hopkins' influence on Thomas; and some would attribute to the latter a revitalisation of poetic language similar to that which Hopkins effected. This, I believe, is to over-state the likeness, as well as to over-estimate Thomas.

D. S. Savage[8] has commented upon the "moral passivity" behind the poet's verse; and it is just this lack of tension (generated when an ethical passion clashes with a strong natural instinct) which limits Thomas' poetic vision. In all his work, there is nothing equal to the exaltation of *The Wreck of the Deutschland* or the inquisition of the 'terrible' sonnets. It is not with Hopkins that he must be compared.

The name of Gray, in this context, has been previously mentioned; and I think it is rather with such a poet that Thomas must be stationed. Gray's complete poetic work contains a little over half the number of pieces included in Thomas' *Collected Poems;* and his fame rests on a mere handful of these: *The Elegy, The Bard* four of his six *Odes,* and possibly *The Progress of Poetry.* With this slender contribution, Gray helped to turn the taste of his age towards a warmer and more colourful style, and to free poetic language from the weary spell of Pope. The parallels with Thomas are not hard to seek; and if Thomas should prove equal to this measure, his fame and its longevity will be assured.

[8] See his essay on the poet in *Little Reviews Anthology 1947–1948.*

from The Wisdom of Poetry

WILLIAM ARROWSMITH

The *Collected Poems* of Dylan Thomas should be the occasion for a genuine reassessment; it is certainly high time. If Thomas is, as some claim, the finest living poet in the English language, we deserve to have made clear the prejudices which permit such a judgment; if he is, alternatively, only a compulsive babbler (as some still think), we need to be shown why the babble is so successful as poetry. In the meantime, I should like to push several observations which seem to me to touch Thomas' poetry in the area of its typical risks and advantages, and its promise in particular.

To begin with, Thomas is a poet of severe limitations, and those limitations are crucial as a bar to his further development. Thomas' debt to primitivism is well known; no need here to speak of his debt to Frazer or Welsh primitive custom or germane symbolisms. For all his apparent debt to Donne and Herbert and the English metaphysicals, Thomas is only in the most distorted sense a metaphysical poet himself. He is in fact our most consistently and extravagantly primitive poet, and I mean no dispraise by this just yet. He came to poetry with a natural Eleusinian sense of life, and he has done his best to deepen that sense as the matrix of his poetry. His own poetry is all explicitly in praise of a life-process which bears less relation to Bergson than to Heraclitus or to Empedocles. It is overtly prelogical; in Thomas' process, logical opposites like Being and Not-Being fold naturally into one another; death and life are directly interchangeable terms by virtue of the process which throws them up as merely different specifications of itself. To insist that Thomas *thinks* as, say MacNiece thinks, is to ignore the fact that the language in which Thomas' "thought" is carried on belongs to those fine days before

Reprinted from *The Hudson Review,* VI, No. 4 (Winter 1953–54), 597–600.

Plato's *Parmenides* when Not-Being still Was. I am not, of course, saying that Thomas "babbles"; he doesn't. But he has anachronized the world back into his process with little concern for the cost. Christ, for instance, is in Thomas no Christian Christ, but amoral and pre-Christian: all Adonis. Moreover, his process is not only prelogical (which doesn't matter in a poet of Thomas' skills) but also premoral (which, I think, does matter).

Put it this way. Thomas' poetry is in praise of Process ("the force that through the green fuse drives the flower"); his typical problem has been the reconcilation of the individual with the process: how can a man have a history or destiny apart from the process, especially when his relation to it is one of making second-order statements about it, like the artist? Up to now, the artist-participant whose vision gives form to the process itself has been Thomas' answer. In the new poem, *Over Sir John's hill,* for instance, there is an unusually magnificent statement of a common Thomas idea: the celebration of the Process in equal praise of the destroying "hawk on fire" and the murdered "small birds of the bay"; standing aside, neither wholly within the process nor wholly apart from it, are the linked figures of the "holy heron" and Dylan as the fabling Aesop of the Process, singing both a paean and a dirge, i.e., a "paeanodirge." Elsewhere Thomas is the Noah of the small animals with whom he sets sails against the flood; there, lonely at first, he finds the sea blossom with "a multitude of arks" (cf. "alone in a multitude of loves") which signify creature-communion and common love in the great flux. All creatures by living and dying celebrate the process; their poem is in their living the process out, incarnating it, while the poet (who is with them, but not of them, like Noah and Aesop) lives in his poetry his informing second-order praise.

It is, for obvious reasons, not altogether easy to come to terms with this Eleusinian apocalypse and its passionate prophet. It has, after all, generated poetry of extraordinary vitality in the hands of a poet who lives it as a matter of faith. And for all its rigorous prelogicality, it is not therefore philosophically invalid. But there are, I think, two major objections, one concerned with the method of its carrying out, and the other concerned with its human cost. To celebrate life means to celebrate its particularities as much as the universal behind them; and given the apparent strength-in-particularity of Thomas' poetry, it is perhaps imprudent to suggest that Thomas is more in love with Process than the small creatures who have to live it. But for all the flurry of creatures, mice, foxes, badgers, etc., who clamber on to

Dylan's ark, it seems clear to me that if Thomas is a Franciscan, he is the Francis of symbols, without tenderness. These animals are heraldic; they are not foxes *qua* foxes, but Process-foxes, and what Thomas loves in them is not their individual lives but the smell of the processed fox. This point, if granted, leads directly to the second. The Process is an abstraction of Life, and to give your heart to an abstraction means the eventual truncation of the humane emotions. If it does not mean that, then it must mean the falsification of the animals and creatures in whom Process is felt to be immanent. For instance: in *Over Sir John's hill,* the poet speaks explicitly of "praise to the hawk on fire!" and equally of grief for the hawk's victims ("we grieve . . . for the sake of the slain birds sailing"). To celebrate Process means celebrating both destroyer and destroyed as being essentially one; but Thomas fools himself if he thinks that grief, real grief, for the victim is compatible with the oppressor's glory, even in the matter of birds. If the grief is genuine, it is because it is not grief for real birds at all, but for the emblem-birds of Process. And elsewhere it is the same; what is true of birds is true of men. Truly to celebrate Process means not to be able to afford the human luxury of grief or pity or pride; they are irrelevant to Process or its waste-products. I have the constant impression in Thomas that his devotion to Process has resulted in a genuine truncation of the emotions or has forced him to artificialize his grief and his creatures so they can carry the intolerable weight of the life-process. What makes him a magnificent poet, that thudding vitalism in which winds whack and hills bounce, cuts him off from the completion of his poetic and human skills. Thomas is a primitive poet, and the cost of that primitive celebration is the loss of the civilized virtues and the problems of civilized men. The cost is, I think, already taking its toll; at least I find in these late poems a renewed belligerency about Life which shows itself in increasing rage and self-disgust, the rage of a man who feels that Morality or a Christian Christ is on the point, despite all his efforts, of getting a foothold in the Process via the back door. A lover's quarrel with Process should be worth watching; not until then will these mysteries be either moralized or civilized.

Replies to an Enquiry*

1. Do you intend your poetry to be useful to yourself or others?

   To both. Poetry is the rhythmic, inevitably narrative, movement from an overclothed blindness to a naked vision that depends in its intensity on the strength of the labour put into the creation of the poetry. My poetry is, or should be, useful to me for one reason: it is the record of my individual struggle from darkness towards some measure of light, and what of the individual struggle is still to come benefits by the sight and knowledge of the faults and fewer merits in that conrete record. My poetry is, or should be, useful to others for its individual recording of that same struggle with which they are necessarily acquainted.

2. Do you think there can now be a use for narrative poetry?

   Yes. Narrative is essential. Much of the flat, abstract poetry of the present has no narrative movement, no movement at all, and is consequently dead. There must be a progressive line, or theme, of movement in every poem. The more subjective a poem, the clearer the narrative line. Narrative, in its widest sense, satisfies what Eliot, talking of "meaning," calls "one habit of the reader." Let the narrative take that one logical habit of the reader along with its movement, and the essence of the poem will do its work on him.

3. Do you wait for a spontaneous impulse before writing a poem; if so, is this impulse verbal or visual?

   No. The writing of a poem is, to me, the physical and mental task of constructing a formally watertight compartment of words, pref-

* These replies [by Dylan Thomas] to questions submitted by the editor were published in *New Verse,* October, 1934.

erably with a main moving column (*i.e.*, narrative) to hold a little of the real causes and forces of the creative brain and body. The causes and forces are always there, and always need a concrete expression. To me, the poetical "impulse" or "inspiration" is only the sudden, and generally physical, coming of energy to the constructional, craftsman ability. The laziest workman receives the fewest impulses. And vice versa.

4. Have you been influenced by Freud and how do you regard him?

Yes. Whatever is hidden should be made naked. To be stripped of darkness is to be clean, to strip of darkness is to make clean. Poetry, recording the stripping of the individual darkness, must, inevitably, cast light upon what has been hidden for too long, and by so doing, make clean the naked exposure. Freud cast light on a little of the darkness he had exposed. Benefiting by the sight of the light and the knowledge of the hidden nakedness, poetry must drag further into the clean nakedness of light more even of the hidden causes than Freud could realise.

5. Do you take your stand with any political or politico-economic party or creed?

I take my stand with any revolutionary body that asserts it to be the right of all men to share, equally and impartially, every production of man from man and from the sources of production at man's disposal, for only through such an essentially revolutionary body can there be the possibility of a communal art.

6. As a poet what distinguishes you, do you think, from any ordinary man?

Only the use of the medium of poetry to express the causes and forces which are the same in all men.

Is Dylan a Fake?

HENRY TREECE

No one who has followed his progress from the position of editor of an advanced Little Magazine to that of author of a 'highbrow' thriller would call Julian Symons an irresponsible writer. Strongly biased, yes; but usually seeming to know what he is about, and moreover, often too interested in critical truth to perjure himself for the sake of a few clever words. Therefore, in view of his early praise of Dylan Thomas, his indictment that Dylan's poems are "Jokes, rhetorical, intellectual fakes of the highest class",[1] is especially interesting.

Is Mr. Symons renouncing his earlier judgment, admitting a critical instability at the time when he first praised the poet?[2] Or, is he announcing, like Louis MacNeice, who censured Dylan's 'adolescence', that he has grown up?

Whatever the answer, I think that it may be worth while to consider Mr. Symons's criticism here more fully, which we may best start to do by examining the meaning of this word "fake".

What is a fake? According to Chambers' *Dictionary*, it is a "counterfeit, swindle or sham".

Now it seems to me that the first definition: "counterfeit, swindle or sham", presupposes in the performer of the swindle a desire to deceive others, to deprive them of their rightful possessions by the exchange of goods which are much less than what they seem, for his own profit. A second person must come into the examination, otherwise Mr. Symons's criticism falls flat, since no one may be suf-

From *Dylan Thomas* by Henry Treece (London: Lindsay Drummond, Ltd., 1949), pp. 129–135.

[1] Quoted by Marshall W. Stearns in *Transformation* 3 (Lindsay Drummond).
[2] "No modern poet except Thomas is, for me, more affecting, more able to twist words to the shape of the reader's tears" (Julian Symons, writing on Hart Crane in *Twentieth Century Verse*).

ficiently omniscient to decide whether or not the poet is deceiving *himself*. That is something only a psychoanalyst could assure us of: nor would his assurance be of great interest critically. Furthermore, in view of Dylan's belief in his power to strip clean what had previously been hidden, to bring up to the light those elements of thought and feeling which he had not been conscious of before, it seems unlikely that he would at the same time, with the same movement, as it were, *expose* and *deceive*.

I believe, then, that Dylan Thomas is not swindling himself, consciously at least.

Is he, therefore, swindling his readers, asking their tolerance and appreciation of work which is counterfeit and sham? It is true that his nature is such that he wishes to make an impression on his audience, to parade before them a striking personality. But, if he does this legitimately, that is, by *being* such a personality, and by producing such poems as will elucidate this personality, where then is the swindle? The audience knows the sort of thing it is going to be shown: if they like it, well and good; if they don't, then they should go to another playhouse. There can be no question of swindle, though.

Nor do I see anything in Thomas's work which, judged relatively to his own personality, could be called "sham" or "counterfeit". If there is a deficiency in his work, this deficiency grows from a similar deficiency in the poet's personality, I believe. But that work seems to be the sincere expression of his personality, good or ill, and therefore no sham.

What, then, are these deficiencies which have caused Mr. Symons to suspect the poet? He is fond of the *dramatic gesture*, for instance; which he habitually produces by a mouthful of fine words:

> And father all nor fail the fly-lord's acre,
> Nor sprout on owl-seed like a goblin-sucker,
> But rail with your wizard's ribs the heart-shaped planet;
>
> *25 Poems*

The ability to roll such words on his tongue may be an elemental childlike ability, born of a desire for magnificence, created from a sense of glory, that same desire and sense which cause the poet so often to introduce the names of heroes (Caesar, Nansen, Blake) into his lines; but the gravest charge one may bring is that it is empty rhetoric; a primitive Celtic mechanism, and in no way a deception. Only a court set up in these times of rationing, utility and austerity could condemn a Romantic poet for indulging in the extravagant taste of fine words! And on that reckoning Hopkins, Keats, Shelley, Tennyson, Swinburne and a dozen others would stand convicted. A variant of this capacity for rhetoric, and, as it well may be, possibly part of it, is such a passage as:

> If my head hurt a hair's foot
> Pack back the downed bone. If the unpricked
> ball of my breath
> Bump on a spout let the bubbles jump out.
>
> *The Map of Love*

which seems to me a *verbal compulsion,* almost a psychopathic phenomenon, musical-rhythmic automatism, with a possibly unconscious sexual reference thrown in to emphasise the primitive source of the word-group.

If that is a joke, or a fake, or a swindle, I do not think the poet knows it. And what is it counterfeiting? It is like nothing that is not itself. And who, by such a piece of spontaneity, is the poet deceiving, and why? I do not think an answer can be found.

It is true that the poet has a *limited vocabulary* (that is, he has set limits to the number and types of words which he feels appropriate to his poetry), and that he must in consequence make one word serve many purposes of meaning, which, in its turn, may produce an obscurity, since the reader at times may not be certain of the word's connotation. That, however, is a fault of technique very possibly, and not one which denounces the integrity of the poet as poet, in distinction to the poet as craftsman.

What is more reprehensible, but still not sufficiently so to expose Thomas to his critic's charge of "counterfeit", is what seems to be a deliberate obscurity, as though the poet were boyishly teasing his readers rhythmically and musically:

> Now
> Say nay,
> Man dry man,
> Dry lover mine
> The deadrock base and blow the flowered anchor,
> Should he, for centre sake, hop in the dust,
> Forsake, the fool, the hardiness of anger.
>
> *25 Poems*

A pattern of sounds, a musical exercise, verbal 'doodling', perhaps: maybe not worth recording, or if worth recording, not worth printing —but a swindle, no! A piece of poetic high-spirits, yes!

In the above-quoted passage, I was not concerned overmuch about meaning though, admittedly, occasions do occur when this 'teasing' irritates, particularly when it happens alongside a passage of clarity, or on an occasion when the reader may be caught up in the magic of the poem concerned. And especially is this so when Dylan chooses for himself a difficult way of saying something which is essentially simple, or when, by his music and rhetoric, he magnifies a triviality. He seems naturally apt to make a tremendous pronouncement of something that is essentially commonplace. Just as an intoxicated man might:

> When it is rain where are the gods?
> Shall it be said they sprinkle water
> From garden cans, or free the floods?
>
> *25 Poems*

In this respect, one may partially agree with another statement made by Julian Symons: "What is said in Mr. Thomas's poetry is that the seasons change: that we decrease in vigour as we grow older; that life has no obvious meaning; that love dies . . ." Very true, too, and fine subjects for poetry these are. Mr. Symons is quite right; it is only when he goes on to say, "His poems mean no more than that. They mean too little", that I disagree. Mr. Symons is, in effect, denying Thomas a right which all poets have exercised, that of "reducing multitude to a unity of effect", which Blake was summing up in poetic language when he spoke about seeing the world in a sand-grain.

Thomas, like any other poet, has every sanction to put his pen to paper and write a whole sonnet-sequence, if he so wishes, on the fact that love dies, or that the seasons change. Why should these subjects mean "too little"? Shakespeare has done it and so has Keats.

Take away Thomas's right to state a simple, fundamental theme, in his own way, and you take away his whole method of working; for this method is based on the statement of an elemental truth in his first stanza, and the re-statement of this truth, with appropriate varieties, in each subsequent stanza. That is to say, he states a thesis, and repeats that thesis without development, a process which can best be seen at work in the poem, *The force that through the green fuse drives the flower* . . . from *18 poems,* in which each verse is a duplication in different words of the last.

And this is the only point at which I can agree with Mr. Symons, that his word "fake" may have derived from the German "fegen", which means "to furbish", that is, to polish up or decorate.

As it appears to me, however, it is a fault in the critic to use such a term as "fake". A poet, or any other artist, will achieve only that which is in him to achieve. If that achievement does not come up to the critic's self-imposed standards, is the poet then to be labelled as counterfeiter or swindler?

It is, like everything else I have been saying in this chapter, a commonplace that the perfect poet must be perfectly balanced. That is, that he should have that balance of intellect, emotion, experience and technique which will make him a fully-developed man. T. S. Eliot, who, in his *Introduction* to the Poems of Ezra Pound, stresses the supreme poetic importance of this balance between *experience* and *technique,* is one of the few poets writing to-day with this balance.

And it is possible that this balance may be an unknown and unsuspected factor in the working life of most poets. (Nor may a poet, by taking thought, cultivate it; though he may, in a certain degree, develop each separate element which is combined in that balance.) And a poet may write for years, unconscious of his mal-balance; this is, until such a time in his development when he is able to look objectively and coldly, impersonally, like a second person, at his own poems. And that occasion may be years in arriving, if it arrives at all.

I feel that Dylan Thomas is extremely (and unconsciously) ill-balanced; yet, in that unbalance, lies much of his 'charm', and most of his function as a 'Dog among the Fairies'; that is, a cataclysmic force among those poets deadened by traditionalism, or made ineffectual by hypersensitivity. His choking verbalisms, his fixations on certain threadbare or obscure epithets, his inability to resist inorganic alliterations, his wilful obscurity, his deafness to certain obviously poor rhymes, his preponderating rhythmic monotony, his careless use of words, the overstress or understress created by his rhetorical mechanisms, the overemphasised pathos and arrogance, the self-pity, the lack of humour, the poverty of historic background (reflected in his self-sufficiency), all these are evidence, and to spare, of a lack of *maturity.* But, unless such unbalance is known to the poet, it is less than just that he should be called a forger, and his works fakes.

It is more probable that Thomas writes impulsively, almost instinctively, his technique conditioned by certain semi-automatic and habitual verbal mechanisms, initially *for his own benefit* (to strip things clean, as he says). His desire will not be to deceive anyone; in fact, the beginning of the poems will visualise no other reader. When the first impulse has passed, however, it is likely that the poet comes to consider an audience, and so restates and decorates the original germ of his poem with this audience in mind, and with full consciousness of the especial effect which he wishes his own personality to make on the audience.

Review of *Collected Poems* and *Under Milk Wood*

WILLIAM EMPSON

The most interesting question about the poetry of Dylan Thomas, it seems to me, is raised by Cyril Connolly on the back of the dust-cover of the collected edition. He says that Dylan Thomas "distils an exquisite, mysterious, moving quality which defies analysis as supreme lyrical poetry always has and—let us hope—always will." This assertion has a certain truth, because the arts are a great mystery, but we must remember that the logic of it applies equally to Wordsworth. The suggestion of it is something quite different, that you needn't worry if you can't make any sense of the early Dylan Thomas poetry; you had better just be pleased, because you know you are in the fashion if you say you like it, and if it makes no sense that only shows it is profound. But this theory is dispiriting to good readers and a positive encouragement to the practice of bad reading; one ought not to rest content with it. And yet a good deal of his poetry does give countenance to this lethal formula; perhaps more so than any other top-grade poetry in the language. During his lifetime he was frequently attacked for (in effect) tossing the juice around so smudgily, though this has been ignored in the very deserved acclaim immediately after his death.

In any case, he had been changing. (And, incidentally, the early verse turns on rather few fundamental ideas, so that once you know what to expect you can find them with less effort; this makes it unlike the obscurity of Shakespeare when tearing on the tripod, which it otherwise resembles.) There is a period of sag in his work, already just feelable perhaps in the second book of poetry, where the succes-

From *The New Statesmen and Nation,* May 15, 1954.

sion of trilling magical lines, each practically a complete poem in itself, fails to add up. The sonnet sequence called *Altarwise by Owl-light* in the collected edition is a fair example, because a lot of it is undoubtedly wonderful and yet one can't help feeling that the style has become a mannerism. Evidently he became conscious of this, and most of the poems written during the Second World War are concerned to develop a particular theme. He went on to descriptions of his childhood, as in the splendid *Fern Hill,* which is not obscure at all; and meanwhile he was writing plays and stories which are fully externalised, though of course steeped in his particular tone or vision. He was just getting ready to be a dramatist, and knew he needed to, though the superb but rather static survey of *Under Milk Wood* was (as it happened) all he had time for. For that matter, as I have mentioned Wordsworth just to give the contrast of an author wishing to be simple in style, it is as well to point out that Wordsworth felt the need of the same process; he talks a good deal about the loss of his first inspiration and the struggle to become a greater poet as a result of that. We need not think of Dylan as a deluded or self-indulgent author. But, all the same, it is the first inspiration, the poems the young man hit the town with (overwhelmingly good, though one resisted them because one couldn't see why), which are the permanent challenge to a critic and in a way the decisive part of his work. I was disinclined to review the *Collected Poems* when it came out during his lifetime, because I would have had to say I liked the early obscure ones best, and I was afraid this would distress him; so I now have one of those unavailing regrets about my timidity, because he knew all that kind of thing very well and could be distressed only by a refusal to say it.

Many people recently have described their personal contacts with this entrancing talker. What I chiefly remember is hearing him describe how he was going to do a film of the life of Dickens, showing how he was determined to escape from the blacking factory and determined to send his children to Eton and finally killed himself by insisting on doing public performances of readings of the Murder of Nancy and so forth (not needed for money, only needed to make his life dramatic enough) when his doctors had told him it would kill him. You can't exactly blame the top chaps in the films for not hiring Dylan at his own valuation then; it was a question of time and one would think there was time in hand; but still the film he wanted to make about Dickens was very profound and very box-office. If Dylan had lived a normal span of life it would have been likely to mean a considerable improvement of quality in the entertainment profession; he ought not to be regarded as The Marvellous Boy who could not grow up.

Let us go back then to the early poems and their obscurity. It is quite true that they hit you before you know how, but that is no reason for not wanting to know how. When Dr. Johnson went to the Hebrides he took with him Cocker's *Arithmetic*, because (he said) you get tired of any work of literature, but a book of science is inexhaustible. When I was refugeeing across China (in 1937–9) I too had a little book of school Problem Papers, but it was worth carrying the poems of Dylan Thomas as well because they were equally inexhaustible. This was not in the least because I thought a smart critic only tastes them and knows better than ever to wonder what they mean; they would have been no use to me in such a case if I had taken up this silly attitude. All the same, there is still a lot of his poetry where I can feel it works and yet can't see why. I have no theory at all about the meaning of the line:

> The two-a-vein, the foreskin, and the cloud,

though I am sure there is a reason why it seems very good; and indeed I don't much like the poem (called *Now*) it's the last line of, so I don't bother about it, but I assume on principle there is something there which I feel and can't see, but could see. On the other hand, of course, there are cases where a footnote would make no difference. Since I got back to England recently I have been asking about Mnetha in the tremendous verse:

> Before I knocked and flesh let enter,
> With liquid hands tapped on the womb,
> I who was shapeless as the water
> That shaped the Jordan near my home
> Was brother to Mnetha's daughter
> And sister to the fathering worm.

Miss Kathleen Raine has at last told me that Mnetha is a suitable character in one of Blake's Prophetic Books; but this acts only as a reassurance that the line meant the kind of thing you wanted it to, not really as an explanation of it—"That'll do very well," as Alice said when she was told the meaning of a word in the *Jabberwocky;* because she knew already what it ought to fit in with. I think an annotated edition of Dylan Thomas ought to be prepared as soon as possible, and that a detail like that ought to go in briefly, but it would be hard to decide what else ought to go in.

The political poets of the early 1930's had good luck for poets in being able to recommend something practical (more socialism at home, a Popular Front against Hitler abroad) on which almost the whole country had come to agree with them by 1940. The idea that they ought to be ashamed of it, which is now creeping about, seems to be farcical. If they changed their minds they did so like other citizens; they were right at the time, as the country soon came to agree. It is untrue (and I gather that the mistake is liable to be made nowadays) to think that, when Dylan Thomas broke in, it meant a change of politics. He had much the same political opinions as Auden, and was very ready to say so; but he was not interested in writing about them. What hit the town of London was the child Dylan publishing *The force that through the green fuse* as a prize poem in the *Sunday Referee,* and from that day he was a famous poet; I think the incident does somes credit to the town, making it look less clumsy than you would think. The poem is more easily analysable than most early Dylan Thomas poems, and we need not doubt that the choosers knew broadly what it meant (I would not claim to know all myself); but it was very off the current fashion. It centres on comparing the blood-stream of the child Dylan to the sea-cloud-river cycle by which water moves round this planet, and he is united with the planet, also personally guilty of murder whenever a murderer is hanged, and so forth. The mining term *vein* for a line of ore was naturally a crucial pun for the early Dylan, because of his central desire to identify events inside his own skin with the two main things outside it, the entire physical world and also the relations with that of other men. Such was the main thing he was talking about, and the point of vision was set too high for him to let the current politics into the structure of metaphors. There was no other reason for not letting it in. He really was a "mystic," as the term is used, but he would have been very cross with anybody who supposed that this meant Right-wing politics.

I am trying to consider a reader who is doubtful whether to read this poetry, so I am thinking whether I could give any useful advice. You must realise that he was a very witty man, with a very keen though not at all poisoned recognition that the world contains horror as well as delight; his chief power as a stylist is to convey a sickened loathing which somehow at once (within the phrase) enforces a welcome for the eternal necessities of the world. It is particularly important to realise this at the end of the sequence *Altarwise by Owl-*

light, which I mentioned earlier as bad, but when it is good it is ragingly good. It ends:

> Green as beginning, let the garden diving
> Soar, with its two bark towers, to that Day
> When the worm builds with the gold straws of venom
> My nest of mercies in the rude, red tree.

I hope I do not annoy anyone by explaining that the Cross of Jesus is also the male sexual organ; Dylan would only have thought that tiresomely obvious a basis for his remark. But when you get to the worms instead of the birds able to build something valuable in this tree, and the extraordinary shock of the voice of the poet in his reverence and release (at the end of the whole poem) when he gets to his nest, you do begin to wonder whether he meant something wiser than he knew.

How Much Me Now Your Acrobatics Amaze

GEOFFREY GRIGSON

Whoever has the power of creating, has likewise the inferior power of keeping his creation in order.

W. W. LANDOR

Suppose one were compelled to decide between "reason" and "romance"; it is, surely, no more the reason of 1700 that one would choose than the romance of 1800 one would easily reject. "Romance" is too simple a pejorative. In the eighteenth century one could be "romantic" under reason, and in the nineteenth century one could be rational under romance. The "romance" we are drifting back to in England is a romance without reason: it is altogether self-indulgent and liquescent. An Inky Cap mushroom grows up white and firm and then flops down into a mess of ink—which is our new romance, something once alive which avoids no longer the decay into death. It is so much easier to flop, so much easier to give up the metabolism of life and literature, in a time which is contemptuous of law, and when there is no body of opinion at all clear about what is true and untrue, possible and impossible, probable and improbable. And so now a poet (Mr. George Barker) can fill nine-tenths of a book with such lines as:

> O Dolphins of my delight I fed with crumbs
> Gambading through bright hoops of days,
> How much me now your acrobatics amaze
> Leaping my one-time ecstasies from Doldrums. . .

From *The Harp of Aeolus and Other Essays on Art, Literature and Nature* by Geoffrey Grigson (London: George Routledge and Sons Ltd., 1947), pp. 151–160. Reprinted by permission of the author.

and another (Mr. Stephen Spender) declare

> And there was many another name
> Dividing the sun's light like a prism
> With the rainbow colours of an "ism"

—not only without critical eyebrow-raising, but with the evocation of the highest praise. If, in the most public way possible, in some periodical of the widest circulation and the highest repute, one were to examine such poetry, turn it inside out, expatiate with the greatest clarity and skill on the nature of poetry and its function in life, prove the awkwardness, limpness, and absurdity of these crumb-fed dolphins, nothing would happen, no one would notice. Objection, reason, proof—all would be swamped and swallowed in the universal mess.

Thinking of some of Gerard Hopkin's strictures on Browning, I have collected a number of pieces from another book of recent poems, full of lions and amber and dust and dew:

1. ... bird-blood leaps within our veins
   And is changed to emeralds like the sap in grass.
2. And you are the sound of the growth of spring in the heart's deep
   core.
3. And I would that each hair on my head was an angel
   O my red Adam.
4. O heed him not, my dew with golden feet
   Flying from me.
5. But the sap in these dry veins sang like a bird:
   "I was the sea that knew the siren song
   And my veins heard
   A planet singing in the Dorian mode. . ."
6. Another old man said:
   "I was a great gold-sinewed King, I had a lion's mane
   Like the raging sun. . ."
7. Were those the veins that heard the Siren's song?
8. So changed is she by Time's appalling night
   That even her bone can no more stand upright.
9. . . . but the long wounds torn by Time in the golden cheek
   Seem the horizons of the endless cold.
10. . . . and the first soundless wrinkles fall like snow
    On many a golden cheek
11. The kiss that holds . . . the rose that weeps in the blood.
12. But now only the red clover
    lies over the breath of the lion and the mouth of the lover.

All these—it is Hopkins's phrase—are frigidities, all of them untruths to nature, the emerald blood jumping in the veins, the angelic coiffure, dew with feet, veins with ears, sinews made of gold, cheek wounds like landscapes, wrinkles falling like snow, the rose weeping in the veins, the earth and plants on top of the dead lion's breath—frigidities except 2 and 8 (heart's deep core—heart's deep heart), which are specimens of the undiluted art of sinking. The poetry they come from is chimerical. The chimera has a lion's head, a goat's body, and a serpent's tail. The lion's head is a lion no longer real (as the lions of Dryden were real:

> And still for him the Lioness stalks
> And hunts her lover through the lonely walks).

The goat's body (and hair) is the absence of form; the serpent's tail the lines elongating into nothingness. Gerard Hopkins found it monstrous (his word once more, and I am speaking of the chimerical)—monstrous in Browning's *Instans Tyrannus*, that the sky was written of as a shield protecting the just man from the tyrant—"The vault of heaven is a vault, hollow, concave towards us, convex upwards; it therefore could only defend man on earth against enemies above it; an angry Olympus for instance." He held that Browning had "all the gifts but the one needful and the pearls without the string; rather, one would say raw nuggets and rough diamonds". His turning of concave into convex was a "frigidity", an "untruth to nature". It came of "frigid fancy with no imagination"; and frigid fancy describes the gilded stringless writing from which I have panned these dozen samples, writing of an order lower than that of Browning, and more full of untruths to nature.

Two signs of our drift into "romance" are the writing of such poetry, and the reception of it. The reception of these poems has been marked with the epithets of greatness in a hallelujah of reviews. If the poet (who is Miss Sitwell) adds to the reassembly, to the reiteration of the great truisms of the life and time and youth and age and decay and death, to the repetition of adjectives (golden, etc.) no longer valid for our sense of wonder, she has added nothing from nature. In fact, it is the ubiquitous confidence of the day that anything, any first impression, can be crammed into formless verse without the self-discipline and self-criticism which are the sources of form; the sources of that composition in which, Henry James declared, exists the "principle of health and safety". And that, exactly is where our new "romance", in all its guises, is decadent and different to, shall one say, the romance of Coleridge. It is dragging the past for verbiage, for words out of their setting, nature not at all, and the self for disorderly nonsense. Coleridge was a scientifically-minded poet, curious about self, the past, and the given nature around him. If the glitter and the excellence of a phenomenon in nature appealed to him, he did not crawl like a spaniel to its charm or mystery. He had seen, for example, the Glory, described in the *Memoirs of the Literary and Philosophical Society of Manchester,* in 1790, by a Fellow of the Royal Society. The Glory is the rainbow which surrounds the shadow of your head upon mist when the mist is in the right place below you, and the sun in the right place behind you. But instead of using the Glory as an ornament (as I have explained in writing of the Aeolian Harp), Coleridge used it in *Dejection,* and again in *Constancy to an Ideal Object,* to express his deepest exploration into the relation of man to nature:

> . . . would we aught behold of higher worth,
> Than that inanimate cold world, allow'd
> To the poor, loveless, ever-anxious crowd,
> Ah! from the soul itself must issue forth
> A light, a glory, a fair luminous cloud
> Enveloping the earth—
> And from the soul itself must there be sent
> A sweet and potent voice of its own birth.

Nature to Coleridge and Wordsworth, as romantics, may have been very different to nature as uniformity and commonsense for Dryden and for Pope. For an image, Dryden and Pope might never have used such a phenomenon as the Glory, so much outside the general experience of mankind. Yet even if Coleridge was a poet of the age of spontaneity and of expression of the individual self, his intellect never abdicated; he was born in the eighteenth century, he lived within the influence of its controls. Even if he drugged himself with opium, if he only published Kubla Khan, it is at least worth recalling now, at someone else's request, "and, as far as the Author's own opinions are concerned, rather as a psychological curiosity, than on the ground of any supposed *poetic* merits". "Psychological curiosity": this is perhaps the point for reminding oneself of Mr. Dylan Thomas, who has become one of the "greater" poets of our grey time, and before whom (so much have things changed since Sir John Squire greeted *The Waste Land* with "a grunt would serve equally well") even the conventional critics have begun abasing themselves. Mr. Eliot's poems have their seldom-mentioned shortcomings, as of some half-man who has escaped with a few guarded fragments of humanity, or divinity, from what Mr. Edward Dahlberg has called "the most clinkered land in the world for the artist to live in"; but one would not name Mr. Eliot's poems "psychological curiosities". Mr. Eliot's poems live tightly above the waist—rather higher than that, above the heart; Mr. Thomas's live, sprawl loosely, below the waist. Mr. Eliot is a reasoning creature. The self in Mr. Thomas's poems seems inhuman and glandular. Or rather like water and mud and fumes mixed in a volcanic mud-hole, in a young land. Those who admire his poems, one concludes, are fascinated because there is something primal and universal in the underground fury by which they are generated; but not to worry the metaphor too far, one would prefer a man's poetry to break out of the common fury at least like a geyser, at least with the force and cleanness of form, at least with the meaning of a pillar; and not with the meaningless hot sprawl of mud.

Mr. Thomas is a poet, Miss Edith Sitwell has remarked, whose work is "on a huge scale both in theme and structurally". She must imply, not just that his poems are about birth, death, and love, in his newest book, but that Mr. Thomas says something about his theme, says something on a *huge* scale, and by "huge" again Miss Sitwell must imply a scale of meditation to Wordsworth's in *The Prelude,* Blake's upon the contrary states of the human soul, Shakespeare's in *The Tempest,* or Goethe's in *Faust.* One cannot demolish Mr. Thomas's poems by demolishing Miss Sitwell's critical discernment; but one can say that even Mr. Thomas's most recent book, *Deaths and Entrances,* shows, not a theme, not meditation, but simply obsession;—obsession with birth, death, and love, and obsession mainly in a muddle of images with only the frailest ineptitude of structure. Rhyme schemes begin and break. Rhythms start off and falter, into incoherent prose. Image repeats image, in a tautology of meaning. If a poet rhymes, he must twist his rhymes to the exigencies of impulse, or illumination; not, as Mr. Thomas very often does, twist, and so falsify, his illumination to the exigencies of rhyme. And when he determines to keep his purpose, being too unskilful in words, he nearly-rhymes. Near rhymes have their virtue, but only if they come as deliberately as true rhyme, and have, against each other, the proper weight, accent, and length; but Mr. Thomas's ineptitude licenses him to write

> Lie still, sleep becalmed, sufferer with the *wound*
> In the throat, burning and turning. All night *afloat*
> On the silent sea we have heard the *sound*
> That came from the wound wrapped in the salt *sheet*

Afloat-sheet is Mr. Thomas's skill. Here, too, is Mr. Thomas faltering into prose (though perhaps one should characterize his poems as attempts to falter out of prose). Some movement begins:

> Friend by enemy I call you out.
>
> You with a bad coin in your socket,
> You my friend there with a winning air

—then smash:

> Who palmed the lie on me when you looked
> Brassily at my shyest secret.

To display most kinds of Mr. Thomas's formal awkwardness, it would be most fair to read through a short poem, since in three stanzas the difficulties of form are easier to resolve (and in this poem, *On a Wedding Anniversary,* see again the rhythm smashed in the third line):

> The sky is torn across
> This ragged anniversary of two
> Who moved for three years in tune
> Down the long walks of their vows.
>
> Now their love lies a loss
> And Love and his patients roar on a chain;
> From every true or crater
> Carrying cloud, Death strikes their house.
>
> Too late in the wrong rain
> They come together whom their love parted:
> The windows pour into their heart
> And the doors burn in their brain.

Clouds with craters are like veins with ears; more ridiculous, in fact, than Nat Lee's night-raven with huge wicker wings, and strange eyes: "In each black Eye there rolls a Pound of Jet." Syntactically Mr. Thomas makes wonders of awkwardness; not, one feels, from theory, but because his words are nearly automatic, his words come up bubbling in an automatic muddle,

> Never until the mankind making
> Bird beast and flower
> Fathering and all humbling darkness
> Tells with silence the last night breaking
> And the still hour
> Is come of the sea tumbling in harness

—construable—just, but made none the more active or effective by the confusion (or by *darkness:harness*).

No more, no less construable is:

> There was a saviour
> In the churches of his tears
> There was calm to be done in his safe unrest
> Children kept from the sun
> On to the ground when a man has died
> To hear the golden note turn in a groove,
> Silence, silence to do, when earth grew loud
> In the jails and studies of his keyless smiles

—a stanza upon which Mr. Thomas's explorers and admirers should meditate, for reasons which I shall give later. And like a child, learning to talk, or a journalist, Mr. Thomas deals in the striking, but rootless image, and in the cliché turned—*once below a time, all the sun long, happy as the heart was long—a bad coin in your socket:* word-tumbling without either gravity or point, or point of fun (as when Lewis Carroll writes "Either you or your head must be off, and that in about half no time.")

Mr. Thomas does indeed work, as a child works, towards form and coherence. From the shape of one poem he must have been *looking* at George Herbert. But otherwise his poetry as near as may be is the poetry of a child, volcanic, and unreasoning, who has seldom read, and little cared for, the poets of his own language, and allowed them little power over his own manipulation—or rather automatism:

> How soon the servant sun
> (Sir morrow mark)
> Can time unriddle, and the cupboard store
> (Fog has a bone
> He'll trumpet into meat)
> Unshelve that all my gristles have a gown
> And the naked egg stand strange. . .

The power which these poems appear to exercise over readers does not reside in sense, demonstrably; it does not reside in music, it does not reside in an ordered, musical non-sense. The unit, one realizes, in Mr. Thomas's poetry, is neither poem, nor stanza; it is phrase or line, which by accident suggests the next phrase, or the next line, the solipsist image which suggests the next solipsism; power resides in the novel suggestion, in these massive solipsisms, of the strange, the magical, the profound; and in fact their strangeness is little else than the strangeness of Mr. Thomas, their profundity little beyond the Indian-ink deepness of an individual, their magic little else than what appears to be a black magic. (Here perhaps I should interpolate that the second, just-construable piece which I quoted from Mr. Thomas, is one made up by myself of disconnected lines from three stanzas of one poem. But between then and now, I hope any idolater will have taken his time to admire it, and to meditate upon it; for it reads, I am convinced, as authentically as most of Mr. Thomas's stanzas.)

Mr. Thomas, as I say, cannot help what bubbles into him and bubbles out; but to invest these black magical bubblings, as critics feel them to be, with greatness,—in spite of here and there a fancy, even a "sublime" fancy (though often it is "the sublime dashed in pieces cutting too close with the fiery four-in-hand round the corner of nonsense"), here and there even a poem—to do that deserves many descriptions, of which I will mention only one, that it seems a little out of date. The "new romanticism", of which Mr. Dylan Thomas's poetry is the exemplar, became articulate and "new" some twenty years ago in the hey-day of *Transition;* and as Mr. Wyndham Lewis made plain in attacking *Transition* in *The Diabolical Principle,* it was not new even then. Muddled up with politics, the "new romanticism" of *Transition* was based considerably upon Lautréamont, whose diabolism, minus the politics (and minus a clear sense of the devil, and minus the will to be devilish) soaked into Mr. Dylan Thomas in his Welsh childhood. "That this bric-à-brac", wrote Mr. Lewis of Lautréamont, "should be seriously represented as the exemplar of the best or newest seems possible. That it should be . . . published to catch *l'homme moyen sensuel,* on account of its blood-dripping fangs associated with the milk-white bodies of virgins, is as natural and harmless as that *Fanny Hill* should never be quite out of print, or that the *History of a Flea* or even the 'bourgeois' pornography of Paul de Kock's *Ten Pairs of Drawers* should remain scandalous best-sellers. But there, you would suppose, the joke would end—once the gull's money was safely transferred from his bank to that of the sagacious . . . literary publishers. . . . But that is not the case." Mr. Thomas once defined his notion of poetry: "Whatever is hidden should be made naked. To be stripped of darkness is to be clean, to strip of darkness is to make clean. Poetry, recording the stripping of individual darkness must, inevitably, cast light upon what has been hidden for too long, and by so doing make clean the naked exposure." "Whatever is hidden. . . ." It suggests the disinfection of psychological ordure—as if, in Ananda Coomaraswamy's words, "as if the artist had nothing better to do than make an exhibition of himself to his neighbour." And what self-adulation, what absence of humility, what insolence (even if Mr. Thomas is not altogether to be blamed for it), to believe in the importance to others of the stripping of one's own dirty, individual darkness, which must be made clean! Art, yes, as the peeling off of the ten pairs of drawers!

Yesterday's heresy has become with the middlemen, and *les hommes moyen sensuels,* today's provincial orthodoxy. The poetry of the unpeeled drawers is now acceptable. But we should take care. What I believe should be our concern in all this war and post-war drift back into a decayed romance is not, first of all, to use "romance" pejoratively because of any such examples, not to throw away everything that genuine "romance", everything that poets and artists, everything that psychologists from Coleridge to Freud, everything that anthropologists have curiously revealed about the source and nature of the arts. Dryden's poetry, and Poussin's painting (even if one does not need to underwrite all the views of Dryden's age or Poussin's age about nature and reason), are always there, as models of control. It is ironic to think that we can once more read Boileau with profit; that Boileau at whom Keats had to make a long nose:

> A Poem, where we all perfections find,
> Is not the work of a Fantastick mind:
> There must be Care, and Time, and Skill, and Pains;
> Not the first heat of unexperienc'd Brains.
> Yet sometimes Artless Poets, when the rage
> Of a warm Fancy does their minds ingage,
> Puff'd with vain pride, presume they understand,
> And boldly take the Trumpet in their hand;
> Their Fustian Muse each accident confound;
> Nor can she fly, but rise by leaps and bounds,
> Till their small stock of learning quickly spent
> Their poem dyes for want of nourishment.
> With impudence the Laurel they invade
> Resolv'd to like the Monsters they have made.

But still, as I say, we do not want to throw away the discoveries of the last hundred and fifty years, or the last forty years; we do not want to waste them because so many writers and artists, and so many critics, now are debasing themselves to a new exclusive set of dogmas derived from the very things discovered. Art—being an artist—is subject to entropy; or is a perpetual walking across a tight rope, with death and disaster on either side and below. And the Enlightenment of

Dryden and Pope tailed off, too, by making reason's light a dogma when nothing was left to enlighten.

No one has added up and analysed the whole romantic slide with more skill and more power, than W. H. Auden, in an essay, *Criticism in a Mass Society,* which was little noticed in the England of neo-romance. To the critic, he wrote, "Slogans like Art for Art's sake, or Art for Politic's sake, will be equally objectionable." The critic "will flatter neither the masses by assuring them that what is popular must be good, nor the highbrows by assuring them that what is *avant garde* must be superior. Further, he will conceive of art, like life, as being a self-discipline rather than a self-expression . . . he will distrust the formless, the expansive, the unfinished, and the casual."

But in combatting the slide into romance, into idiot romance, we have to be careful not to encourage the white and dry which sterilize the creative impulse. Even that danger does not mean that we should be afraid to recover our wits and our honesty, and speak out now and then, afraid because we may seem to be betraying a cause to the old enemy, and assuring Sir John Squire, or whoever carries his mantle in these later years, that he was right.

POSTSCRIPT: As I read this in proof, I discover that Mr. Thomas has also published a recipe for the writing of his poems: "I let an image be made from my subconscious, and from that first image I let"—this is peculiar—"its opposite emerge. These two images then war with each other, producing a third; the poem becoming a water-tight column of images." Wyndham Lewis once defined art as "a constant stronghold of the purest human *consciousness.*" This definition of Mr. Thomas's is making art the constant stronghold of certainly not the purest (since purity implies sifting and discernment) human, or sub-human, consciousness.

Dylan Thomas

EDITH SITWELL

"Even in religious fervor," said Whitman in his *Notebooks*, "there is always a touch of animal heat." Both religious fervor and animal heat were in the poetry of Dylan Thomas, to a high degree. His poetry was the "pure fire compressed into holy forms" of which one of Porphyry's Oracles spoke.

His was a language "fanned by the breath of Nature, which leaps overhead, cares mostly for impetus and effects, and for what it plants and invigorates to grow." (Whitman, *Notebooks*.) He strips from words their old, used, dulled sleepiness, and gives them a refreshed and awakened meaning, a new percussion.

His voice resembles no other voice, the spirit is that of the beginning of created things: there is here no case of a separate imagination, of invention. From the depths of Being, from the roots of the world, a voice speaks.

Boehme said, "The sap in the tree denoteth pure Deity." So it was with Dylan Thomas. He loved and praised "The force that through the green fuse drives the flower" and the

> animals thick as thieves
> On God's rough tumbling ground.

(He saw the world as God's rough tumbling ground, as a ground for joy and the holy wars of the Spirit.)

With him, all is prayer and praise. Poetry to him is prayer. "When we pray," said the Curé d'Ars, "we should open our heart to God, like a fish when it sees the wave coming." "I am so placed and submerged in his great love, that I seem as though in the sea entirely under water, and can on no side touch, see, or feel anything but water." So said Saint Catherine of Genoa. And so might have said Dylan Thomas.

His earliest poems are of great strangeness. From the obscure beauty of those early poems, he went to the miraculous concentration of such lines as "A grief ago" and to the poignance of "In the white giant's thigh."

In William James' *Principles of Psychology* he quotes Condillac as saying that "the first time we see light, we are it rather than see it." In my *Poet's Notebook* I have a quotation from a painter who paints a tree, becoming a tree. This condensation of essence, this power of "becoming a tree" is one of the powers that make Dylan Thomas a great poet. His poems, at first sight, may appear strange. But if we heard a tree speak to us in its own voice, would not that voice seem strange? His is always the voice of Nature. In the exquisite exactness of the lines—

> my ruffled ring dove. . .
> Coo rooing the woods' praise,
> Who moons her blue notes from her nest
> Down to the curlew herd. . .

—you see the misty softness of the sweet dove's feathers, you hear the misty softness of her cooing.

Though he felt, I think, and perhaps dreaded the conquering hand of Time, and knew that he must die young, he defied, always, death and the world's dust:

> A cock-on-a-dunghill
> Crowing to Lazarus the morning is vanity
> Dust be your saviour under the conjured soil.

His pity for the outcast, his love for those who have received no mercy from life, are great:

> I see the tigron in tears
> In the androgynous dark,
> His striped and noon maned tribe striding to holocaust,
> The she mules bear their minotaurs.

In that great poem *A Refusal to Mourn the Death, by Fire, of a Child in London,* with its dark, magnificent, proud movement, we see Death in its reality—as a return to the beginning of things, as a robing, a sacred investiture in those who have been our friends since the beginning of Time.

Bird, beast, and flower have their part in the making of mankind.

The water drop is holy, the wheat ear a place of prayer. The "fathering and all-humbling darkness" itself is a begetting force. Even grief, even tears, are a begetting. "The stations of the breath" are the stations of the Cross.

from the Introduction to *The New British Poets*

KENNETH REXROTH

If Auden dominated the recent past, Dylan Thomas dominates the present. There can be no question but that he is the most influential young poet writing in England today. The unanimity with which everyone except unreconstructed Stalinists and tame magazine versifiers points to him as the outstanding phenomenon in contemporary poetry is simply astonishing. Considering that something like this was once the case with Auden, it bodes ill for Thomas' reputation some ten years hence. However, it was not always thus. When he first appeared, he was greeted with tolerant but embarrassed consternation, as though he had just made a muss. Spender said his poems dripped like water out of a tap. Symons said he twisted words to the shape of his reader's ears. He reminded Hugh Gordon Porteus of an unconducted tour of Bedlam, or a night out in a land of gibbering highbrows. And so on down the line. It was as though something had escaped that had been locked up in Wild Wales since the Synod of Whitby, and was clanking its chains and yammering in the Rectory drawing room. Something terribly unbritish seemed to be happening. It was.

Thomas is far more shameless than [George] Barker. He doesn't wear his heart on his sleeve. He takes you by the neck and rubs your nose in it. He hits you across the face with a reeking, bloody heart, a heart full of worms and needles and black blood and thorns, a werewolf heart. This is the hairy wenid that has been peeping through the shutters since the Saxon drew his lines in Shropshire. In the old age of the English, it has burst in the door and settled down on top of the Sunday dinner. At first the noise was deafening, adders, she-bears, witches on the mountain, exploding pit-heads, menstruating babies, hounds with red ears, Welsh revivalists throwing dynamite and semen in all directions. Thomas smote the Philistines as hard a blow with one small book, *Eighteen Poems,* as Swinburne had with *Poems and Ballads.*

The terrific racket has long since died down. It is possible now to inspect the early Thomas coolly and discover what he is saying and what he is talking about. Many elements went to form his idiom, all bound together by the reeling excitement of a poetry-intoxicated schoolboy. First, I would say, Hopkins' metric and his peculiar, neurasthenic irritability of perception; second, Hart Crane, whom Thomas greatly resembles; third, possibly, translations of Rimbaud and *Maldoror,* though he could have got most of this from Crane; fourth, Welsh poetry and mythology, with its gnarled metrics and its imagery of a barbaric and forested country, a land literally wild; fifth, the Old Testament, as it came to him through the savage Welsh Nonconformity; sixth, a mass of uncontrolled, boyish omnivorous reading: detective stories, translated Surrealism, "science fiction," horror tales, sex books, occultism, Shakespeare, Blake, Lawrence, Henry Miller, A. E. Waite, Arthur Machen, an orgy of literary sensationalism. Yeats once said of somebody that he remained a barbarian because he was born in the provinces and never had a chance to associate with a man of real culture until he was grown. Thomas wrote as though he had never met a human being who had ever bathed or used a toothbrush. On the other hand, there is nothing squalid about it. Thomas wrote like a savage chief on a scalp-taking expedition amongst the palefaces. He definitely belonged to the heroes of Toynbee's "external proletariat," not to the drudges and tramps of his "internal proletariat."

The early Thomas does not add up to just another barbaric yawp, however heroic. It all meant something. Possibly it was a raucous and primitive cry, but it was the most primitive and terrible cry in the world, the cry of parturition, the dual cry of mother and child. If Jung served to elucidate Barker somewhat, Rank can serve even better for Thomas. Most of his early poetry is about the agony and horror of being born and of childbirth. The substance of Rank's *The Artist* is that the artist is, psychologically, his own mother. Few have ever realized this as thoroughly and as violently as Thomas. For him the crucifixion and the virgin birth are one simultaneous process, archetypes of the act, or rather catastrophe, of the creative consciousness. Other men, Baudelaire for instance, have talked about their agonies as creators. Thomas discovered poetry on his hands like blood, and screamed aloud.

I mentioned that Thomas resembled Hart Crane. This is as far as Crane was able to go—the horror of creative birth. I once heard a preacher say that Christ's agony in the garden and his relations with his mother showed the terrible responsibility of sonship. Certainly this phrase can be applied to the early Thomas and to Crane. Crane's solution, his myth, the Bridge, did not work. It is possible to worship the mother, the father, the self, but a saving symbol cannot be made of the umbilicus alone; it must be connected to something. So Crane's poetry and his personality began to break up and deteriorate. This has not happened to Thomas. His recent work has developed in the only way that it could from such antecedents, towards a deeper mystical insight. He has moved away from the old, excited, tempestuous possession, and toward the humility and calm of ecstatic vision. So his influences have been, in his later poems, those entranced Welshmen, Vaughan and Herbert.

The Romantic Heritage of Dylan Thomas

HORACE GREGORY

The literary heritage out of which the poetry of Dylan Thomas emerges may be given the general title of "neo-romanticism," in which the later poems of W. B. Yeats and of Edith Sitwell (and it is not without grace of temperamental affinity that Miss Sitwell praised Thomas' *25 Poems*) provided a precedent for the arrival of Dylan Thomas. Other precedents exist in the richness of Welsh poetry itself, and the annual festivals in Wales of poetry read aloud in which the survivals of the North Druid myths are as vivid as they were a thousand years ago. Still other sources are to be found (particularly in Thomas' recent devotional poems, the "Vision and Prayer" cycle in *Deaths and Entrances*) in *The Temple* of George Herbert, for *The Temple* is not unknown to Welsh readers of English devotional poetry. Nor should a true "ancestor" of younger Welsh writers in England be forgotten—Arthur Machen, whose imaginative writings have gone through at least four cycles of neglect and appreciation, and are as cheerfully alive today as ever. But the "neo-romantic" scene has still other figures, among which Walter de la Mare extends a heritage from Beddoes, John Clare, Poe and Darley; and as one turns from the elder poets, the American, Hart Crane, and the Anglo-Irish George Barker seem to be immediate forerunners of the kind of lyricism that Dylan Thomas found congenial to his gifts. One should also include Henry Treece and Vernon Watkins among Thomas' immediate contemporaries, who, like Barker, reach toward a richness of expression that had been denied such poets as MacNeice and C. Day Lewis who are

From the *Yale Literary Magazine*, November, 1954, pp. 31–34. Reprinted with special permission of the *Yale Literary Magazine*.

often betrayed by their facility into the charms of writing "magazine verse," or colorful epithets, which may amuse or shock the eye, but fail to attach their brilliance to profound centers of human emotion or intellectual meaning. If I seem to imply that the overtly journalistic and admittedly "neo-classic" school which discovered *A Hope for Poetry* before 1939 has suffered reverses, that is the impression I wish to convey. Of that still "young" and yet "elder" generation, W. H. Auden, by virtue of his gifts and his imagination, is the sole survivor of what was fashionable not many years ago.

II

The term "neo-romanticism" does not, of course, define the specific nature of Dylan Thomas' or any other poet's poems, but it does indicate the more general atmosphere and heritage to which a poet's writings may belong; such terms as "classical" and "romantic" are always in danger of being used as weapons of abuse or as tarnished laurels, and as we come closer to an actual reading of Thomas' poems, another term, "Symbolism," rises into view. This is all very well, but since Arthur Symons published *The Symbolist Movement in Literature* in 1899, conscious elements of Symbolism and the techniques employed by the Symbolists have entered the main streams of poetry in English on both sides of the Atlantic. In respect to Thomas' poems one can say this: "That which so closely resembles the technique of Symbolist poetry in his poems is of the same nature that guided W. B. Yeats in his re-creations of the Celtic myth that he drew from the lives of those around him and himself, and drew also from the writings of Dr. Douglas Hyde and Standish O'Grady. In Yeats' poems, those that had been written before 1912, the French Symbolists served as examples, as 'guides,' rather than 'masters'—and it is safe to conclude that he did not follow them literally, but in a more active sense, attracted some features of their technique to the centers of his imaginative being. Anyone who has read the sources of a literature sprung from 'the myth,' and particularly the North Druid myth, soon becomes aware of their likeness to some features of so-called 'modern' Symbolist poetry in English. Thomas' poems, including "The Hunchback in the Park" and "Among those Killed in the Dawn Raid was a Man Aged a Hundred," show something of the same method that Yeats employed, a 'drawing power,' a fusion of 'mythological' reality with individual perception. And it is to be noted that Thomas' word order often carries within it characteristically Welsh phrasing.

One index to Thomas' poetry is found in his book of autobiographical short stories, *Portrait of the Artist as a Young Dog* and its first story, "The Peaches," is a view of things seen and heard in many of Thomas' poems. The "place" of the story is a countryside in Wales, and the "time" is childhood, literally the "time" when things are seen for the first time and at first hand. The description of "the best room" in a farm house has the very elements, the "keepings," and one almost says the "furnishings" of a number of Thomas' poems; they are the centers out of which Thomas' characteristic imagery springs and to which it returns.

> The best room smelt of moth-balls and fur and damp and dead plants and stale, sour air. Two glass cases and wooden coffin-boxes lined the window wall. You looked at the weed-grown vegetable garden through a stuffed fox's legs, over a partridge's head, along the red-paint-stained breast of a stiff wild duck. A case of china and pewter, trinkets, teeth, family brooches, stood beyond the bandy table; there was a large oil lamp on the patchwork tablecloth, a Bible with a clasp, a tall vase with a draped woman about to bathe on it, and a framed photograph of Annie, Uncle Jim, and Gwilym smiling in front of a fern-pot. On the mantelpiece were two clocks, some dogs, brass candlesticks, a shepherdess, a man in a kilt, and a tinted photograph of Annie, with high hair and her breasts coming out . . .

Another paragraph from the same story has other characteristic "keepings" which are brought to light again in Thomas' poems:

> I remembered the demon in the story, with his wings and hooks, who clung like a bat to my hair as I battled up and down Wales after a tall, wise, golden, royal girl from Swansea Convent. I tried to remember her true name, her proper, long, black-stockinged legs, her giggle and paper curls . . .

And still another scene from the story has a farm boy preaching a sermon from a wagon used as a pulpit. It is perhaps gratuitous to remark the well sustained prose rhythm, the shrewd, yet innocent blasphemy, and the wit that is contained in the following passage:

> I sat on the hay and stared at Gwilym preaching and heard his voice rise and crack and sink to a whisper and break into singing and Welsh and ring triumphantly and be wild and meek. The sun, through a hole, shone on his praying shoulders, and he said: "O God, Thou art everywhere all the time, in the dew of the morning, in the frost of the evening, in the field and the town, in the preacher

and in the sinner, in the sparrow and the big buzzard. Thou canst see everything, right down deep in our hearts; Thou canst see us when the sun is gone; Thou canst see us when there aren't any stars, in the gravy blackness, in the deep, deep, deep, deep, pit; Thou canst see and spy and watch us all the time, in the little black corners, in the big cowboys' prairies, under the blankets when we're snoring fast, in the terrible shadows, pitch black, pitch black; Thou canst see everything we do, in the night and the day, in the day and the night, everything, everything; Thou canst see all the time. O God mun, you're like a bloody cat."

In the above quotations one also begins to see the limitations and ranges of Thomas' vocabulary: "black" is among Thomas' favored adjectives, and the subjective associations of the "Ballad of the Long-legged Bait" (which is included in *Deaths and Entrances*) are clearly shown in the phrase, "proper, long, black-stockinged legs." The "myth" of the "Ballad" is taken from a familiar group of North Druid myths, and the "myth" or story is also implied in one of Walter de la Mare's poems.[1] Thomas, by drawing it to the center of his own imagination—an example offered by the poems of de la Mare as well as Yeats—has made the "myth" his own. The mock-sermon provides a precedent for the "Vision and Prayer" cycle in *Deaths and Entrances,* for blasphemy, whether in the best or worst sense, always admits the consciousness and the reality of religious being—and therefore, T. S. Eliot's "The Hippopotamus" has its place in forecasting the arrival of *Ash-Wednesday.* The relationship between Thomas' prose and poetry may be shown by comparing the first passage I have quoted with a few lines from his poem, "In Memory of Ann Jones":

> Morning smack of the spade that wakes up sleep,
> Shakes a desolate boy who slits his throat
> In the dark of the coffin and sheds dry leaves.
> That breaks one bone to light with a judgment clout,
> After a feast of tear-stuffed time and thistles
> In a room with a stuffed fox and a stale fern.

There has been some talk of "Freudian imagery" in more than a few of Thomas' poems, and certainly Thomas has shown no fear in

[1] The title of de la Mare's poem is *The Old Angler,* and the story behind it is glimpsed at in William Morris's poem. *A Garden by the Sea* and in W. B. Yeats' *Song of the Wandering Angus.* This is not to say that Thomas did no more than follow in the wake of Morris, Yeats and de la Mare, for the poem is his own poem whatever its inspiration may have been. Undoubtedly the story as it is known by four poets is a romantic one.

employing sexual imagery of which the elegy, *The Tombstone Told When She Died* is a magnificent illustration:

> The tombstone told when she died.
> Her two surnames stopped me still.
> A virgin married at rest.
> She married in this pouring place,
> That I struck one day by luck,
> Before I heard in my mother's side
> Or saw in the looking-glass shell
> The rain through her cold heart speak
> And the sun killed in her face.
> More the thick stone cannot tell.
>
> Before she lay on a stranger's bed
> With a hand plunged through her hair,
> Or that rainy tongue beat back
> Through the devilish years and innocent deaths
> To the room of a secret child,
> Among men later I heard it said
> She cried her white-dressed limbs were bare
> And her red lips were kissed black,
> She wept in her pain and made mouths,
> Talked and tore though her eyes smiled.
>
> I who saw in a hurried film
> Death and this mad heroine
> Meet once on a mortal wall
> Heard her speak through the chipped beak
> Of the stone bird guarding her:
> I died before bedtime came
> But my womb was bellowing
> And I felt with my bare fall
> A blazing red harsh head tear up
> And the dear floods of his hair.

Is this poem more "Freudian" than a poem by Blake or by D. H. Lawrence or some passages that may be found in the poetry of Coleridge? I would say no more and no less. This is not to underestimate the general influence of Freud upon the poetic imagery of twentieth-century writings in both prose and verse—but the influence, as it exists in Thomas' poems, is more general and more diffuse than Thomas' relationship to the romantic tradition. And I may as well add, as a matter of opinion, that twentieth-century claims for the "modernity" of sex have been greatly exaggerated.

III

In the foregoing paragraphs I have attempted to show something of Dylan Thomas' regional identities, the charm of his highly individual imagination as well as his affinity to a larger, unevenly gifted body of "neo-romantic" literature. Among his elders only Yeats and Edith Sitwell and Walter de la Mare are poets of great and more accomplishment than he; the others, including George Barker and Henry Treece, who seem to have responded to the same impulses that have moved Thomas (and Barker's early poems preceded Thomas' and were in print before Thomas' style had taken form) have fallen prey to the forces of "easy writing" and a tendency towards disintegration. *Death and Entrances* is, I think, his best single book of poems and it also represents a tendency, unlike that of his younger contemporaries, toward a great integration of his imaginative life. That tendency has evidence in the way he has rewritten such poems as "Into Her Lying Down Head" and "When I Woke," for the changes are those that unify time and place in the two poems and increase the attraction of their central imagery.[2] There can be little doubt that Thomas is becoming an excellent critic of his own work, which is a distinction he has gained above many of his contemporaries. I regret that in a paper as short as this the last poem, "Fern Hill", in *Death and Entrances* is too long to quote in full and I have no desire to give the reader less than the complete view of its fine proportions—it is one of Thomas' superlative poems, and for its pastoral qualities alone, it deserves a place in the near company of Wordsworth's early poems.[3]

Two shorter and no less characteristic quotations must take the place of "Fern Hill," the first because of its implied debt to George Herbert, and the second because it shows that in wartime England, Thomas has lost none of his early power to write "When all my five

[2] The reader may contrast and compare versions of the same poems published in *Poetry* before 1943, in *New Poems* (New Directions, 1943), and in *Deaths and Entrances* (J. M. Dent, London, 1946).

[3] In particular I am referring to Wordsworth's *Tintern Abbey*, one of the best poems of its kind in English. In our day Thomas' *Fern Hill* has the same accents of an immortality. Both are rare in their power to recreate the spell of memory and the world of nature seen through the eyes of childhood. In this respect both poems convey similar emotions to the reader.

and country senses see." The first quotation is from his *Vision and Prayer*.

In
The spin
Of the sun
In the spuming
Cyclone of his wing
For I who was lost am
Crying at the man drenched throne
In the first fury of his stream
And the lightnings of adoration
Back to back silence melt and mourn
For I who was lost have come
To dumbfounding haven
And the finding one
And the high noon
Of his wound
Blinds my
Cry

The second is "Among Those Killed in the Dawn Raid was a Man Aged a Hundred":

When the morning was waking over the war,
He put on his clothes and stepped out and he died,
The locks yawned loose and a blast blew them wide,
He dropped where he loved on the burst pavement stone,
And the funeral grains of the slaughtered floor.
Tell his street on its back he stopped a sun
And the craters of his eyes grew springshoots and fire,
When all the keys shot from the locks, and rang.
Dig no more for the chains of his gray-haired heart.
The heavenly ambulance drawn by a wound,
Assembling waits for the spade's ring on the cage.
O keep his bones away from that common cart,
The morning is flying on the wings of his age,
And a hundred storks perch on the sun's right hand.

The poem with its clear reflection of an incident that commonly happened in Europe and Asia since 1914 has none of the usual attributes of war poetry and talk of war. It is, first of all, a poem, and what it has to say is conveyed with greater immediacy than all speculations of comparative safety and of disaster, and in "Fern Hill" Thomas purges his images of "Dawn Raid" with the sight of peace in childhood "Under new made clouds and happy as the heart was long." His immediacy is of a kind that is rare in contemporary writing—its only danger lies in its inability to relax the eye and ear—and it has achieved the unities of time and place, speech and accent.

POSTSCRIPT: In saying a few words about the romantic heritage of Dylan Thomas, I have reprinted with a few changes, a short essay I wrote for *Poetry* (Chicago) in 1947. The main point of the essay was to insist on, however briefly, the timelessness of Thomas' poetry. At that time Thomas was regarded in some quarters as a war poet and a somewhat violent Freudian, and I was in disagreement with these views. The incident of Thomas's death which came with a sense of loss to all serious readers of contemporary poetry has not changed my opinion, but has convinced me that his best poems are, if anything, more alive today than they were seven years ago.

The best possible tribute to Thomas's memory is to reread *Portrait of the Artist as a Young Dog* as well as the poems included in *Death and Entrances.* The stories and the poems still serve to clarify and complement one another; as the stories so eloquently show, he balanced passionate utterance with Welsh humours and excellently native wit. The best of his recordings of poetry deserve a further chapter to be written of him and his accomplishment.

Dylan Thomas and the Religion of the Instinctive Life

STUART HOLROYD

Man's world is no more nature. It is hell
Made by Man-self of which Man must grow well.

STEPHEN SPENDER

I

The religious life, as we have seen, consists in a quest for unity, for a release from the limits of selfhood and a participation in some larger life which invests the particular individual life with meaning. This unity can be realised on a number of different levels. Many men find it by pursuing the life of instinct. Behind what D. H. Lawrence called the "cerebral consciousness" of modern man, deep down in his unconscious mind, lies the matrix of life itself, a condition of being whereon all things share a mystical common identity. Lawrence believed that if a man could draw the sap of his daily existence from these roots, if, in other words, he could direct his life uninhibitedly according to the dictates of instinct, he would break through all the pettiness and superficiality which has accumulated like a crust on the life of modern man. Thereby he would realise an authentic existence.

Lawrence was a dialectician and what he preached was the practice of the poet Dylan Thomas. When he was not catching queer fish in the stream of the unconscious, Thomas was singing the praises of the instinctive life. His finest poems are those in which he conveys a feeling of man's co-existence with nature. His radio play *Under Milk*

From *Emergence from Chaos* by Stuart Holroyd (Boston: Houghton Mifflin Company, 1957), pp. 77–94. This selection is reprinted by permission of and arrangement with Houghton Mifflin Company, the authorized publishers.

Wood describes the life of a Welsh fishing village from sunrise to nightfall, and his characters, brilliant and authentic though they are, never come out of the dream state of unconscious existence. Life proceeds guided by the rhythm of the rising and setting of the sun, and not one of the inhabitants of the village is able, by an act of will, to assert man's autonomous existence, his independence of nature. Nature, the mother of all, broods over all the poems Thomas wrote, and shelters man with her dark wing. In a note to his *Collected Poems* Thomas said that they were written "for the love of Man." No doubt they were, but Man is as variously interpreted a word as God. Man, in fact, is not present in Dylan Thomas's poetry. The lusting blood, the dreaming unconscious mind are present; but man the creator, the being fully conscious of his high destiny, is an alien figure.

D. H. Lawrence always stood apart from the literary movements of his day. He regarded such poets as Rilke and Eliot as too intellectual, over-cultivated to the point of ignoring the primal elements in the constitution of the human animal. . . . Here we might justifiably ask whether Lawrence's emphasis on the physical fact did not result in his committing the fault for which he criticised others, the fault of presenting only one aspect of human life to the exclusion of other equally important aspects. The same question could be asked about Dylan Thomas. Thomas never expressed in print his attitude towards his contemporaries. He was content to be a poet in his own way and to allow others the same liberty. And his way was different from the prevailing fashions of the time. He was never an intellectual poet. His glorification of the instinctive life came from within him; given his psychological constitution it was inevitable. It was not, as with Lawrence, conceived as a panacea for the present ills of society. In fact Thomas was as little concerned with society as he was with the poets who were his contemporaries. But although in his lifetime he stood apart from his contemporaries, in the eyes of posterity he will stand alongside them, for he lived in the same world, was influenced by the same conditions and experienced the same problems. In his poetry there is implied a distinct attitude towards these problems, and to life generally, which criticism will abstract from its literary context and compare with the attitudes of Rilke, Eliot and other poets who were so different from him.

Dylan Thomas has come nearer than anyone else in recent years to being a popular poet. We cannot ignore this fact; it compels us to ask whether his attitude is not more valid for modern man than that of the more intellectual poets. But first we must decide whether that attitude represents a confrontation of or an escape from the problems of existence. The phrase "the problems of existence" is to be taken in a dual sense throughout this [essay]. It refers both to the particular problems of the individual living in the modern world and the eternal problems encountered by man when, face to face with destiny, he poses the metaphysical questions of his own and God's nature and the purpose of life. Putting aside literary standards of judgment for a time, we shall take Dylan Thomas as an example of the psychological type whose religion is that of the instinctive life. We will then try to discover to what extent this attitude fulfils the functions of a religion, which are to give to man a sense of meaningful existence, of unity with a higher, divine principle, and, above all, a vision of the ultimate truth and reality which lies behind appearances.

II

One of the truest things ever said about Dylan Thomas was said by himself when he began one of his early poems with the line

> I, in my intricate image, stride on two levels.

The one level, he said, was that of the "brassy orator", and the other that of "my half ghost in armour"—an image which may be translated prosaically as "my spirit imprisoned in flesh." Of course we all move, not only on two, but on several levels of existence, but with most of us the contrast is not so great as it was in Dylan Thomas between the wild, loud-mouthed, drunken Celt and the painstaking poetic craftsman. Thomas, the libertine, made excellent copy for the journalists and made quite a reputation for that other man, Thomas the poet. When he died, the Thomas legend, which had been growing slowly during the last years of his life, chanced to capture the public imagination and he was elevated to the position of Popular Poet No. 1.

The legend of "fierce, fine and foolish Thomas, poet, roisterer and lover of mankind", as one popular journalist described him, is a falsification of the facts for it ignores an important aspect of the man's character—his weakness. The Celt often hides his true self beneath a mantle of his own fashioning, and very often his brilliance, boastfulness, wildness and bravado conceal an inability to deal with life and to shape his own destiny. Dylan Thomas's finest poems are a triumph over his native weakness of character. He himself has told how he had to labour over them to give them such permanence as they may possess. In such a way he created some half-dozen perfect and immortal poems—an achievement sufficient to absolve any man.

I do not mention the poet's weakness in order to slight his character. It is a psychological fact, and as such not open to criticism. I mention it here because in his use of language there is a certain imaginative vigour, and in his attitude to death a simple courage, which gives the impression of his being a man of strong character. What strength he had resulted from the simplicity of his vision. He was a poet of faith, and it is in those simple but subtly-wrought poems in which he affirms his faith that he is at his best. Faith came easily to him, but it did not come often; at least the passionate faith that gave birth to *Poem in October, A Winter's Tale, Fern Hill,* and *A Refusal to Mourn the Death, by Fire, of a Child in London,* was the exception rather than the rule with him. It was a transfigured Dylan Thomas who wrote these poems, quite a different man from the legendary figure, who, though he would not be dictated to by men or the institutions of men, was nevertheless a slave to his instincts and suffered from that indetermination which is characteristic of his brilliant race.

Yet in a way the two beings who inhabited the body beneath Dylan Thomas's grubby fisherman's jersey were not so contradictory. The one lived, the other celebrated, the instinctive life. I have already stated that he was a poet of faith, and he himself said that his poems were written "in praise of God", but now we must examine these statements a little more carefully. What were the attributes of the God whom Thomas celebrated in his poems? Certainly he was not a stickler for morality. Indeed, Thomas's religious attitude may be compared with that of primitive man in the ages before moral concepts became associated with religion. Nor was he an ideal, if we are to understand by that word a Being, conceived as perfect, towards whom human effort is orientated. Dylan Thomas's god had little in common with the God of the Christians. He demanded no sacrifice of man. No particular effort of will was required in order to attain to the condition of unity with him. Only a complete absorption in the life of the senses:

> And taken by light in her arms at long and dear last
> I may without fail
> Suffer the first vision that set fire to the stars

says the poet at the end of *Love in the Asylum.* Here is a doctrine which directly contradicts the tested truth of all the great religions, that man can only attain to union with God by the complete submission of his own will and the purification of the soul which follows the suppression of the sensual appetites. The contradiction disappears when we realise the two quite different gods are involved. The great gods of the world are transcendent as well as immanent, and they are apprehended by man's conscious mind. The god of Dylan Thomas is wholly immanent, felt along the bloodstream or in the sexual organs, buried in the unconscious. He possesses no attributes, is capable neither of love nor anger, but is conceived rather as a vague Force or Power which is responsible for the harmony of the world and is most clearly discernible in that harmony.

Pantheism has its place in all religions, but it does not constitute a religion in itself because it gives man nothing to live by. It provides neither a code of conduct nor a solution to the question of the goal of life. Nevertheless, people who are not given to metaphysical questioning find it sufficient for their needs, and indeed more congenial than the genuine religions which demand sacrifices of them. However, pantheism is not a word which covers one easily definable attitude to life. Generally speaking, it represents the belief or feeling that all creation has a common identity because all things are manifestations of God. But men may arrive at such a belief in various ways and act upon it differently. Most pantheists are content to exult in the feeling of a mystical and harmonious relationship existing between themselves and the natural world. A few, not content to be identified with the part, seek the whole, and try to be at one with God, the fountainhead of all. Such was the endeavour of the mystic Jacob Boehme, who made a penetrating observation, though one with which most pantheists would disagree, when he wrote: "If thou wilt be like all things, thou must forsake all things; thou must turn thy desire away from them all."

Dylan Thomas's pantheism directly contradicted this statement of Boehme's. Far from forsaking all things, Thomas found that the complete absorption in the particular which attends sexual union was for him the gateway to the unitive life. It led him into the depth of the unconscious, a sticky world where blindly the life force pursued its task of genesis. Genesis was the predominant theme in his first published volume, *Eighteen Poems*. That is partly the reason why much of his early work is obscure: in attempting to probe into the mystery of its first stirring, he had recourse to almost impenetrable imagery. He viewed not only man, but the whole of the natural world, in sexual terms. A process analogous to the human sexual relationship was responsible for the harmony in nature, and indeed in the cosmos. *In the beginning* is a poem in which he gives a symbolically sexual account of the creation of the universe. Though in his later work he developed a wider range of subject matter, the habit of describing things in sexual terms never left him, and in one of his very last poems we find the lines:

> At last the soul from its foul mousehole
> Slunk pouting out when the limp time came;
> And I gave my soul a blind, slashed eye,
> Gristle and rind, and a roarers' life,
> And I shoved it into the coal black sky
> To find a woman's soul for a wife.

If we say that Dylan Thomas was wholly preoccupied with sex we are in danger of giving the wrong impression that he was an erotic poet. He was in fact far less erotic than D. H. Lawrence. His attitude to sex, in his poetry at any rate, was almost clinical. Sex was for him the overwhelming mystery. Without it no living thing could overcome its separateness; by it all things were made as one. Whereas the pantheist normally sees God in all things, Thomas saw sex in all things. In fact sex, together with the processes analogous to it in the natural world, was Dylan Thomas's god. The sexual act between man and woman was therefore invested with a grave significance. The act that created life was symbolical of the moment of death; for death was the entry into the womb of the universe, and as man and woman surrender their separate identities at the moment of union, so does man give up his identity when submerged by death.

Dylan Thomas's attitude to death was similar to that of Shelley when he wrote on the death of Keats in *Adonais* that "He is made one with nature." One of Thomas's finest poems celebrates this fact:

> And death shall have no dominion.
> Dead men naked they shall be one
> With the man in the wind and the west moon;
> When their bones are picked clean and the clean bones gone,
> They shall have stars at elbow and foot;
> Though they go mad they shall be sane,
> Though they sink through the sea they shall rise again;
> Though lovers be lost love shall not;
> And death shall have no dominion.

Death was a return to the matrix of life, to the

> mankind making
> Bird beast and flower
> Fathering and all humbling darkness.

The darkness of which Thomas speaks is different from that meant by T. S. Eliot in the two lines from *East Coker*: "I said to my soul, be still, and let the dark come upon you/Which shall be the darkness of God". Thomas's darkness is not the darkness of God, but rather that of the unconscious mind. Out of that darkness man emerges into consciousness, and when the brief span of his life is completed he returns to it. For what purpose he emerges and what he accomplishes during the period of consciousness, are questions the poet never asked. The implication in his poetry seems to be that man fulfils his function in this life at those moments when he absorbs himself in nature and thus returns to the state of pristine unconsciousness.

Death is one of the major themes in Dylan Thomas's poetry. The first impression we get from reading his more popular and easily understandable works is that he is a perfectly healthy-minded writer. But on reading him with more attention we are forced to reconsider our first impression when we come across lines like:

> I sit and watch the worm beneath my nail
> Wearing the quick away.

> I smell the maggot in my stool.

> When, like a running grave, time tracks you down.

It is notable that all these lines appear in his first volume of poems. In *25 Poems* he wrote *Death shall have no dominion*, and in *Deaths and Entrances*, his third and last volume, a serene and reconciled *Poem on his Birthday*. It is as though in his second book he became more confirmed in his pantheistic faith. His poetic starting-point was an attempt to get to "the sensual root and sap" of life. He discovered that it was a force of dynamic attraction operative in the human animal in the form of the sexual instinct. This force manifested itself in all living things. When he wrote:

> The force that through the green fuse drives the flower
> Drives my green age; that blasts the roots of trees
> Is my destroyer.

he had already taken the easy and natural step from his original position to that of the pantheist. But, as the second part of the quoted lines shows, he was not yet reconciled to the fact of mutability and death. Perhaps the impact of the war brought from him the affirmation that "Death shall have no dominion", a statement which he confirmed with the sonorous last line of the magnificent *Refusal to Mourn the Death, by Fire, of a Child in London:*

After the first death, there is no other.

By the time he came to write the poems which were published in *Deaths and Entrances* the note of morbidity had quite disappeared from Thomas's poems about death. It was replaced first by the promethean defiance of *Do not go gentle into that good night,* then by the joyful acceptance which found expression in one of his last poems, namely, *Poem on his birthday*:

. . . the closer I move
To death, one man through his sundered hulks,
The louder the sun blooms
And the tusked, ramshackling sea exults;
And every wave of the way
And gale I tackle, the whole world then,
With more triumphant faith
Than ever was since the world was said,
Spins its morning of praise,
I hear the bouncing hills
Grow larked and greener at berry brown
Fall and the dew larks sing
Taller this thunderclap spring, and how
More spanned with angels ride
The mansouled fiery islands! Oh,
Holier than their eyes,
And my shining men no more alone
As I sail out to die.

Equally important as, and in a way complementary to, the theme of death, there runs through Dylan Thomas's poetry another theme: that of pre-natal life. Coupled with the genesis theme it was predominant in *18 Poems.* It is perhaps expressed most clearly in the poem *Before I knocked and flesh let enter*, where the condition of pre-natal life is described in terms similar to those used when he speaks of life after death.

Dylan Thomas's mind had no metaphysical proclivities, otherwise he would have been obliged to find an answer to the question, Why does man proceed from a state of absorption in nature through earthly life and then back to the same state? Preoccupied as he was with the phenomenon of life, he never had time to ask questions about it. With the problems which we . . . see tormenting the minds of other poets

. . . he was blissfully unconcerned. He arrived at the paradise of faith without passing through the hell of despair or the purgatory of doubt. He saw man's situation in the universe in the simplest terms. And his own position too was clear to him: he was here to sing the glory of life. When he was not probing into the unconscious he became what he really was: a bard in the old sense of the word, a descendant of Chaucer or Villon or of his own great mediaeval compatriot Dafydd Ap Gwilyn. His lack of interest in metaphysical issues was responsible at once for his limitations and for his greatness. His simple vision invested his poems with a certain grandeur and enabled him to divine what Hopkins called "the freshness deep down things".

As he grew older Dylan Thomas seemed to recapture the undivided consciousness of the child or the animal. His relationship with nature was one of immediate response. There are no Wordsworthian mystical overtones in his poems. Nature-mysticism is only possible for a civilised mind. It is a means of bridging a gap between man and nature which was non-existent for primitive man. For Thomas, too, such a gap did not exist. On his thirtieth birthday he rose early and went from the town into the country, where he had passed the days of his youth. And there he remembered that:

> These were the woods the river and sea
> Where a boy
> In the listening
> Summertime of the dead whispered the truth of his joy
> To the trees and the stones and the fish in the tide.
> And the mystery
> Sang alive
> Still in the water and singingbirds.

"The mystery sang alive still": never throughout his life did Dylan Thomas lose the freshness and immediacy of the child's vision of nature. In most men the sense of wonder is blunted by the passing years and the capacity for delight diminished. Not so with this poet. With Thomas Traherne he could have said:

> I seemed as one brought into the Estate of Innocence. All things were spotless and pure and glorious: yea, and infinitely mine, and joyful and precious. I knew not that there were any sins, or complaints or laws. . . . I was entertained like an Angel with the works of God in their splendour and glory, I saw in all the peace of Eden; Heaven and Earth did sing my Creator's praises, and could not make more melody to Adam, than to me.

For Thomas everything in the natural world was infinitely his, for, living on the level of the instinctive life, he felt no barrier between himself and that life in its other manifestations.

Thomas, like D. H. Lawrence, was surrounded in his youth by a debased form of Protestant Christianity, and, also like Lawrence, he rebelled against it. Christian teaching was for him a "spent lie" from which he wished to dissociate himself. Yet he was by nature a man of faith and for that reason he was far less capable than Lawrence of completely rejecting Christianity. He wrote:

> I have longed to move away but am afraid;
> Some life, yet unspent, might explode
> Out of the old lie burning on the ground,
> And, crackling into the air, leave me half-blind.

So his religion became a personal one, a blending of his indigenous paganism and those aspects of Christianity which he found acceptable. In the poem *Find meat on bones,* which appeared in his second volume, he declares with typical pagan pride and high spirits

> War on the destiny of man!
> Doom on the sun!

but in the very next line, the last one of the poem, there is a sudden reversal of thought, and, either frightened by the vehemence of his cursing or suddenly becoming aware of his own insignificance, he says to himself:

> Before death takes you, O take back this.

Such poems are rare in Dylan Thomas's work. As a rule his poems have neither development nor conclusion, but consist of a series of images grouped around a central mood or feeling.

It was while writing his second volume, *25 Poems,* that Thomas finally determined his attitude towards Christianity and moved towards that assured personal faith which was to stamp some of the poems in *Deaths and Entrances* with the seal of immortality. Throughout his first two books of poems the themes of time's irrevocable passage and death's inexorable approach constantly recur. It was this fear of death which kept him bound to Christianity, even though he longed to move away from it. He admits the fact in the first line of one of his more obscure poems:

> It is the sinners' dust-tongued bell claps me to churches.

We have seen how his attitude to death gradually changed, and as it did so he moved further away from the Christian attitude to life, which he could never find congenial, and became more confirmed in his pantheism.

Unconcerned as he was with religion in the moral sense, Dylan Thomas was unable to appreciate the full significance of the dogma of original sin. Occasionally he alluded to it, but if we examine the poems in which he does so we find that his interpretation of the dogma is unorthodox. It is, however, quite consistent with his character. It is just what we might expect from a person whose religion is that of instinctive life. Of course, he appreciates that there existed before the Fall a state of innocence in which man lived unconsciously in harmony with nature. In just such a state he lived himself, and he is eloquent in speaking of it as:

> . . . the morning
> Of man when
> The land
> And
> The
> Born sea
> Praised the sun
> The finding one
> And upright Adam
> Sang upon origin!

But when he attempted to describe the cause of the Fall, as he does in the poem *Incarnate Devil* in *25 Poems*, he significantly changes the Christian account of it. According to Thomas there was no original sin, no momentous human action which transgressed for the first time the laws of nature. The change came about without human agency when

> . . . the garden gods
> Twined good and evil on an eastern tree.

The knowledge of the distinction between good and evil was indeed a consequence of the Fall, but its cause was not an accident as Thomas seems to suggest, but a deliberate human *action*. Man chose to emerge from the state of unconscious goodness that he might himself be like a god, and, blessed and cursed with consciousness, might lord it over the other living creatures and over the material world. By denying that it was an action on man's part that effected the change, Thomas missed the whole point. It is because he deliberately chose to taste of the forbidden fruit of the tree of knowledge that man is responsible for all the sins of the world and is burdened with the task of atoning for those sins and of winning through to that higher state of consciousness which is a second "Estate of Innocence". Dylan Thomas did not believe in any such higher state of consciousness; for him the greatest imaginable felicity lay in never emerging from the pristine state of unconscious and instinctive participation in the life of nature. He said so much in one of his last poems, *In Country Sleep,* where the phrase "country sleep" represents the condition of man before the dawn of consciousness:

> The country is holy: O bide in that country kind,
> Know the green good,
> Under the prayer wheeling moon in the rosy wood
> Be shielded by chant and flower and gay may you
> Lie in grace.

Tracing the course of Dylan Thomas's poetic development, we detect an increasing tendency towards objectivity. The probing into the unconscious of *18 Poems* and the self-questioning of *25 Poems* were succeeded by the radiant outward vision of the best poems in *Deaths and Entrances.* When he died he was beginning to turn his attention to dramatic writing, a field in which his exuberant spirit, his feeling for life and his lively sense of humour served him well. He was a humanist with an eye quick to perceive and to note those superficial idiosyncrasies of human character which are the stuff of popular drama. Mr. Donald Taylor, whose idea it was to write a film scenario about the Burke and Hare murders, states in his Introduction to *The Doctor and the Devils* that he "had been searching for some years to find a story which would pose the question of 'the ends justifying the means.'" It was no less a subject than that which had inspired Dostoevsky's *Crime and Punishment,* but when Dylan Thomas came to write the scenario he neglected this moral issue entirely. The result was a very colourful and entertaining piece of dramatic writing, but far less important a drama than might have been written if the author had concentrated more on the situation of Dr. Rock, who knowingly paid money for murdered corpses in order to advance medical science, than on the two loutish, stupid and uninteresting murderers, Fallon and Broom.

Thomas wrote always out of a sense of delight. Sometimes it was only delight in the sound of words, as in much of his obscurer poetry where we often feel that he has sacrificed sense to sound; in his best poems it was delight in nature and in his own feeling of identity with it that inspired him; in his dramatic writings it was delight in human character and in his own irrepressible sense of humour. Delight abounds in his writings and humbles the critic who might approach him too academically. His attitude to life and its problems may appear to some of us to be too facile, but we must remember that it developed naturally out of his psychological and physical constitution. And whatever criticism may be levelled against him there will always remain something quite beyond criticism: the perfection of *Fern Hill* and *Poem in October* and the assured mastery of poetic craftsmanship which he revealed in writing *A Winter's Tale* and *In Country Sleep.*

III

What can we say now of general relevance about the type of religious experience which this poet represents? Is the religion of the instinctive life the panacea that Lawrence imagined it to be? Does it satisfy a man's needs on all levels of his being? What effect does it have on his thought and on his capacity for apprehending an ultimate reality? I have already hinted at the answers to some of these questions; it remains for these to be enlarged upon and for the advantages and limitations of the religion of the instinctive life to be comprehensively reviewed.

It is conscious man who has conquered the world of matter and bent it to his purpose, who with the sciences developed by his intellect has explored the microcosm and the macrocosm and released the mighty forces which for so long had lain dormant in nature. If those forces now threaten to overwhelm him he cannot find an escape by attempting to return to his original state of unconscious co-existence with nature. His only hope of salvation lies in his raising himself to a higher state of consciousness, which involves a profounder understanding of himself and of the universe in which he lives. An individual may find his needs best satisfied by the religion of the instinctive life, but he will not find therein any positive solution either to his own or to mankind's problems. He will declare with Thomas that

> What's never known is safest in this life

and seek to avoid knowledge and thought lest he should burden himself with too heavy a sense of responsibility. In such a condition he will probably live and die happily, but he will not contribute one iota to man's great work of winning from nature, from unconsciousness, a little ground which may henceforth partake of the singular nature of conscious human existence.

Nature is a great balm and comfort to man, and there undoubtedly exists a certain *rapport* between it and important aspects of our own being. Granted that the condition of being alienated from it is bad, but to be wholly immersed in it is equally bad. Man pursues his life, when he lives it fully, on two levels, whereas the life of nature is on one level and is a monotonous affair. The eternal alternation of the seasons and of day and night is quite meaningless unless man is there to give it meaning. It is just those things which distinguish him from other forms of natural life that constitute man's greatness, and that establish a relationship between himself and the God of the higher religions, whom he apprehends not only with his instinctive faculties but with his mind.

The life of instinct obliterates personality. Personality does not consist in superficial peculiarities, but in those triumphs of a man's moral character over his natural self which are the distinctive features of his manhood. When he lives in the security of instinct his latent potentialities are forced into abeyance. He fails to realise himself as a man. He lives without problems and without that tension which urges man to create beyond himself. But the problems remain: the metaphysical problems of human existence and its relationship with time, the universe, and with God, and the practical or political problems of how best to conduct human life on the planet so that it finds conditions conducive to its optimum development. These problems can only be solved by man acquiring a deeper knowledge of himself, which he will do by an effort of consciousness involving the exercise of his higher facilities, and probably aided by the disciplines which have enabled religious men in all lands and ages to free themselves from the tyranny of nature and instinct.

America and Dylan Thomas

ELIZABETH HARDWICK

He died, grotesquely like Valentino, with mysterious, weeping women at his bedside. His last months, his final agonies, his utterly woeful end were a sordid and spectacular drama of broken hearts, angry wives, irritable doctors, frantic bystanders, rumors and misunderstandings, neglect and murderous permissiveness. The people near him visited indignities upon themselves, upon him, upon others. There seems to have been a certain amount of competition at the bedside, assertions of obscure priority. The honors were more and more vague, confused by the ghastly, suffering needs of this broken host and by his final impersonality. No one seems to have felt his wife and children had any divine rights but that they, too, had each day to earn their place on the open market in the appalling contest of Thomas's last years. Could it have happened quite this way in England? Were his last years there quite as frenzied and unhealthy as his journeys to America? He was one of ours, in a way, and he came back here to die with a terrible and fabulous rightness. (Not ours, of course, in his talents, his work, his joys, but ours in his sufferings, his longings, his demands.) "Severe alcoholic insult to the brain," the doctors said.

Dylan Thomas was loved and respected abroad, but he was literally *adored* in America. Adored, too, with a queer note of fantasy, a baffled, psychic force that went beyond his superb accomplishment as a poet, his wit, amazing and delightful at all times, his immense abilities on the public platform. He was first-rate: one need not be ashamed to serve him or to pursue him. He was also, and perhaps this was more important to some of his admirers, doomed, damned, whatever you will, undeniably suffering and living in the extremest reaches of experience. As Eliot observed about Byron: after the theatricalism, the posing, the scandals, you had to come back to the fact that Byron

From *The Partisan Review,* Spring, 1956, pp. 258–264.

was, nevertheless, genuinely disreputable. And so it was with Thomas. Behind his drinking, his bad behavior, his infidelities, his outrageousness, there was always his real doom. His condition was clearly critical. It couldn't go on much longer.

There was a certain element of drama in Thomas's readings that had nothing to do with his extraordinary powers. His story preceded him wherever he went; the perverse publicity somehow reached every town before he did and so the drama of his visit started before he arrived. Would he, first of all, really make it? (Awful if he didn't, with the tickets sold, hall hired, cocktail canapes made in advance.) Would he arrive only to break down on the stage? Would some dismaying scene take place at the faculty party? Would he be offensive, violent, obscene? These were alarming and yet exciting possibilities. Here, at last, was a poet in the grand, romantic style, a wild and inspired spirit not built for comfortable ways. He could be allowed anything. They would give him more drinks when he was dying of drink; they would let him spit in the eternal eye of the eternal head of the department, pinch the eternal faculty wife, insult the dull, the ambitious, the rich, tell obscene stories, use four-letter words. It did not make any difference. Thomas was acknowledged, unconsciously perhaps, to be beyond judgment, to be already living a tragic biography, nearing some certain fatality.

And he could make all the passes he chose, have all the love affairs, since the unspoken admission always was that he was doomed, profoundly ill, living as a character in a book, and his true love, beyond all others at this time, was alcohol. Yet so powerful and beguiling was his image—the image of a self-destroying, dying young poet of genius —that he aroused the most sacrificial longings in women. He had lost his looks, he was disorganized to a degree beyond belief, he had a wife and children in genuine need, and yet young ladies *felt* they had fallen in love with him. They fought over him; they nursed him while he retched and suffered and had delirium; they stayed up all night with him and yet went to their jobs the next morning. One girl bought cowboy suits for his children. Enormous mental, moral and physical adjustments were necessary to those who would be the companions of this restless, frantic man. The girls were up to it—it was not a hardship, but a privilege.

Apparently no one felt envious of Thomas or bitter about the attention he received. Even here he was an interesting exception. The explanation for the generosity lay first of all in the beauty and importance of his verse: this circumstance was the plain ground from which the elaborate and peculiar flowering of Thomas's American experience sprang. The madness of the infatuated is, after all, just an exaggeration of the reasonable assent of the discriminating. And so Thomas's personal greatness began it all, and the urgency of his drinking, his uncontrollable destructiveness seemed to add what was needed beyond his talents. He was both a success and a failure in a way we find particularly appealing. What he represented in the vividness of his success and failure was real and of irresistible power to certain art-conscious Americans. He had everything and "threw it all away." In him sophisticated schoolteachers, bright young girls, restless wives, bohemians, patrons and patronesses, found a poet they could love. He was not conservative, not snobbish, not middle-class, not alarmingly intellectual; he was a wild genius who needed caring for. And he was in a pattern we can recognize all too easily—the charming young man of great gifts, willfully going down to ruin. He was Hart Crane, Poe, F. Scott Fitzgerald, the stuff of which history is made, and also, unexpectedly, something of a great actor; indeed he was actually a great actor in a time when the literary style runs to the scholarly and the clerical. He satisfied a longing for the extreme. He was incorrigible and you never knew what he might do. He was fantastically picturesque. His Anglo-Welsh accent delighted everyone who heard it. Every college girl had her Dylan Thomas anecdote and it was usually scandalous, since he had a pronounced gift for that. His fees were exceeded only by the Sitwells, *tous les deux,* and by Eliot. His drinking had made him, at least superficially, as available as a man running for office. Everyone knew him, heard him, drank with him, nursed him. He was both immoderately available and, in the deepest sense, utterly unavailable too. His extraordinary gregariousness was a sign of his extremity. He knew everyone in the world, but for a long time he had perhaps been unable to know anyone. Oddly enough, at the end Thomas was more "fashionable" than he had ever been in his happier days. Even excess, carried off with so great a degree of authenticity and compulsiveness, has a kind of *chic.*

John Malcolm Brinnin's book, *Dylan Thomas in America,* has been praised by some critics, but many others have felt a good deal of moral annoyance about the work. They have found Brinnin a false friend, and they have decided his material might better have gone unpublished. Thomas's widow was much disturbed by the "intimate journal" and, one hears, has written a book-length "answer" to it. It seems unfair to accuse Brinnin of treachery or of the commercial exploitation of his friendship with Thomas—the most astonishing aspect of his record is just the wild and limitless nature of his devotion to his subject. It has, at times, almost the character of an hallucination.

"The sharpest scrutiny is the condition of enduring fame," Froude said as he set out to tell all he knew about Carlyle. This is the dominion of history and scholarship. And yet Brinnin's book does not seem to be a product of the historical impulse as we usually think of it. His journal is truly an obsessive document and is most unusual for that reason. It is not easy to think of anything else quite like it, anything one might justly compare it with. His commitment to his subject is of such an overwhelming degree that he cannot leave out anything. He treats Dylan Thomas as a great force of nature and would no more omit an infidelity or a hangover than a weatherman would suppress the news of an ugly storm. In certain respects, the book is not a piece of composition at all, but is rather the living moment with its repetitions, its naïveté, its peculiar acceptance of and compulsive attachment to every detail of Thomas's sad existence. It is as flat and true as a calendar. As a record, it is oddly open and marked by a helpless, uncomfortable fascination on Brinnin's part. For him Thomas was an addiction. Having once taken on the friendship, Brinnin was trapped, spell-bound, enlisted in a peculiar mission. Here are sentences from the early pages of the journal which tell of Thomas's first American visit: "He slept, breathing heavily, as I fingered through some English magazines he had brought with him, and watched the early lights of Manhattan come on through the sleet. As I contemplated Dylan's deep sleep, I tried first to comprehend and then to accept the quality (it was too early to know the dimensions) of my assignment . . . no one term would serve to define a relationship which had overwhelmed my expectations and already forced upon me a personal concern that was constantly puzzled, increasingly solicitous and, I knew well by now, impossible to escape."

Although Brinnin was the business agent for Thomas's American performances, his presence is due, not to business concerns, but to the notion of a mysterious and compelling destiny, a fatigued and yet somehow compulsory attendance. The "too late now to turn back" theme is heard again and again. "I knew that, above all now, I wanted to take care of him. . . . Just as certainly, I knew that I wanted to get rid of him, to save myself from having to be party to his self-devouring miseries and to forestall any further waiting upon his inevitable collapses." Reading such passages, you are reminded of the fatal commitments in Poe's work, of those nightmares of the irresistible and irrational involvement. Even Thomas's first visit was anticipated by Brinnin as a gloomy necessity; he approached the arrival with a painful and helpless alarm, and yet with a feeling of the inevitable. The commitment was of a quality impossible to analyze. It went beyond any joy that might or might not be found in Thomas's company, beyond mutual interests and personal affinity. It was so deep and so compelling that despair was its natural mood. Because of the fabulous difficulty of Thomas's character, this mood of despair seems more appropriate than the carousing, robust tone some others fall into when they talk of Thomas. In Brinnin's book it is always, in feeling at least, the dead, anguished middle of a drunken night. The despair, the wonder and the helplessness start the book and lead up to the grim, apoplectic end. There is no pretense that it was fun. It was maddening, exhausting, but there it was. And after Thomas died there was no release from the strain because the book had to be written, fulfilled with the same dogged, tired fascination the author felt in the case of the actual events. The self-effacement of the style seems a carry-over from the manner one adopts when he sits, sober, exhausted and anxious, with a drunken friend whose outbursts and ravings he is afraid of. The lists of guests at a party, the lecture dates, the financial details —the reader takes these in nervously, flatly, with the sense of a strange duty being honored. The girls, the quarrels, the summers and winters, the retchings, the humiliations, the heights and the depths— they are all presented in the same gray, aching tone. The writing of the book seems to have been the same sort of hallucinated task as the planning of the lecture tours. There is a unique concentration upon the elemental, upon how much Thomas slept, how much he could be made to eat, upon the momentary predicaments. Of character analysis or literary analysis, there is very little. This is the terrifying breath of life, but of a life without words. "He was ill and downcast again in the morning. . . ." "We broke our trip to Connecticut by a stop in Sturbridge, to drink ale before the wood-burning fireplace of an old inn, and arrived at the University just in time to spend an informal hour with the fourteen students of my graduate seminar." To spend *an hour* with the *fourteen* students! One does not know what to make of the inclusion of so much fact and figure. Thomas's conversation, so rare and beautiful, is not captured at all. The record is of another kind. It is certainly bemused and depressed and yet it is outlandishly successful as a picture of the prosaic circumstances of some months in a dramatic life.

Near the end: "There he ate an enormous dinner—a dinner which, in the course of events, was to be his last full meal." Dylan Thomas died in St. Vincent's Hospital in New York City. His death was miserable and before he passed into the final coma he had delirium tremens, horrors, agonies, desire for death, and nearly every physical and mental pain one can imagine. Brinnin does not try to render the great denouement, but again it is, in an odd and indefinable fashion, rendered by the dazed and peculiarly accurate and endless detail. "His face was wan and expressionless, his eyes half-opening for moments at a time, his body inert." The actual death: "Dylan was pale and blue, his eyes no longer blindly searching but calm, shut, and ineffably at peace. When I took his feet in my hands all warmth was gone. . . ." The final line of the record does fly upward in intention, but it is more clumsy, more earthbound than all the repetitive detail of all the thousands of preceding lines and it does not even seem true. "Now, as always, where Dylan was, there were no tears at all."

Could it have happened quite this way in England? It is an unhappy circumstance for us that Thomas should have died here, far from his family, far from the scenes he had lived in and written about. The maniacal permissiveness and submissiveness of American friends might, for all we know, have actually shortened Thomas's life, although he was ill and driven in England too. But there was a certain amount of poison in our good will. In the acceptance of his tragic condition there was a good deal of indifference and self-deception. The puzzling contentiousness and the ugly competition remain coldly in our mind. According to Brinnin, Thomas made these frantic flights to America because of his "conviction that his creative powers were failing, that his great work was finished." He feared he was "without the creative resources to maintain and expand his position." The financial benefit was destroyed by the familiar condition of our economic life: he spent every penny he made just as soon as he had it in his hands. His wife and his mother wanted him to stay at home *in order* to earn a living for his family. Furthermore Caitlin Thomas felt he had been "spoiled" in America, that he came here for "flattery, idleness and infidelity." Perhaps one shouldn't read too much between the lines, but it is hard to get the idea that Thomas's American friends, with a cynical show of piety, treated these accusations and feelings as outrageous. They, sinking sensuously into their own suspicious pity, flattered and allowed and encouraged right to the brink of the grave.

In England we have Brinnin's own observation that the deference shown to Thomas was of a quieter, less unreal and unbalancing sort. It might almost have passed for a lack of interest. In a London pub with Thomas, Brinnin was impressed that the poet was, for once, "not the object of everyone's attention." Here in America the approbation was extreme, the notice sometimes hysterical, the pace killing. The cost of these trips was "disproportionate to the rewards." The trip before the last one was felt to be "too exhausting to contemplate," and still it was not only contemplated, it was arranged, it happened, and was followed by an unbelievable another, the last of the three. In these tours Thomas seems like nothing so much as a man in the films, addressing the audience cheerfully, but with a gun in his back. It was a ghastly affair, preserved faithfully and grimly by Brinnin. There is an element in this story of ritual and fantasy, a phantasmagoria of pain and splendor, of talent and untimely death. And there is something else: the sober and dreary fact of the decline of our literary life, its thinness and fatigue. From this Thomas was, to many, a brief reprieve.

from These Be Your Gods, O Israel!

ROBERT GRAVES

I was never one to stroll down the street with a catapult and break windows just for the fun of hearing the tinkle of glass and seeing furious faces peering out as I scuttle away. But to break windows *from the inside* amounts, at times, to a civic duty. One smells gas, bursts open the kitchen door, turns off the oven-tap, wraps a towel around one's fist and breaks every pane in the kitchen window; for which a commendatory word or two may be expected from the magistrate—or from the coroner, according as the suicide is successful or not.

An anonymous leader-writer in *The Times Literary Supplement,* discussing the poetry of today, has described ours as an 'Age of Consolidation'. I find 'Consolidation' too active a word, and should prefer 'Age of Acquiescence' or 'Age of Acceptance'; which, of course, in the Welfare State, covers a wider range of subjects than poetry and literature in general. Most of my younger contemporaries have been acquiescing in an organized attempt, by critics, publicists, and educationalists, to curtail their liberty of judgement, and make them bow the knee before a row of idols, whose rites are quite incompatible with devotion to the Muse herself.

Idolatry is nothing new. The Goddess, or the God, being held too mysterious and exacting a figure for public worship, idols are set up as intermediaries—like the hero-images in Classical Greece—to focus the vague yearnings and aspirations of the unenlightened mass. As Isaiah remarks:

From *The Crowning Privilege* by Robert Graves (London: Cassell & Company Ltd., 1955), pp. 119–122, 138–142. Reprinted by permission of the author, Cassell & Company Ltd. and Doubleday & Company, Inc.

> He maketh a god even his own graven image and falleth down unto it and prayeth unto it and saith: 'Deliver me, for thou art my God!'

Yet the ancients at least waited until Homer and Virgil were decently dead before they paid them heroic honours. The living poet hero is a modernism; I think I am right in saying that Petrarch was the first poet to receive quasi-divine honours during his lifetime. And once an idol is set up it cannot easily be removed; but slowly moulders down the years, as Byron's and Wordsworth's have done. Tennyson's idol began to moulder soon after his death, because it had become identified with much that was unpopular in Victorianism. Thus Thomas Hardy wrote in his *An Ancient to Ancients* twenty-five years later:

> The bower we shrined to Tennyson,
> Gentlemen,
> Is roof-wrecked; damps there drip upon
> Sagged seats, the creeper-nails are rust,
> The spider is sole denizen;
> Even she who voiced those rhymes is dust,
> Gentlemen!

In 1910, when I first made poetry the most important thing in my life, no idols were forced upon me. English literature did not form part of the curriculum at Charterhouse, and I could go foraging for myself in blessed freedom. Moreover, war broke out just when I should have gone to Oxford; I volunteered and took a commission in an unliterary line-regiment, where I spent the next four and a half years. I had never met a poet of my own generation until, by a stroke of luck, Siegfried Sassoon was posted to my battalion; and through him and Edward Marsh (who had befriended me while I was still at school) I came to know several of the real poets then extant—including Hardy, William Davies, and Wilfred Owen.

A wave of popular excitement had been raised, two or three years before the War, by Masefield's bold use of the word 'bloody' in his *Everlasting Mercy;* but so dim were the other poetic lights of the period that he was the only modern poet whom Max Beerbohm found topical enough for inclusion in his *Poet's Corner*—except the insufferable Kipling (swapping 'ats with 'is gal Britannia on 'Amstead 'Eath). Max wrote:

A swear word in a rustic slum
A simple swear word is to some,
To Masefield, something more.

A second wave of popular excitement was raised by the death of Rupert Brooke during the Dardanelles campaign. Brooke's patriotic sonnet 'If I should die . . .' was included in Edward Marsh's *Georgian Poetry,* and the subsequent three volumes set poetical taste for the duration of the War, and for some years after.

But there were no living idols even in the early 'twenties. Thomas Hardy was known mainly for his novels; Charles Doughty for his *Arabia Deserta;* William Davies for his *Autobiography of a Super Tramp;* A. E. Housman for his Latin scholarship. I was still young then, yet could regard them as my friends and colleagues; simply because the current text-books of English literature stopped at Tennyson and Swinburne—we were all equally post-Canonical. Thus, though I had been attracted at the age of sixteen by the soft music of Yeat's *Countess Cathleen* and *Wanderings of Oisin,* he was not yet a 'required' poet; and I had felt no compunction about going behind him to literal translations of the Irish texts from which he quarried.

How things have changed since those days! Contemporary English literature has insinuated itself into the Public School and Secondary School Curriculum. It is now recognized by the English faculty here too. Even I have my niche in the popular text-book: I am briefly mentioned with the Georgian War Poets of 1914–1918. . . . , successors to the Imagists . . . and themselves superseded . . . by the Modernist Movement of the 'twenties; which merged . . . into the Left Wing Movement of the 'thirties; which was suffocated . . . by the 1939–45 War; which gave a pause for reflection, the new poets being few and inhibited. And for the setting up of five living idols—namely Yeats, Pound, Eliot, Auden, and Dylan Thomas . . . .

Are you men and women of culture? Then you are expected not only to regard these five as the most 'significant' modern writers but to have read all the 'significant' literature that has grown up about them; because 'Age of Consolidation' implies 'Age of Criticism'. The educational emphasis is now on appreciation of contemporary as well as ancient literature, and since to appreciate no longer means 'to evaluate', as it did in earlier days, but has become a synonym for 'to admire', there must be recognized objects of official appreciation—namely idols.

Ladies and gentlemen, relax! None of this lore is necessary for your salvation, once you have satisfied the examiners. There are only poems, very few of these in any generation, and there are periodic verse-fashions. And as for the old-clothesman of literature, the critic who starts by writing D. Phils. on such subjects as *W. H. Auden and the Freudian Theory of Transference*, or *T. S. Eliot as Anticipated by Duns Scotus;* and who then applies for a Foundation Research Fellowship, because he is compiling a scholarly edition (with cancelled first drafts) of all Dylan Thomas's advertisement copy for Messrs. J. Walter Thompson's *Night Custard* account; or perhaps a polyglot concordance to Pound's *Pisan Cantos*—as for the old clothesman, leave him to his industry! Waste no money on books *about* poetry; not even on mine. Build up a library of plain texts: the poet who pleads his case before Dame Occupacyon is expected to present a plain, unannotated text of his poems, and no supporting documents or testimonials whatsoever. I am here to remind you that poets are not idols, nor are idols poets; and that the Muse alone deserves your love. The idols are well swaddled against anything less destructive than a cobalt bomb; and all my iconoclastic zeal, so far from turning the whole temple blue, will not so much as dent a protective sandbag. Nevertheless, here it comes.

. . . . .

. . . At what interval after the death of a young poet is it decent to tell the truth about him? Despite the splendid orations spoken at his grave, more eulogistic than any poet has earned since Byron's death at Missolonghi, was Thomas either a master-poet or a 'great Christian gentleman'? He himself never pretended to be anything more than a young dog—witty, naughty, charming, irresponsible, and impenitent. But he did give his radio-audience what they wanted.

Thomas had all the rich musical eloquence of a South Welshman. Did anyone ever hear a Welsh choir, either in a concert hall, or a chapel, or when fortuitously assembled in a motor-bus or railway carriage, sing out of tune? It is a Welsh national characteristic to sing in tune and be eloquent; just as the Egyptian *fellah* lays a tennis-court dead flat without the aid of a spirit-level, or the old Majorcan shepherd never misses his mark with a sling-stone. But the Welshman seldom really cares what the tune is, whether *Marchog Jesu,* or *Saspan Fach,* or *Roll out the Barrel,* so long as he can sing it as a part-song.

Dylan Thomas was drunk with melody, and what the words were he cared not. He was eloquent, and what cause he was pleading, he cared not. He had a rich voice, could put on the *hwyl* like any Rev.

John Jones, B.A., Bangor, albeit in English as spoken in Langham Place; and, when I listened to him broadcasting, I had to keep a tight hold on myself to avoid being seduced. As when once, in 1916, I listened to a war speech given by Lloyd George to the Honourable Society of Cymrodorion.

I never met Thomas; but when he was sixteen, he sent me from Swansea a batch of his early poems. I wrote back that they were irreproachable, but that he would eventually learn to dislike them. I forgot what more I said; but I remember thinking that whereas musical prodigies like Mozart, or mathematical prodigies like William Rowan Hamilton, are not uncommon (and, when they grow up, continue happily as they began), poetic prodigies are monstrous and ill-omened. Young poets tumble and make a thousand clumsy errors, and though one may hope or guess that they will be something in the end, there is only promise, not performance. A sense of poetic protocol develops very slowly indeed. (The sole exceptions are such inspired young women poets as Juana de Asbaje, or Christina Rossetti; but a girl is often a women when her elder brother is still a child.) Even experts would have been deceived by the virtuosity of Dylan Thomas's conventional, and wholly artificial, early poems.

In order to conceal this defect in sincerity, he learned to introduce a distractive element. He kept musical control of the reader without troubling about the sense. I do not mean that he aimed deliberately off-target, as the later Yeats did. Thomas seems to have decided that there was no need to aim at all, so long as the explosion sounded loud enough. The fumes of cordite would drift across the target and a confederate in the butts would signal bull after bull. Nevertheless, as in double-talk, a central thread of something like sense makes the incrustations of nonsense more acceptable. Listeners, as opposed to readers, are easily convinced, in such cases, that they are obtuse and slow to follow the workings of the interlocutor's mind, especially when the musical content is so rich. But professionally-minded English poets ban double-talk, except in satire, and insist that every poem must make prose sense as well as poetic sense on one or more levels. The common report that most of Thomas's poems came out of the beer barrel cannot be accepted. It is true that he drank a great deal of beer, and that beer is a splendid drink before one takes one's place in a male voice choir; but the poems show every sign of an alert and sober intelligence. The following typical stanza is nonsense, but Dylan's golden voice could persuade his listeners that he was divulging ineffable secrets:

If my head hurt a hair's foot
Pack back the downed bone. If the unpricked ball of my breath
Bump on a sprout let the bubbles jump out.
Sooner drop with the worm of the ropes round my throat
Than bully ill love in the clouted scene.*

Stephen Spender, who often prognosticates next year's poetic skirt-length or waist-line long before the autumn collections, wrote of Thomas in 1946:

> He is a poet who commands the admiration of all [sic] contemporary poets. He has influenced a number of writers who see in him an alternative to the intellectual [sic] writing of Auden. Of the poets under forty-five, he is perhaps the only one capable of exercising a literary influence as great as that of Auden.

Yeats, Pound, Eliot, Auden, and Thomas are credited with having delivered English poetry from the shackles of the past. And the people said: 'These be thy gods, O Israel, which brought thee up out of the land of Egypt!'

* When I delivered this lecture, I offered a £1 note to anyone who could make sense of these lines. The ingenious Mr. M. J. C. Hodgart of Pembroke, a member of the Cambridge English Faculty, has since come forward to claim the award. He suggests that the child about to be born is here addressing his mother. The child cries out that if he is to cause her any pain by his birth, let him not be born at all. 'If I were to hurt so much as a hair of your head in process of birth push my downy, but bony, head back into the womb'. . . . Birth (Mr. Hodgart adds) is represented here as a violent movement like a bouncing ball; and the child's breath before birth is compared to an unpricked bubble. Therefore: 'If even this soft bubble of breath should hurt you by bouncing on your spouting blood, prick it and let my life run out in bubbles.' And: 'I would sooner be born hanged with my navel-string coiled around my throat than bully you when I appear on a scene made wretched by baby-clouts, or clouts on the head.'

There are flaws in this argument. The hair's foot, misleadingly identical in sound to *hare's* foot, is not a hair's *root*. Also, the physical situation is blurred by the apparent contact of the baby's downy head with the mother's hairy one, and by the description of the navel-string as 'the worm of the ropes'—why 'ropes' in the plural? And by the metaphor of an unpunctured ball bouncing on the top of a spout—as in pleasure fountains; how the bubble of breath could bounce on the flow of lochial blood is not easy to see (blood is not mentioned in the poem). And why should the unpricked bubble become 'bubbles'? And is the infant experienced or ignorant? If ignorant, how can it anticipate baby-clouts, and balls bouncing on fountains? If experienced, how can it make so absurd a suggestion as that the mother should push its head back again to relieve her labour pains? And if it is so considerate and saintly as Mr. Hodgart suggests, why should it ever turn bully?

I have a conscience about paying my debts, but though Mr. Hodgart may have identified the thin thread of sense on which the enormous and disgusting hyperboles of the child's address are strung, this is not enough; the five lines taken as a whole remain nonsensical.

Need I also dwell on the lesser idols now slowly mouldering: on sick, muddle-headed, sex-mad D. H. Lawrence who wrote sketches for poems, but nothing more; on poor, tortured Gerald Manley Hopkins?

Despite the great spate of commercial jazz, there has always been a small, clear stream of living jazz music; despite the great outpouring of abstract or semi-abstract art (the more abstract, the more imitative and academic) there has likewise been a thin trickle of admirable painting and sculpture. The same is true of poetry. To take only the United States: Robert Frost, E. E. Cummings, John Crowe Ransom, Laura Riding, have all written living poems in their time. I refrain from invidiously singling out their English counterparts still alive, who are no fewer in number. But I do find it remarkable that the extraordinary five years of Siegfried Sassoon's poetic efflorescence (1917–21) should be utterly forgotten now. For the rest it will be enough to say that William Davies, though at times his simplicity degenerated into artfulness, put his near-contemporary Yeats to shame; and that Norman Cameron, who died last year within a month or two of Thomas, and worked in the same office for a while, was indisputably the truer poet; and that so was Alun Lewis, killed during the Second World War.

This is Alun Lewis writing for the Welsh Regiment in Burma to his Muse in Wales:

> . . . My longing is more and more for one thing only, integrity, and I discount the other qualities in people ruthlessly if they lack that fundamental sincerity and wholeness.
>
> . . . And although I'm more engrossed with the *single* poetic theme of Life and Death, for there doesn't seem to be any question more directly relevant than this one, of what survives of all the beloved, I find myself quite unable to express at once the passion of love, the coldness of Death (Death is cold), or the fire that beats against resignation, 'acceptance'. Acceptance seems so spiritless, protest so vain. In between the two I live.

With this quotation, I make my bow, and thank you for your continued patience. If, in the course of these lectures, I have said anything out of order, pray forgive me doubly; I am no longer a stranger here.

Dylan Thomas

KARL SHAPIRO

The death of Dylan Thomas a year and a half ago was the cause of the most singular demonstration of suffering in recent literary history. One searches his memory in vain for any parallel to it. At 39 Thomas had endeared himself to the literary youth of England and America, to most of the poets who were his contemporaries, and to many who were his elders; he was the master of a public which he himself had brought out of nothingness; he was the idol of writers of every description and the darling of the press. Critics had already told how Thomas became the first poet who was both popular and obscure. In an age when poets are supposed to be born old, everyone looked upon Thomas as the last of the young poets. When he died, it was if there would never be any more youth in the world. Or so it seemed in the frenzy of his year-long funeral, a funeral which, like one of Thomas' own poems, turned slowly into a satanic celebration and a literary institution.

When Yeats and Valéry died, old and wise and untouchable, there were held, so to speak, the grand state funerals. It was civilization itself that mourned. When Thomas died, a poet wrote wildly how, to get him up in the morning, he plugged Thomas' mouth with a bottle of beer,—"this wonderful baby." All the naughty stories were on everybody's lips; all the wrong things began to be said, and the right things in the wrong way. Someone quoted bitterly: Kill him, he's a poet! and this childishness was the signal for a verbal massacre of the bourgeoisie, reminiscent of the early decades of our century.

The death of a young poet inflicts a psychic wound upon the world and is the cause among poets themselves of frightening babbling and sooth-saying. These doings may be likened to a witches' sab-

From *In Defense of Ignorance* by Karl Shapiro (New York: Random House, 1960), pp. 171–186.

bath, and some have seen in these morbid celebrations the very coming-to-life of Thomas' poems. It is his death as an occasion for literary and psychological insurrection that must interest us today, if we are to understand the meaning of Thomas' poetry and the significance his contemporaries have given it. It is one thing to analyze and interpret poetry and keep it all in a book: it is another to watch that poetry enter an audience and melt it to a single mind. I want to speak about the second thing, the live thing, the thing that touched the raw nerve of the world and that keeps us singing with pain. We want to know what kind of audience that is. The poetry of Thomas is full of the deepest pain; there are few moments of relief. What is the secret of his pain-filled audience? How are we to place Thomas among the great impersonal poets of our time, when this one is so personal, so intimate and so profoundly grieved? Thomas was the first modern romantic you could put your finger on, the first whose journeys and itineraries became part of his own mythology, the first who offered himself up as a public sacrifice. Hence the piercing sacrificial note in his poetry, the uncontainable voice, the drifting almost ectoplasmic character of the man, the desperate clinging to a few drifting spars of literary convention. Hence, too, the universal acclaim for his lyricism, and the mistaken desire to make him an heir to Bohemia or to the high Symbolist tradition.

Writers said of Thomas that he was the greatest lyricist of our time. The saying became a platitude. It was unquestionably true, but what did the word mean? It meant that, aside from the epic pretensions of many of the leading modern poets, there was only one who could be called a singer: Thomas. To call him the best lyric poet of our time was to pay him the highest, the only compliment. Nearly everyone paid him this splendid compliment and everyone knew its implications. But no one, I believe, fully understood that this compliment marked a turning-point in poetry. I doubt that Thomas himself knew how personal poetry might become after him.

During his life there were also the armed camps who made him honorary revolutionary general; and I cannot be sure Thomas refused the home-made epaulets of these border patrols. I rather think he was proud to be taken in. Who were these people? First there are those we can call the Blankety-Blank School of modern poetry, the remnant of Bohemia. These are people who exist in the belief that everyone is dead except themselves. I saw one of these poets lately; he had just come from England and he informed me casually that everyone in England is dead. To change the subject I asked him if he was glad to be home; but it turned out that everyone in America is also dead. Among these poets there is a sincere fascination for all things dead; and it is interesting to speculate upon their adoption of Thomas as a leader and a patron saint. In the same way nearly all critics and lovers of Thomas' poetry have spoken of him in connection with Symbolism. The similarity between the Symbolist position and that of the Bohemian remnant is noteworthy. The Remnant poets are clearly materialistic and social revolutionary; the Symbolist critics praise the love of death as the highest order of poetic knowledge. The two positions are really one: one is a vulgarization of the other.

All the same, this theory of posthumous vitality seems to make sense when we speak of Thomas. How much did Thomas subscribe to official Symbolism? Just enough to provide ammunition for those people. How much did he love death as his major symbol? As much as any poet I know in the English language. These factions have a claim on Thomas which we cannot fully contradict.

Thomas is in somewhat the relation to modern poetry that Hopkins was to Tennyson and the Victorians; this is a relation of anti-magnetism. Thomas resisted the literary traditionalism of the Eliot school; he wanted no part of it. Poetry to him was not a civilizing maneuver, a replanting of the gardens; it was a holocaust, a sowing of the wind. But I do not think we can compare Thomas, say, with Auden, because they are different in kind. Thomas' antithesis to Auden, as to Eliot, and his school is significant. Thomas grew up in a generation which had lost every kind of cultural leadership. The poets who began to write during the Depression, which was worse in Wales than in America, were deprived of every ideal. The favorite poem of this generation was Yeats' *The Second Coming*. Yeats' poems gave to a generation of prematurely wise young poets an apocalypse, a vision of anti-Christ and a vision of the downfall of civilization. The theatricality of the Yeats poems was a great convenience to a poet like Thomas who, having nothing of true philosophical or religious substance to fall back upon, could grasp this straw. The acknowledged precedence of Yeats in modern English literature—in world literature perhaps—has been a consolation to all poets. Yeats with his cruel forcing of the imagination—his jimmying of the spirit—is an heroic figure in modern poetry. One thinks of him as brute imagination holding off the forces of speed—the historical speed-up of the spool of film that goes faster and faster and faster and ends up flipping around idiotically on the reel. Like every whole poet he tried to stop this runaway by opening a more grand and more distant prospect. . . . And this is where Thomas looked in.

The romantic poets who were the new poets of Thomas' generation, had one moment of intellectual generalship: to bring about a change of heart, as Auden said, in mankind. The official name of this philosophy: Marxism. But the belief betrayed the believers; and war, always a natural setting for poets, threw down not only the remaining gods but their statues. The poets went leaping through the flames. This was the apocalypse that Yeats prefigured after the first World War; the horror of the second war surpassed the historical imagination; the prescience of the third war paralyzed thought. In this atmosphere the poetry of Dylan Thomas was composed.

Thomas suffers from the waifishness imposed upon his generation. The so-called Apocalyptic poets, which he was supposed to be a member of, never existed. One can see that he plays around with copying the superficies of Vaughan and Herbert and Traherne and maybe David ap Gwilym (who in English is not much better than James Whitcomb Riley) and Yeats and Hopkins. But Thomas was outside the orbit of the English poets who succeeded Eliot and cannot easily be placed in their tradition. He was anti-tradition by nature, by place, by inclination. Certainly Thomas' love for America can also be seen in this light; America is the untraditional place, the Romantic country par excellence.

Thomas' technique is deceptive. When you look at it casually you think it is nothing. The meter is banal. It is no better and no worse than that of dozens of other poets of his age. There is no invention and a great deal of imitation. There is no theory. Yeats and Auden and Pound have developed this aspect of English poetry almost single-handed, each for his followers. But despite the lack of originality, the impress of Thomas' idiom on present-day English poetry is incalculable. One critic said not many years ago that Thomas had visited a major affliction on English poetry. This was an unfriendly way of saying that Thomas had captured the young poets, which he certainly had. How did Thomas do this? He did it through the force of emotion. He did it with the personal idiom, the twists of language, the bending of the iron of English. Once he had bent this iron his way everybody else tried it. Thomas has more imitators today than any other poet in the literature. Whether this excitement will last a year or a hundred years, no one can tell. But it is a real excitement. Except for Yeats, Eliot, Pound and Auden, and perhaps Stevens, no one else has had this power over the language in our day.

Even when we examine the texture of his language we fail to find anything original. But at the same time, we find something completely distinctive. It is hard to locate the distinctiveness of Thomas' idiom. There are a few tricks of word order, a way of using a sentence, a characteristic vocabulary, an obsessive repetition of a phrase, and so on—things common to many lesser poets. Again, if we analyze his images and metaphors, which are much more impressive than the things I have mentioned, we frequently find over-developing, blowziness and euphemism, on the one hand, and brilliant crystallization on the other. But no system, no poetic, or practice that adds up to anything you can hold on to. The more you examine Thomas as a stylist the less you find.

What does this mean? It means that Thomas is a quite derivative, unoriginal, unintellectual poet, the entire force of whose personality and vitality is jammed into his few difficult half-intelligible poems. To talk about Thomas as a Symbolist is dishonest. Not long ago in Hollywood Aldous Huxley introduced a Stravinsky composition based on a poem of Thomas. Huxley quoted that line of Mallarmé's which says that poets purify the dialect of the tribe. This, said Huxley, was what Thomas did. Now anybody who has read Thomas knows that he did the exact opposite: Thomas did everything in his power to obscure the dialect of the tribe—whatever that expression may mean. Thomas sometimes attempted to keep people from understanding his poems (which are frequently simple, once you know the dodges). He had a horror of simplicity—or what I consider to be a fear of it. He knew little except what a man knows who has lived forty years, and there was little he wanted to know. There is a fatal pessimism in most of his poems, set off by a few bursts of joy and exuberance. The main symbol is masculine love, driven as hard as Freud drove it. In the background is God, hard to identify but always there, a kind of God who belongs to one's parents rather than to the children, who do not quite accept Him.

I went through the *Collected Poems* recently to decide which poems I would keep if I were editing the best poems of Dylan Thomas. Out of ninety poems I chose more than thirty which I think stand with the best poems of our time. If this seems a small number, we should remember that there are not many more poems upon which the fame of Hopkins rests; of Rimbaud; or, for that matter, John Donne. And yet we expect a greater volume of work from such an exuberant man. And it is a point of pride with many modern classicists that they have written so little. Thomas' sixty poems that I would exclude are short of his mark; but they are not failures. Even within the past fifteen years the critical consciousness of our time, which is of the most sensitive temper, has noticed the best in Thomas. I would like to name by name those poems which I think belong to the permanent body of any poetry—or most of them anyway: *I see the boys of summer; A process in the weather of the heart; The force that through the green fuse drives the flower; Especially when the October wind; When like a running grave; Light breaks where no sun shines; Do you not father me; A grief ago; And death shall have no dominion; Then was my neophyte; When all my five and country senses; We lying by seasand; It is the sinner's dust-tongued bell; After the funeral; Not from this anger; How shall my animal; Twenty-four years; A Refusal to Mourn; Poem in October; The Hunchback in the Park; Into her lying-down head; Do not go gentle; A Winter's Tale; The Marriage of a Virgin; When I woke; Among those killed in the dawn raid; Fern Hill; In Country Sleep; Over Sir John's Hill;* and *Poem on His Birthday.* I leave out the sonnets, which I think are rather forced, and the *Ballad of the Long-Legged Bait* and the *Prologue,* and many others. My list is probably off here and there but I think it is the substantial list of works by which Thomas will be remembered.

The "major" poems, that is the more pretentious poems, such as the ten sonnets (called *Altarwise by Owl-light*) reveal most of what we know of Thomas' convictions and what we can call his philosophy. He believed in God and Christ; the Fall and death; the end of all things and the day of eternity; while everything living carries in it its own germ of destruction, and one can envisage life as an insane mockery, there will yet be Mercy. This is very conventional religion but Thomas was uncritical about it. Add to this the puritanism which runs through his whole work. And, finally, the forced optimism in the last poems such as *In Country Sleep,* in which, although the whole sequence is unfinished, there is a recognizable affirmation of faith in life. But one feels that these matters are not of paramount importance in the poetry of Dylan Thomas. Thomas was not interested in philosophical answers. Religion, such as he knew it, was direct and natural; the symbolism of religion, as he uses it, is poetry, direct knowledge. Religion is not to be used; it is simply a part of life, part of himself; it is like a tree; take it or leave it, it is there. In this sense, one might say that Thomas is more religious than Eliot, because Thomas has a natural religious approach to nature and to himself. The language of Thomas is very close to that of Hopkins, not only in obvious ways, but in its very method. Hopkins, however, arrived at his method philosophically, abstractly, as well as through temperament, and the twist of his personality. Thomas, with no equipment for theorizing about the forms of nature, sought the "forms" that Hopkins did. The chief difference between the two poets in terms of their symbols is that Hopkins draws his entire symbology from the God-symbol; Thomas draws his symbology almost entirely from the Sex-symbol. God, in various attributes, is the chief process in Hopkins' view of the world; sex is the chief process in Thomas' view of the world.

Thomas' idea of process is important. The term itself is rather mechanistic, as he intends. He always takes the machine of energy rather than some abstraction, such as spirit or essence. Hence the concreteness of his words and images; obscurity occurs also because of the "process" of mixing the imagery of the subconscious with biological imagery as in Hopkins. But there is also a deliberate attempt to involve the subconscious as the main process: Thomas' imagination, which is sometimes fantastic, works hard to dredge up the images of fantasy and dreams. Very often the process fails and we are left with heaps of grotesque images that add up to nothing. I would equate the process in Thomas' poetics with his rather startling views of the sexual process. Aside from those poems in which sex is simply sung, much as poets used to write what we called love poems, there are those poems in which sex is used as the instrument of belief and knowledge. I do not know how to make this clearer, but perhaps there is a comparison between Thomas and Baudelaire's description of physical love as a surgical operation. Using the cliché of modern literature that everyone is sick and the whole world is a hospital, Thomas wants to imply that sex will make us (or usually just him) healthy and whole again. And there are suggestions of Druidism (which I know nothing about) and primitive fertility rites, apparently still extant in Wales, all mixed up with Henry Miller, Freud, and American street slang. But sex kills also, as Thomas says a thousand times, as in a dream, and he is not sure of the patient's recovery. In place of love, about which Thomas is almost always profoundly bitter, there is sex, the instrument and the physical process of love. The activity of sex, Thomas hopes in his poems, will somehow lead us to love in life and in the cosmos. As he grows older, love recedes and sex becomes a nightmare, a Black Mass.

Thomas moves between sexual revulsion and sexual ecstasy, between puritanism and mysticism, between formalistic ritual (this accounts for his lack of invention) and irresponsibility. In his book one comes, on one page, upon a poem of comparative peace and lucidity, and on the next page, upon a poem of absolute density and darkness. His dissatisfaction with his own lack of stability is reflected in his devices which intend to obscure even the simple poems: he leaves out all indications of explanation—quotation marks, punctuation, titles, connectives, whether logical or grammatical. In addition he uses every extreme device of ambiguity one can think of, from reversing the terms of a figure of speech to ellipsis to over-elaboration of images. There is no poetic behind these practices—only an undefined mystique. One is always confused in Thomas by not knowing whether he is using the microscope or telescope: he switches from one to the other with ease and without warning. It is significant that his joyous poems, which are few, though among his best, are nearly always his simplest. Where the dominant theme of despair obtrudes the language dives down into the depths: and some of these complex poems of the depths are among the most rewarding, the richest in feeling, and the most difficult to hold to. But, beyond question, there are two minds working in Thomas, the joyous, naturally religious mind, and the disturbed, almost pathological mind, of the cultural fugitive or clown. On every level of Thomas' work one notices the lack of sophistication and the split in temperament. This is his strength as well as his weakness. But it is a *grave* weakness because it leaves him without defense, without a bridge between himself and the world. Thomas begins in a blind alley with the obsessive statement that birth is the beginning of death: it is the basic poetic statement but it means nothing unless the poet can build a world between. Thomas never really departs from this statement, and his obsession with sex is only the clinical re-statement of the same theme. The idealization of love, the traditional solution with most poets, good and bad, is never arrived at in Thomas. He skips into the land of love, like somebody else's garden, and skips out again. And he is too good a poet to fake love. He doesn't feel it; he distrusts it; he doesn't believe it. He falls back on the love-process, the assault, the defeat, the shame, the despair. Over and over again, he repeats the ritualistic formulas for love, always doubting its success. The process is despised because it doesn't really work. The brief introduction to the collected poems sounds a note of bravado which asserts that his poems "are written for the love of Man and in praise of God." One wishes they were; one is grateful for the acknowledgment to God and Man, but in the poems we find neither faith nor humanism. What we find is something that fits Thomas into the age:

the satanisms, the vomitous horror, the self-elected crucifixion of the artist.

In the last few years of his life Thomas was beginning to find an audience. No one, I think, was more surprised than he at this phenomenon, because most of the poems which the audience liked had been in books for five or ten years already. Thomas was the one modern poet who by his presence created an audience. His audience was the impossible one: a general audience for a barely understandable poet. His way of meeting this audience, at the end, was no solution for Thomas as a poet. He became a dramatist, a writer of scenarios, a producer. What he wrote in this phase was not negligible by any means; but it was probably not what he wanted and not what his audience wanted. His audience wanted the poetry; they wanted the agony of the process. The frenzy that attended Dylan Thomas' death was a frenzy of frustration. Many times, in his stories and letters and his talk, Thomas tried to leap over this frustration into a Rabelaisian faith; but it never rang true enough. After the gaiety came the hangover, the horrible fundamentalist remorse. Yet through the obscurity of the poetry everyone could feel the scream of desperation: not a cry of desire; on the contrary, it was the opposite; it was the cry of the trapped animal; the thing wanting to be man; the man wanting to be spirit.

He is a self-limited poet; and an exasperating one. He runs beyond your reach after he has beckoned you to follow; he arouses you and then slumps into a heap. He knows, more than his readers, that he has no bridge between life and death, between self and the world; his poetry is absolutely literal (as he himself insisted all the time.) But its literalness is the challenge to literature which is always significant. Thomas sought to keep poetry in his hand, like a boy who has captured a bird. Sometimes the bird is squeezed to death. He is too honest to rhapsodize or to intone over the great symbols: rather he growls or rages or more often hypnotizes himself by the minute object, which he is likely to crush in his anger. Unlike Hopkins, he has no vision of nature and cannot break open the forms of nature; he cannot break open words. He focuses madly on the object, but it will not yield. He calls a weathercock a bow-and-arrow bird. Metaphor won't come and he resorts to riddle, the opposite of metaphor. A good half of his poetry is the poetry of rage: not rage at the world of society or politics or art or anything except self. He is impatient for a method and the impatience early turns into desperation, the desperation into clowning. Consider the enormous patience of Yeats or Pound or Stevens in stalking their prey: these are great hunters of the word. Thomas falls off his elephant and ends up by thinking it funny. But not really. Because he was not a member of the hunting party in the first place; he just happened to wander that way. He was not the kind of poet who knew what was meant by the tradition; he was another naïf, like Rimbaud, a countryman, who having left the country wanders over the face of the earth seeking a vision. He is running away from his fame, which he does not feel equal to. He is running away from the vision of self, or keeping the integrity of self by fleeing from the foci of tradition. I interpret the life and work of Thomas this way: the young poet of natural genius and expansive personality who recoils from the ritual of literary tradition and who feels himself drawn into it as into a den of iniquity. (This is both the puritanism and the provincialism of Thomas.) Such a man can never acquire the wisdom of the world which is called worldliness, and he turns to the only form of behavior, literary and otherwise, permissible both to society and to self. That is buffoonery. All the literary world loves a buffoon: the French make a saint of the clown. But folklore always says the clown dies in the dressing-room.

It is the most certain mark of Thomas' genius that he did not give way to any vision but his own, the one authentic source of knowledge he had—himself. And it is the most certain mark of his weakness that he could not shield himself from the various literary preceptors who buzzed around his head like a helmet of bees. He became immobile, I think, out of pure fright. He wrote personal letters (which are now being published) apparently meant for publication, in which he adopted the modern clichés about modern life. He pretended to be horrified by the electric toaster (or maybe really was).

The doctrinaire impersonality of our poetry demands allegiance to a tradition: any tradition, even one you rig up for yourself. Thomas represents the extreme narrowness of the individual genius, the basic animal (one of his favorite symbols) in man. The animal to Thomas is everything and we listen because he calls it animal, not spirit or essence or potentiality or something else. It is the authentic symbol for a poet who believes in the greatness of the individual and the sacredness of the masses. It is Whitman's symbol when he says he thinks he could turn and live with animals: because they are natural and belong to nature and do not try to twist nature out of its socket. They do not try to believe anything contrary to their condition.

But Thomas is drawn away from his animal; he becomes brute. And this he knows. In the brute phase of his poetry (which is the phase loved by the modernists who picked up his scent) the poetry is a relentless cutting down to the quick, surgery, butchery and worse. And as Thomas is the one and only subject of his poems, we know what is being destroyed.

It is some of the saddest poetry we have. It leaves us finally with grief. The pathos of Thomas is that he is not diabolical, not mystical, not possessed; he has not the expansive imagination of Blake nor the fanatical self-control of Yeats, nor the suicidal gaiety of the accursed poet. He is the poet of genius unable to face life. Like D. H. Lawrence he is always hurling himself back into childhood, and the childhood of the world. Everyone speaks of Thomas as a child. He became a child.

It is easy to dismiss him but he will not be dismissed. He was a tremendous talent who stung himself into insensibility because he could not face the obligations of intellectual life. He could not take the consequences of his own natural beliefs; and he could not temporize; there was no transition, no growth, only the two states of natural joy and intellectual despair, love of trees and fascination of the brute process. He said everything he had to say: it had little to do with wars and cities and art galleries. What he said was that man is a child thrust into the power of self; an animal becoming an angel. But becoming an angel he becomes more a beast. There is no peace, no rest, and death itself is only another kind of disgusting sex. Yet man must not believe so little. He must invent a belief in love, even if it doesn't exist. For Thomas it did not exist. Other writers knew that here was his Achilles heel.

But something happened. Somehow the spark escaped; it leapt out of the hands of literature and set a fire. Thomas, I think, did the impossible in modern poetry. He made a jump to an audience which, we have been taught to believe, does not exist. It is an audience that understands him even when they cannot understand his poetry. It is probably the first non-funereal poetry audience in fifty years, and an audience that has been deprived of poetry by fiat. It bears certain characteristics to the mob—but that, under the circumstances, is also understandable. The audience understands Thomas instinctively. They know he is reaching out to them but doesn't quite know how to effect the meeting. The reaching ends in a tantalizing excitement, a frenzy. It is not a literary frenzy, the kind that ends in a riot with the police defending Edith Sitwell after a reading of *Facade*. On the contrary, it is the muttering of awakening, a slow realization about poetry, a totally unexpected apocalypse. This audience sees Thomas as a male Edna St. Vincent Millay, or perhaps a Charlie Chaplin; they hear the extraordinary vibrato, a voice of elation and anguish singing over their heads like a wind that tears all the blossoms off the trees. They know this is poetry and they know it is for them.

He is like the old cliché of vaudeville in which a tragi-comic figure engaged in some private act (such as keeping his pants from falling down) wanders onto a stage where a highly formal cultural something is in progress. Naturally the embarrassed clown steals the show. One must remember Thomas' own story about himself—there are many variations—the story in which he gets his finger stuck in a beer bottle and can't get it out. He goes from place to place, beer bottle and all, meeting new people. The beer bottle becomes Thomas' symbol of his natural self: it is his passport from the common people to the literary life, and back again. It is both his symbol of self and his symbol of other-self. But to Thomas it is mainly a horror symbol. It is the key to No-Man's Land. Because Thomas is an uncivilizable puritan and a hardshell fundamentalist of some indefinable kind, the puritanism sets up the tension in his poetry—a tension based upon love and fear of love—the basic sexual tension, the basic theological tension. The greatness of Thomas is that he recognizes the equation; and the weakness of Thomas is that he takes to his heels when he tries to grapple with it.

Everything I have said can be said better in the little poem by Thomas that takes nine lines. The last line of the poem is so much like a line of Whitman's that I have searched through Whitman's poems to find it. I am sure it is there and yet I know it isn't. The line reads "I advance for as long as forever is."

Twenty-four years remind the tears of my eyes.
(Bury the dead for fear that they walk to the grave in labour)
In the groin of the natural doorway I crouched like a tailor
Sewing a shroud for a journey
By the light of the meat-eating sun.
Dressed to die, the sensual strut begun,
With my red veins full of money,
In the final direction of the elementary town
I advance for as long as forever is.

Return Journey

DYLAN THOMAS

NARRATOR. It was a cold white day in High Street, and nothing to stop the wind slicing up from the Docks; for where the squat and tall shops had shielded the town from the sea lay their blitzed flat graves marbled with snow and headstoned with fences. Dogs, delicate as cats on water, as though they had gloves on their paws, paddled over the vanished buildings. Boys romped, calling high and clear, on top of a levelled chemist's and a shoeshop; and a little girl, wearing a man's cap, threw a snowball in a chill deserted garden that had once been the Jug and Bottle of the Prince of Wales. The wind cut up the street with a soft sea-noise hanging on its arm, like a hooter in a muffler. I could see the swathed hill stepping up out of the town, which you never could see properly before, and the powdered fields of the roofs of Milton Terrace and Watkin Street and Fullers Row. Fish-frailed, netbagged, umbrella'd, pixie-capped, fur-shoed, blue-nosed, puce-lipped, blinkered like drayhorses, scarved, mittened, galoshed, wearing everything but the cat's blanket, crushes of shopping women crunched in the little Lapland of the once grey drab street, blew and queued and yearned for hot tea, as I began my search through Swansea town cold and early on that wicked February morning. I went into the hotel. "Good morning."

The hall-porter did not answer. I was just another snowman to him. He did not know that I was looking for someone after fourteen years, and he did not care. He stood and shuddered, staring through the glass of the hotel door at the snowflakes sailing down the sky, like Siberian confetti. The bar was just opening, but already one customer puffed and shook at the counter with a full pint of half-frozen Tawe water in his wrapped-up hand. I said "Good morning," and the barmaid, polishing the counter vigorously, as though it were a rare and valuable piece of Swansea china, said to her first customer:

BARMAID. Seen the film at the Elysium Mr. Griffiths there's snow isn't it did you come up on your bicycle our pipes burst Monday . . .

NARRATOR. A pint of bitter, please.

BARMAID. Proper little lake in the kitchen got to wear your Wellingtons when you boil a egg one and four please . . .

CUSTOMER. The cold gets me just here . . .

BARMAID. . . . and eightpence change that's your liver Mr. Griffiths you been on the cocoa again . . .

NARRATOR. I wonder whether you remember a friend of mine? He always used to come to this bar, some years ago. Every morning, about this time.

CUSTOMER. Just by here it gets me. I don't know what'd happen if I didn't wear a band . . .

BARMAID. What's his name?

NARRATOR. Young Thomas.

BARMAID. Lots of Thomases come here it's a kind of home from home for Thomases isn't it Mr. Griffiths what's he look like?

NARRATOR. [*Slowly*] He'd be about seventeen or eighteen . . .

BARMAID. . . . I was seventeen once . . .

NARRATOR. . . . and above medium height. Above medium height for Wales, I mean, he's five foot six and a half. Thick blubber lips; snub nose; curly mouse-brown hair; one front tooth broken after playing a game called cats and dogs in the Mermaid, Mumbles; speaks rather fancy; truculent; plausible; a bit of a shower-off; plus fours and no breakfast, you know; used to have poems printed in the *Herald of Wales;* there was one about an open-air performance of *Electra* in Mrs. Bertie Perkins' garden in Sketty; lived up the Uplands; a bombastic adolescent provincial bohemian with a thick-knotted artist's tie made out of his sister's scarf—she never knew where it had gone—and a cricket-shirt dyed bottle green; a gabbing, ambitious, mock-tough, pretentious young man; and mole-y, too.

BARMAID. There's words what d'you want to find *him* for I wouldn't touch him with a bargepole . . . would you, Mr. Griffiths? Mind, you can never tell. I remember a man came here with a monkey. Called for 'alf for himself and a pint for the monkey. And he wasn't Italian at all. Spoke Welsh like a preacher.

NARRATOR. The bar was filling up. Snowy business bellies pressed their watch chains against the counter; black business bowlers, damp and white now as Christmas puddings in their cloths, bobbed in front of the misty mirrors. The voice of commerce rang sternly through the lounge.

FIRST VOICE. Cold enough for you?

SECOND VOICE. How's your pipes, Mr. Lewis?

THIRD VOICE. Another winter like this'll put paid to me, Mr. Evans.

FOURTH VOICE. I got the flu . . .

FIRST VOICE. Make it a double . . .

SECOND VOICE. Similar . . .

BARMAID. Okay, baby . . .

CUSTOMER. [*Confidentially*] I seem to remember a chap like you described. There couldn't be two like him let's hope. He used to work as a reporter. Down the Three Lamps I used to see him. Lifting his ikkle elbow.

NARRATOR. What's the Three Lamps like now?

CUSTOMER. It isn't like anything. It isn't there. It's nothing mun. You remember Ben Evans' stores? It's right next door to that. Ben Evans isn't there either . . .

[*Fade.*]

NARRATOR. I went out of the hotel into the snow and walked down High Street, past the flat white wastes where all the shops had been. Eddershaw Furnishers, Curry's Bicycles, Donegal Clothing Company, Doctor Scholl's, Burton Tailors, W. H. Smith, Boots Cash Chemists, Leslie's Stores, Upson's Shoes, Prince of Wales, Tucker's Fish, Stead and Simpson—all the shops bombed and vanished. Past the hope in space where Hodges and Clothiers had been, down Castle Street, past the remembered, invisible shops, Price's Fifty Shilling, and Crouch the Jeweller, Potter Gilmore Gowns, Evan Jeweller, Master's Outfitters, Style and Mantle, Lennard's Boots, True Form, Kardomah, R. E. Jones, Dean's Tailor, David Evans, Gregory Confectioners, Bovega, Burton's, Lloyd's Bank and nothing. And into Temple Street. There the Three Lamps had stood, old Mac magisterial in his corner. And there the Young Thomas I was searching for used to stand at the counter on Friday pay-nights with Freddie Farr, Half Hook, Bill Latham, Cliff Williams, Gareth Hughes, Eric Hughes, Glyn Lowry, a man among men, his hat at a rakish angle, in that snug, smug, select, Edwardian holy of best-bitter holies . . .

[*Bar noises in background*]

OLD REPORTER. Remember when I took you down the mortuary for the first time, Young Thomas? He'd never seen a corpse before, boys, except old Ron on a Saturday night. "If you want to be a proper newspaperman," I said, "you got to be well known in the right circles. You got to be *persona grata* in the mortuary, see." He went pale green, mun.

FIRST YOUNG REPORTER. Look, he's blushing now . . .

OLD REPORTER. And when we got there, what d'you think? The decorators were in at the mortuary, giving the old home a bit of a re-do like. Up on the ladders having a slap at the roof. Young Thomas didn't see 'em; he had his popeyes glued on the slab, and when one of the painters up the ladder said "Good morning, gents" in a deep voice, he upped in the air and out of the place like a ferret. Laugh!

BARMAID. [*Off*] You've had enough, Mr. Roberts. You heard what I said.

[*Noise of a gentle scuffle.*]

SECOND YOUNG REPORTER. [*Casually*] There goes Mr. Roberts.

OLD REPORTER. Well fair do's they throw you out very genteel in this pub . . .

FIRST YOUNG REPORTER. Ever seen Young Thomas covering a soccer match down the Vetch and working it out in tries?

SECOND YOUNG REPORTER. And up the Mannesman Hall shouting "Good footwork, sir," and a couple of punch-drunk colliers galumphing about like jumbos.

FIRST YOUNG REPORTER. What have you been reporting today, young Thomas?

SECOND YOUNG REPORTER. Two typewriter Thomas the ace news-dick . . .

OLD REPORTER. Let's have a dekko at your notebook. "Called at British Legion. Nothing. Called at Hospital. One broken leg. Auction at the Metropole. Ring Mr. Beynon *re* Gymanfa Ganu. Lunch. Pint and pasty at the Singleton with Mrs. Giles. Bazaar at Bethesda Chapel. Chimney on fire at Tontine Street. Walters Road Sunday School Outing. Rehearsal of the *Mikado* at Skewen"—all front-page stuff . . .

[*Fade.*]

NARRATOR. The voices of fourteen years ago hung silent in the snow and ruin, and in the falling winter morning I walked on through the white havoc'd centre where once a very young man I knew had mucked about as chirpy as a sparrow after the sips and titbits and small change of the town. Near the *Evening Post* building and the fragment of the Castle, I stopped a man whose face I thought I recognised from a long time ago. I said: I wonder if you can tell me . . .

PASSER-BY. Yes?

NARRATOR. He peered out of his blanketing scarves and from

under his snowballed balaclava like an Eskimo with a bad conscience. I said: If you can tell me whether you used to know a chap called Young Thomas. He worked on the *Post* and used to wear an overcoat sometimes with the check lining inside out so that you could play giant draughts on him. He wore a conscious woodbine, too . . .

PASSER-BY. What d'you mean, conscious woodbine?

NARRATOR. . . . and a perched pork-pie with a peacock feather, and he tried to slouch like a newshawk even when he was attending a meeting of the Gorseinon Buffalos . . .

PASSER-BY. Oh, *him!* He owes me half a crown. I haven't seen him since the old Kardomah days. He wasn't a reporter then; he'd just left the Grammar School. Him and Charlie Fisher—Charlie's got whiskers now—and Tom Warner and Fred Janes, drinking coffee-dashes and arguing the toss.

NARRATOR. What about?

PASSER-BY. Music and poetry and painting and politics. Einstein and Epstein, Stravinsky and Greta Garbo, death and religion, Picasso and girls . . .

NARRATOR. And then?

PASSER-BY. Communism, symbolism, Bradman, Braque, the Watch Committee, free love, free beer, murder, Michelangelo, ping-pong, ambition, Sibelius and girls . . .

NARRATOR. Is that all?

PASSER-BY. How Dan Jones was going to compose the most prodigious symphony, Fred Janes paint the most miraculously meticulous picture, Charlie Fisher catch the poshest trout, Vernon Watkins and Young Thomas write the most boiling poems, how they would ring the bells of London and paint it like a tart . . .

NARRATOR. And after that?

PASSER-BY. Oh, the hissing of the butt-ends in the drains of the coffee-dashes and the tinkle and gibble-gabble of the morning young lounge lizards as they talked about Augustus John, Emil Jannings, Carnera, Dracula, Amy Johnson, trial marriage, pocket money, the Welsh sea, the London stars, King Kong, anarchy, darts, T. S. Eliot and girls . . . Diw, it's cold!

NARRATOR. And he hurried on, into the dervish snow, without a good morning or goodbye, swaddled in his winter woollens like a man in the island of his deafness, and I felt that perhaps he had never stopped at all to tell me of one more departed stage in the progress of the boy I was pursuing. The Kardomah Café was razed to the snow, the voices of the coffee-drinkers—poets, painters, and musicians in their beginnings—lost in the willynilly of the years and the flakes.

Down College Street I walked then, past the remembered invisible shops, Langley's, Castle Cigar Co., T. B. Brown, Pullar's, Aubrey Jeremiah, Goddard Jones, Richards, Hornes, Marles, Pleasance and Harper, Star Supply, Sidney Heath, Wesley Chapel and nothing. . . . My search was leading me back, through pub and job and café, to the school.

[*Fade. School Bell*]

SCHOOLMASTER. Oh yes, yes, I remember him well,
though I do not know if I would recognise him now:
nobody grows any younger, or better,
and boys grow into much the sort of men one would suppose
though sometimes the mustaches bewilder
and one finds it hard to reconcile one's memory of a small
none-too-clean urchin lying his way unsuccessfully out of his homework
with a fierce and many-medalled sergeant-major with three children
or a divorced chartered accountant;
and it is hard to realise
that some little tousled rebellious youth whose only claim
to fame among his contemporaries was his undisputed right
to the championship of the spitting contest
is now perhaps one's own bank manager.
Oh yes, I remember him well, the boy you are searching for:
he looked like most boys, no better, brighter, or more respectful;
he cribbed, mitched, spilt ink, rattled his desk and
garbled his lessons with the worst of them;
he could smudge, hedge, smirk, wriggle, wince,
whimper, blarney, badger, blush, deceive, be
devious, stammer, improvise, assume
offended dignity or righteous indignation as though to the manner
born;
sullenly and reluctantly he drilled, for some small
crime, under Sergeant Bird, so wittily nicknamed
Oiseau, on Wednesday half-holidays,
appeared regularly in detention classes,
hid in the cloakroom during algebra,
was, when a newcomer, thrown into the bushes of the
lower playground by bigger boys,
and threw newcomers into the bushes of the lower

playground when *he* was a bigger boy;
he scuffled at prayers,
he interpolated, smugly, the time-honoured wrong
irreverent words into the morning hymns,
he helped to damage the headmaster's rhubarb,
was thirty-third in trigonometry,
and, as might be expected, edited the school magazine.

[*Fade.*]

NARRATOR. The hall is shattered, the echoing corridors charred where he scribbled and smudged and yawned in the long green days, waiting for the bell and the scamper into the yard; the school on Mount Pleasant Hill has changed its face and its ways. Soon, they say, it may be no longer the school at all he knew and loved when he was a boy up to no good but the beat of his blood; the names are havoc'd from the hall and the carved initials burned from the broken wood. But the names remain. What names did he know of the dead? Who of the honoured dead did he know such a long time ago? The names of the dead in the living heart and head remain forever. Of all the dead whom did he know?

[*Funeral Bell.*]

VOICE

Evans, K. J.
Haines, G. C.
Roberts, I. L.
Moxham, J.
Thomas, H.
Baines, W.
Bazzard, F. H.
Beer, L. J.
Bucknell, R.
Tywford, G.
Vagg, E. A.
Wright, G.

[*Fade.*]

NARRATOR. Then I tacked down the snowblind hill, a cat-o'-nine-gales whipping from the sea, and, white and eiderdowned in the smothering flurry, people padded past me up and down like prowling featherbeds. And I plodded through the ankle-high one cloud that foamed the town, into flat Gower Street, its buildings melted, and along long Helen's Road. Now my search was leading me back to the seashore.

[*Noise of sea, softly.*]

NARRATOR. Only two living creatures stood on the promenade, near the cenotaph, facing the tossed crystal sea: a man in a chewed muffler and a ratting cap, and an angry dog of a mixed make. The man diddered in the cold, beat his bare blue hands together, waited for some sign from sea or snow; the dog shouted at the weather, and fixed his bloodshot eyes on Mumbles Head. But when the man and I talked together, the dog piped down and fixed his eyes on me, blaming me for the snow. The man spoke towards the sea. Year in, year out, whatever the weather, once in the daytime, once in the dark, he always came to look at the sea. He knew all the dogs and boys and old men who came to see the sea, who ran or gambolled on the sand or stooped at the edges of the waves as though over a wild, rolling ashcan. He knew the lovers who went to lie in the sandhills, the striding masculine women who roared at their terriers like tiger tamers, the loafing men whose work it was in the world to observe the great employment of the sea. He said:

PROMENADE-MAN. Oh yes, yes, I remember him well, but I didn't know what was his name. I don't know the names of none of the sandboys. They don't know mine. About fourteen or fifteen years old, you said, with a little red cap. And he used to play by Vivian's Stream. He used to dawdle in the arches, you said, and lark about on the railway lines and holler at the old sea. He'd mooch about the dunes and watch the tankers and the tugs and the banana boats come out of the Docks. He was going to run away to sea, he said. *I* know. On Saturday afternoon he'd go down to the sea when it was a long way out, and hear the foghorns though he couldn't see the ships. And on Sunday nights, after chapel, he'd be swaggering with his pals along the prom, whistling after the girls.

[*Titter.*]

GIRL. Does your mother know you're out? Go away now. Stop following us.

[*Another girl titters.*]

GIRL. Don't you say nothing, Hetty, you're only encouraging. No thank *you*, Mr. Cheeky, with your cut-glass accent and your father's trilby! I don't want *no* walk on *no* sands. What d'you say? Ooh, listen to him, Het, he's swallowed a dictionary. No, I don't want to go with nobody up no lane in the moonlight, see, and I'm not a baby-snatcher neither. I seen you going to school along Terrace Road, Mr. Glad-Eye, with your little satchel and wearing your red cap and all. You seen me wearing my . . . no you never. Hetty, mind your glasses! Hetty Harris, you're as bad as them. Oh, go away and do your homework, you. No I'm not then. I'm nobody's homework, see. Cheek! Hetty Harris, don't you let him! Oooh, there's brazen! Well, just to the end of the prom, if you like. No further, mind . . .

PROMENADE-MAN. Oh yes, I knew him well. I've known him by the thousands . . .

NARRATOR. Even now, on the frozen foreshore, a high, far cry of boys, all like the boy I sought, slid on the glass of the streams and snowballed each other and the sky. Then I went on my way from the sea, up Brynmill Terrace and into Glanbrydan Avenue where Bert Trick had kept a grocer's shop and, in the kitchen, threatened the annihilation of the ruling classes over sandwiches and jelly and blancmange. And I came to the shops and houses of the Uplands. Here and around here it was that the journey had begun of the one I was pursuing through his past.

[*Old piano cinema-music in background.*]

FIRST VOICE. Here was once the flea-pit picture-house where he whooped for the scalping Indians with Jack Basset and banged for the rustler's guns.

NARRATOR. Jackie Basset, killed.

THIRD VOICE. Here once was Mrs. Ferguson's, who sold the best gob-stoppers and penny packets full of surprises and a sweet kind of glue.

FIRST VOICE. In the fields behind Cwmdonkin Drive, the Murrays chased him and all cats.

SECOND VOICE. No fires now where the outlaws' fires burned and the paradisiacal potatoes roasted in the embers.

THIRD VOICE. In the Craig beneath Town Hill he was a lonely killer hunting the wolves (or rabbits) and the red Sioux tribe (or Mitchell brothers).

[*Fade cinema-music into background of children's voices reciting, in unison, the names of the counties of Wales.*]

FIRST VOICE. In Mirador School he learned to read and count. Who made the worst raffia doilies? Who put water in Joyce's galoshes, every morning prompt as prompt? In the afternoons, when the children were good, they read aloud from *Struwwelpeter*. And when they were bad, they sat alone in the empty classroom, hearing, from above them, the distant, terrible, sad music of the late piano lesson.

[*The children's voices fade. The piano lesson continues in background.*]

NARRATOR. And I went up, through the white Grove, into Cwmdonkin Park, the snow still sailing and the childish, lonely, remembered music fingering on in the suddenly gentle wind. Dusk was folding the park around, like another, darker snow. Soon the bell would ring for the closing of the gates, though the park was empty. The park-keeper walked by the reservoir, where swans had glided, on his white rounds. I walked by his side and asked him my questions, up the swathed drives past buried beds and loaded utterly still furred and birdless trees towards the last gate. He said:

PARK-KEEPER. Oh yes, yes, I knew him well. He used to climb the reservoir railings and pelt the old swans. Run like a billygoat over the grass you should keep off of. Cut branches off the trees. Carve words on the benches. Pull up moss in the rockery, go snip through the dahlias. Fight in the bandstand. Climb the elms and moon up the top like a owl. Light fires in the bushes. Play on the green bank. Oh yes, I knew him well. I think he was happy all the time. I've known him by the thousands.

NARRATOR. We had reached the last gate. Dusk drew around us and the town. I said: What has become of him now?

PARK-KEEPER. Dead.

NARRATOR. The Park keeper said . . .

[*The park bell rings.*]

PARK-KEEPER. Dead . . . Dead . . . Dead . . . Dead . . . Dead . . . Dead.

(*1947*)

from *Dylan Thomas Letters to Vernon Watkins*

The poems 'The Tombstone Told When She Died' and 'A Saint About to Fall' accompanied the next letter, and its two paragraphs are concerned with them in that order. The second poem, on which he had been working continuously, was written in anticipation of the birth of his first child in January.

VERNON WATKINS

Monday: [sent 14th October 1938]
Sea View, Laugharne

Dear Vernon,

I'm sorry not to have written before, I've been awfully busy with my own work, with reviewing, & muddled up with trying to get money from a sinister philanthropic society. Here's my new big poem and—with no anger at all—the Hardy-like one. I considered all your suggestions most carefully. A 'strange & red' harsh head was, of course, very weak & clumsy, but I couldn't see that the alliteration of "raving red" was effective. I tried everything, & stuck to the commonplace "blazing", which makes the last line violent enough then, if not exactly good enough, for the last. In the last line you'll see I've been daring, & have tried to make the point of the poem softer & subtler by the use of the dangerous "dear". The word "dear" fits in, I think, with "though her eyes smiled", which comes earlier. I wanted the girl's *terrible* reaction to orgastic [sic] death to be suddenly altered into a kind of despairing love. As I see it now, it strikes me as very moving, but it may be too much of a shock, a bathetic shock perhaps, & I'd like very much to know what you think. No, I still think the womb "bellowing" is all right, exactly what I wanted; perhaps it looks too much like a stunt rhyme with heroine, but that was unavoidable. "Hurried" film I just couldn't see; I wanted it slow & complicated, the winding cinematic works of the womb. I agree with your objection to "small"; "innocent" is splendid, but "fugitive" & "turbulent" are, for me in that context, too vague, too 'literary' (I'm sorry to use that word again) too ambiguous. I've used "devilish", which is almost colloquial.

As to the big poem—only provisionally called "In September", & called that at all only because it was a terrible war month—I'm at the moment very pleased with it, more than anything I've done this year. Does "Glory cracked like a flea" shock you? I think you'll see it *must* come there, or some equally grotesque contrast. The last line of the 2nd verse might appear just a long jumble of my old anatomical clichés, but if, in the past, I've used "burning brains & hair" etc. too loosely, this time I used them—as the only words—in dead earnest. Remember this is a poem written to a child about to be born—you know I'm going to be a father in January—& telling it what a world it will see, what horrors & hells. The last four lines of the poem, especially the last but two, may seem ragged, but I've altered the rhythm purposely; "you so gentle" must be very soft and gentle, & the last line must roar. It's an optimistic, taking-everything poem. The two most important words are "Cry Joy". Tell me about this, please, very soon. I'm surer of the *words* of this poem than of the words in any recent one. I want mostly to know what the general effect of the poem is upon you (though of course you can criticize, as you like, any detail).

Sorry you couldn't come this weekend. Do try to come next. I'm afraid we're much too poor to be able to come up to see you for a long time. So do your best.

All Love,
Dylan.

[Undated: probably May or June 1939]
Sea View, Laugharne

Dear Vernon,

I don't find your way of criticizing at all irritating; you know that. It's the most helpful there is for me, and I want it to go on. About many suggestions of yours we'll always, of course, disagree, especially when they seem completely to misunderstand my meaning; but, as nobody else has done—though this is a late and wrong place for a recommendation of your complete intellectual honesty, a thing we needn't talk about—without rancor, affectation, on the felt need to surprise. I think you are liable, in your criticisms of me, to underrate the value—or, rather, the integrity, the wholeness—of what I am saying or trying to make clear that I am saying, and often to suggest alterations or amendments for purely musical motives. For instance, "Caught in a somersault of tumbled mantime" may (and I doubt it) sound more agreeable—we'll leave out any suggestion of it sounding inevitable because it is, however good the implied criticism, a group of words *outside* the poem—to the "prophesying ear" than "In an imagining of tumbled mantime", a line I worked out *for* its sounds & not in spite of them. My criticism of your critical suggestion in this case is that your 'ear' is deaf to the logic of my poem;

> "Caught in a somersault etc etc
> Suddenly cold as fish"

is an ambiguous tangle, very like nonsense. (I know your suggestion was not meant to be the last substitutive word for my first words, but was meant mainly to suggest further things, allway pointers, to me myself; but the suggestion still does, I believe, show the way your criticism often works: towards the aural betterment (ugh) of details, without regard for their significance in a worked-out, if not a premeditated-*in-detail,* whole). This is certainly one critical way, but when it suggests "withered" for "sheeted" in the last line but one of the first stanza, *I* suggest it cuts across the poem and does not come out of it. It is a poet saying "This is what I would have done"; not a critic saying, "This, I think, is what the poet should have done". I suppose, argumentatively, not randomly speaking, that all criticism which is not an analysis of reasons for praise must primarily be suspicion; and that's stimulating. Nothing but the inevitable can be taken for granted, and it always excites me to find you dealing suspiciously with a word, a line, that I had, in a naturally blind or artificially blinkered moment, taken, myself, with too much trust, trusting too much the fallible creative rush of verse—small or large rushes of verse—that comes, in many cases, between the mechanical preparations for that (in a way) accidental rush. (Wooly writing, I'm afraid; I hope the meaning comes clearly.) With your annoyance at the word "chuck" I agree; and my use of it is sentimental. I have tried "cast", but that is too static a word; I'll find what I really want. And, yes the poem did appear to tire of itself at the end—; (by the way, I resent that 'tire of itself' idea, which arrogantly supposes the self-contained *identity* of the poem even in its forming phases; the poem is not, of course, itself until the poet has left it). The jingle of "abide with our pride" I'm retaining; I wanted the idea of an almost jolly jingle there, a certain carelessness to lead up to the flat, hard, ugly last line of truth, a suggestion of "Well, that's over, O atta boy we live with our joy"; a purposeful intolerance—no, I meant an intolerance on purpose—of the arguments I had been setting against my own instinctive delight in the muddled world. Whether that intolerance, carelessness, etc. is *poetically* effective is another kettle of wishes.

It is very fine news of the masque, and Caitlin and I will be there. We will try to bring Hughes too. Why don't you write to him? You want a big audience, of word-boys as well as theatre boys. Who have you asked? I shall do a review for Life & Letters, but after the show you must let me read the masque. We'll be there for the First Night, I hope.

We want a little poem for Llewelyn.

Love till we see you; and before and after. Can you come & see Norman Cameron? He'll be down for a weekend soon, I'll let you know when.

Write soon. Here is a new short poem, nothing very much.

Dylan

Talks with Dylan Thomas

HARVEY BREIT

I

Recently poets have manifested an increasing tendency toward respectability. They are presentable and well dressed. They hold responsible views on political matters and are the backbones of universities. They support their families. They have even gone into government. In cold weather they wear overcoats and for the rain they have rubbers. They seem to have accepted the dictum of the times (and Thomas Mann): the artist is strange enough inwardly, outwardly he should be anonymous. And so poets read their poems as if they were reading the Sunday newspaper to their wives over the boiled eggs. Interviewed, what they have to say is serious, cooperative and directly illuminating. Their poems may puzzle the public; the poets themselves are proving they are socially viable.

But when Dylan Thomas (pronounced Dillon) arrived on his first visit to America it was obvious that this revolution of respectability had left him "disengaged." The 35-year-old Welsh poet—whose poems are as wild and structural as atoms and who is regarded by critics to be the best young poet writing in English since the extraordinary debut of Wystan Hugh Auden—is one of a passing breed of spiritual anarchists who resist every encroachment of society merely by ignoring it.

Thomas, this observer feels, is a seriously elusive man. He is for chit-chat and verbal games and oblique counters. In social gatherings he gives the impression, fleetingly, of a wary animal of the woods who walks stolidly and boldly into the clearing. When he reads poetry (as everyone knows who has heard him), his wariness and his shyness

Part I from *The New York Times Book Review,* May 14, 1950, p. 19; part II from *The New York Times Book Review,* February 17, 1952, p. 17.

and his stolidness fall away. His stirring and subtle and remarkably clean reading of poetry (read unashamedly as poetry) elicited from a critical listener the judgment, "This is the greatest reading since Yeats" (and, typically, from Thomas himself the comment, "I'm afraid it's second-rate Charles Laughton").

Thomas has just completed a reading tour of the nation that took in some forty university towns, winding up with a thumping reading for the Modern Museum poetry sessions under the direction of Lloyd Frankenberg. On May 15, by popular demand, he makes a farewell appearance at The Poetry Center of the Ninety-second Street Y which, under John Malcolm Brinnin, is chiefly responsible for Thomas' visit here. In celebration of this first "coming," New Directions is publishing this spring some selected poems (about twenty-six) in a limited, signed edition.

One day recently this writer met Dylan Thomas at a Third Avenue bar and grill. "I love Third Avenue," Thomas said, filled with genuine admiration (although the only other landmark he had really visited is the RCA building). "I don't believe New York," he went on. "It's obvious to anyone why. All the same, I believe in New Yorkers. Whether they've ever questioned the dream in which they live, I wouldn't know, because I won't ever dare ask that question."

Thomas is a little short, a little round and round-eyed, a little fair, very unruly-haired. His strongly modeled but no longer cherubic face (as Augustus John drew it . . . bears a male resemblance to Elsa Lanchester's. He said: "Say I am 35 years older, small, slim, dark, intelligent, and darting-doting-dotting-eyed. Say I am balding and toothlessing. I am also well dressed." Mr. Thomas was wearing rumpled tweeds and was coatless. "Do you think that an invisible coat is well dressed? It is absolutely essential that I wear an invisible coat. Visible overcoats make you feel proprietorial."

Avoiding the sartorial question, I asked Thomas if he ever read American poetry. He replied with mock eloquence: "Whenever the day is dull and the rain is falling and the feet of the heron are battering against my window, and whenever the Garnetts (who are a literary family) or the gannets (who I believe are a bird) are gossiping in the bay, then what do I do but count my beads and then: a volume of American verse edited by Oscar Williams!"

What, one wanted to know, were Mr. Thomas' conclusions after such an immersion? "I suddenly have the death wish," he said, "which is what I started with. And then I have to read the poetry again and then I like it. And then it all begins again: the melancholy, gay, euphoric roundabout."

Thomas drank his whisky and beer a little moodily. "Any possible success that could happen to me is bad for me," he said, apparently thinking of his audiences. To pursue the thought: Was it "success" if people liked his work?

"If people like my poetry, if they like my reading of it, if they like me, that is success, and that is bad for me. I should be what I was," Mr. Thomas replied. Did Mr. Thomas mean thirty-five years ago? "No, twenty years ago," he said. "Then I was arrogant and lost. Now I am humble and found. I prefer that other."

II

In 1950 the brilliant, aseptic Welsh poet Dylan Thomas (Dylan rhymes with penicillin) visited us for the first time. He is back a second time now—to read his own and other poets' verses at the Ninety-second Street Y.M.H.A., the Modern Museum and scores of colleges and universities—as much by popular demand as by his own wish. In celebration of this event, New Directions is bringing out his new poems, "In Country Sleep," and in celebration of a more personal sort this writer engaged Mr. Thomas in a repeat performance talk. Though Mr. Thomas—it was an absolutely reliable bet—wouldn't repeat himself, couldn't repeat himself. And so, inexorably, it turned out.

In the course of the first talk (May 14, 1950), Mr. Thomas described himself as "35 years old, small, slim, dark, intelligent, and darting-doting-dotting eyed." He then added, "Say I am balding and toothlessing. I am also well-dressed." Mr. Thomas wasn't slim then, and still isn't, he is still fair, with plenty of unruly hair, enough teeth, and his eyes are round and sleepy-looking. His tweeds are definitely unpressed. Mr. Thomas, as a matter of fact, could easily have stood in for Heywood Broun on the occasion when he was described as resembling an unmade bed. Mr. Thomas, it is nice to be able to report, continues all in all to remain intelligent, imaginative and unreconstructed.

The talk at first was on poetry in general and Thomas Hardy in particular, who turned out to be Mr. Thomas' favorite poet of the century. But Mr. Thomas was also a prose writer of talent, and one wondered how he thought about the two mediums. Did he, for example, care less and less about prose? "No," Mr. Thomas said, "as you grow older they are more and more separate is what you feel. When you are young you are liable to write this bastard thing, a prose-poetry. When you get a bit older you find they get separated, and prose becomes more clean and spare."

One felt that about Eliot's prose. Mr. Thomas nodded. "Eliot does keep them separate. He writes beautiful prose—only because it's nothing to do with the verse. A poet can't write extravagant prose: it would be a slopover. A prose writer can write extravagant poetry. Joyce is the direct reverse. He wrote simple, clean poetry and marvelously imaginative prose. With most people it's the opposite. Writers should keep their opinions for their prose."

Supposing, the interviewer said, you were not you and I were not I——

"I'd believe it," Mr. Thomas said succinctly.

And then not-I asked not-you, why shouldn't poets have opinions in their poetry?

"Opinions," Mr. Thomas proceeded, "are the result of self-argument and as most people can't argue with anybody and especially with themselves, opinions are bloody awful. There are opinions, of course. In dramatic poetry for one, but most of us are lyric poets. It was Eliot in this century who showed that one could talk about any subject in verse, except one's self."

Then wasn't there some sort of discrepancy in what Mr. Thomas was saying? "I suppose," Mr. Thomas said, "the thing about opinion should be qualified." That was precisely what Mr. Thomas had been doing, hadn't he? "The slant," Mr. Thomas went on, "the tilt of the mind informs the poetry."

Mr. Thomas kept his Between-the-Acts little cigar in the corner of his mouth, his head tilted at an angle away from the smoke. "I like to put down the word blood. It's a curious kind of word; it means insanity, among other meanings. It's part of the tilt of my mind that I put it down often."

Mr. Thomas and his guest drank. "What is interesting," he pursued, after a while, "is the way in which certain words either lost their meaning or their goodness. The word honor, for instance. A world fit for heroes. A world fit for Neros is more like it."

Why did words lose their meaning or goodness? "The wrong people crowed about them," Mr. Thomas said, looking like an owl.

How long was he going to be here? "About three months," Mr. Thomas said. "It will be my last visit for some time. I will have had the universities and they will have had me."

The writer wasn't taking that statement seriously at all.

"Well," Mr. Thomas said, "*I* am."

Would he sum up?

"Poetry," Mr. Thomas summed up, avoiding what might have sounded theatrical, "poetry. I like to think of it as statements made on the way to the grave."

Without Apologies

MARTIN SHUTTLEWORTH

The first guests to arrive at Foyle's literary luncheon, held at the Dorchester in honour of Mr. Dylan Thomas last Tuesday week, kept their furs on and pointed one another out to their guests. So and so had brought along a young poet, somebody else a staff officer on N.A.T.O. ("I'm sure he would have been an A.D.C. to Curzon, my dear, if he'd been old enough,") and conversation was general.

"Such a relief to find you at St. Moritz for Christmas, of course the season is getting earlier, but you're just the sort of unpractical person to arrive ten years late when we have all gone to Kitzbühl."

"Personally I went to the Ritz. Rather full for Christmas. Empty on Boxing Day."

"Who's she?"

"Shipping, I believe, or maybe margarine."

"Don't be silly, Willy, margarine was nationalised a long time ago."

"I told Ulrich that we really had to come. He was buying up stock for a sale at his Nottingham branch this morning but I did say, my dear, that these affairs were of so much importance to young poets if people in our position went that we really ought to make an effort and here we are. What did you say his name was?"

"Thomas."

"Not Lottie's boy?"

"Then he really must be a poet; I do think that it is good of them."

And so to lunch when the remainder of the guests arrived in a rush at once. The lifeless pallor of the ballroom walls, a little bit lighter than sauterne, a little darker than chablis, robbed the fur coats of their sheen and rusted the blackest of dresses. We, at the round tables, identified the celebrities from our programme and turned

From *The New Statesman and Nation,* February 7, 1953, pp. 144–145.

away from our unknown neighbours to our private affairs until the toast-master's gavel recalled us to a proper sense of the occasion.

Then A. L. Rowse rose and, after he had told us that he was a Cornishman and that he was unaware of what "a mere don" might contribute to the afternoon's proceedings, settled down to a search for the points that he was about to make. Years ago he had heard in Copenhagen from a particularly intelligent Dane that it was unusual for a nation that was so practical as the English to be so poetic. He thought so too; in fact he was not sure which he admired most, the latest jet bombers, or Mr. Thomas's poetry, but, he repeated, he himself was a hundred per cent a Celt and that had a very important bearing upon the proceedings. He sometimes found his Celtic temperament a nuisance, it was true, but it did lead him on to his second point that French poetry was cerebral and English, at its best, intuitive. Sometimes English poets tried to be intellectual but most of them failed. Men with first-class intellects like himself knew that the reason was because most of them had third (or should he say second) rate minds. Thereupon he commended this man of genius who, as all Celts knew was Dullan, not Dylan, Thomas for, whatever he was, he was truly an intuitive man. . . .

The smoke thickened, the speech ceased and the voice of the much-professed Celt was stilled. There could not have been a better moment to flavour the quality of the poet himself. When, finally, his deep bass voice throbbed through the ballroom for a few seconds to utter his thanks all the choirs of Eisteddfod could not have been more moving.

"Oh, darling," said the woman at the next table when the chairs began to scrape, "I've got a fitting at three. I wonder if I'll have time to go to the library for a copy of that man's poems before Archie's party at six."

from *Dylan Thomas in America*

JOHN MALCOLM BRINNIN

JULY, 1951—JUNE, 1952*

"In Cardiff a few days ago I visited the National Museum where the long history of the land of Wales is told in fragments of stone, bronze, pottery and jewelry, in parchment and in pigment—where, by following the guidebook, one can witness from its primordial beginnings the legend of human enterprise on these shores until, descending the steps, point-blank, one faces into the busy daylight of circling cars and buses, and emerges half-blind into the present. The function of a museum is, of course, to preserve as many evidences of history as is possible in the most compact space, to embalm under glass those traces of time that connect us with preconscious existence. One's visit has much the quality of the reading of a scholarly, illustrated volume in which the text provides perspectives for the pictures. As I came away, I felt the museum had provided me with a metaphor I should like to apply to the subject of my talk, the poet Dylan Thomas of Laugharne, Carmarthenshire, and his reputation and influence in America.

"To qualify my metaphor before I go on with it, I must say that among the work of poets writing in English, that of Dylan Thomas is by all odds the least reminiscent of the still air of a museum. And yet I am aware of no other poet whose work carries with it that sense of having encompassed the stratifications of human history, of possessing the past as well as the present, of having sounded again echoes that make the early darkness alive. And it is just this recreation

* [The first quoted excerpt is a transcript of a broadcast made over the BBC in July, 1951. J.M.B.]

of the living past in the living present that distinguishes him as a poet, and which contributes largely to the wonder and astonishment with which American readers first encounter him.

"Although it is not always consciously felt, Americans, more than any other people on earth, have a basic need for assurances as to their identity. Our history is brief, and our national character, compounded of so many heterogeneous influences, still does not allow of definition. While we have created an American legend recognized by the rest of the world, we ourselves have little real association with it. Most Americans know in their hearts that the American dream is something in which they have but a small part. In spite of the success with which the American myth has been published at home as well as abroad, Americans long for that which other peoples take quite for granted—the simple signs of speech, of place, of character and tradition that might tell them who they are. As a Welshman rooted deeply in his people and his land, Dylan Thomas speaks to us from sources we have lost, and we are drawn by his native accents with nostalgia and the excitement of vicarious participation.

"Other poets may win our attention when they write as analysts or as philosophical victims of the modern world, and may objectify for us the unexpressed thoughts and emotions that move us, but Dylan Thomas touches us alive, not only to our common dilemma in a violent age, but to our common humanity which in his poems is not merely proffered for contemplation, but recreated. He has made of the history in his bones a speech that we come upon with instantaneous enlightenment, as if the barriers of geography and time had fallen away. We know him and respond to what he says because he speaks to us as an ancient who has somehow survived the impositions of time.

"I do not want to imply that Dylan Thomas is a primitive, or that he is so regarded. We know—even without the evidence turned up by our critics and students of literature—that his poetry is not only the work of a man immersed in his native history, but that it is the product of a sophisticated craftsman sharply aware of that literary tradition which his contribution both transforms and continues. We find in him not only the lyrical finesse and delicacy of the seventeenth century, but the vigor and breadth of Walt Whitman. For American readers, this combination is irresistible. We read Whitman when we are young, and he implants in us a lively vision of democracy that persists as part of our belief. But as we grow older, we find less and less satisfaction in his qualities as an artist, and finally tend to remember him as a prophet rather than as a poet. On the other hand, we find that our youthful acquaintance with Donne and Marvell and Herrick and Crashaw grows into a loving knowledge. While Whitman, the laureate of large ideals, lies forgotten on the shelf, we read these earlier poets with new pleasure and are perhaps puzzled by the change that has come over us. When we read Dylan Thomas, then, we feel again not only the breadth and grandeur that Whitman once evoked, but that finely-wrought music of the intellectual eye and ear which charms us back to the seventeenth-century lyricists. In short, I believe we find a combination of democratic expression and aristocratic artistry which satisfies a dual need which we may not have consciously recognized.

"Beyond Whitman, the other major affinity of Dylan Thomas in American literature would, I think, be Herman Melville; and I believe that the recent re-discovery and revaluation of Melville as an American artist has been based upon quite the same premises as our response to Dylan Thomas. I have not the time to deal with similarities between the two men, but it would appear obvious to me that once the notion had been set before them, few readers would be unaware of the whole range of ideas, images and historically-encrusted metaphors which Dylan Thomas shares with the creator of *Moby Dick.* The literary obsession of both men is the confirmation of a basic human identity transcending the mutations of history—and in pursuit of this, both have written with a consciousness of time not as a sequence of events harking backwards and downwards, but as though history itself were a landscape surrounding the houses in which they lived.

"A further aspect of Dylan Thomas's poetry that appeals to Americans is the exotic unfamiliarity of its imagery. This is perhaps a lesser source of appeal, but an important one. While we think, as a rule, of the exotic as something rarefied, and out of reach, and perhaps slightly bogus, the exotic in Dylan Thomas's poems is something that intrigues and charms us because we have every confidence that he is giving us a vision of the world he sees and knows, and that only by the accidents of time and place are we ourselves prevented from confirming the reality of his observations. It has been most revealing to me, for instance, to recognize in Wales something I had known previously only as part of a poem.

"The tangency of literary reality to observed reality is an unimportant consideration in the work of a poet since, after all, in the writing of every poem he is concerned with creating an artifact. But in spite of that critical understanding, we are always delighted when some slight contact with the scene of a poem or a story throws new light on what we felt we had completely known. For years, a particular image from one of Dylan Thomas's poems has always pleased me immensely —and that image is, 'The heron-priested shore.' To me it has always conjured up a druidical series of tall birds standing as if in performance of some ritual along a water's-edge. The picture I saw was large and quite pleasantly satisfying as a glimpse of far-away Wales, but since I had never actually seen a heron in its natural state, my experience of this image was, without my ever knowing it, quite vague and limited. But now that I have seen herons along the very shore where Thomas sees them, I am delighted to find that while my first impression had a literary validity, my new impression is based upon the observation that herons *do* stand in sacerdotal attitudes, as if they were perpetually extending benedictions, and that, when they are surrounded by kitty-wicks and oyster-catchers, they do recall priests crowded about by parishioners. One could find hundreds of such instances in which observed reality expanded the literary reality, or transformed it—so that the point I want to make of my own experience is the fact that while so much of Dylan Thomas's world is strange to the American reader, and shut away from observation, he has invested that world with such conviction and presented it so soundly that we accept his most exotic images with absolute confidence that they do not only grace the iconography of his poems but that they are generic to the landscape of his country. As he himself has written:

> Who in these labyrinths,
> This tidethread and the lane of scales,
> Twine in a moon-blown shell,
> Escapes to the flat cities' sails
> Furled on the fishes' house and hell,
> Nor falls to His green myths?
> Stretch the salt photographs,
> The landscape grief, love in His oils
> Mirror from man to whale
> That the green child see like a grail
> Through veil and fin and fire and coil
> Time on the canvas paths.

"In speaking of Dylan Thomas's influence on poetry written in America, I believe I can say that it has been profound, but that its real force is somewhat difficult to measure. He has been widely imitated, of course, but almost always with disastrous consequence—and I believe this is so because his methods, which offer many possibilities for approximation in texture and rhythm, simply cannot be seized upon and used to any worthy end. Rather, they must be earned in the same rigid process by which Thomas himself has achieved them—which is to say that his methods develop out of a way of discovering and interpreting areas of feeling in which rhythm and texture are determined by the quality of perception. American imitations, as a rule, have seemed synthetic and manufactured because they have been conceived out of a purely literary experience, whereas Thomas's own poems are conceived out of the living experience of a deeply known time and place.

"It is my own impression that Thomas's real influence is evident in what American poets do not do, or in what they have given up. Since his arrival on the literary scene there has been a great decrease in didacticism in American poetry, a newly recovered awareness of the plasticity of the English language, and, most important, a new realization that the individual psyche can be creatively plumbed. He has shown us that exploration of the inner world of the individual need not result in the pale and rarefied poetry we used to label as 'ivory tower,' but that the universal lies deep within the individual and invites his resourcefulness.

"Since all American readers of poetry know Thomas, contemporary standards of judgment have of course been affected by his career. Our best American poets are quite unlike him, but none of them writes without having first taken into account his innovations or without studying the masterful way in which he has himself assimilated strong literary influences.

"It will be years before the breadth of his impact on American poetry can be adequately measured, but there is no question of the tremendous response he evokes from American readers. When he came to the States last year, his progress across the continent was marked by the kind of reception which, in the nineteenth century, would have been described as 'a triumphal tour.' He traveled for three months, reading his poems in colleges and universities and literary societies from Florida to Vancouver and from Los Angeles to Boston, and I do believe that, had he the endurance, he could very well be traveling in America still. As one American poet expressed it, his presence was 'a Dionysian experience for the academies.' In a time when nearly all our poets are tamed by scholarship and professional respectibility as teachers or editors or librarians, when our representative poetry is careful, learned, but quite immovably anchored to acceptable forms and intellectual clichés, his readings and his personality struck us with delight and surprise. We had, for lack of evidence, almost forgotten that even in our day, poetry and the poet could be possessed of the demonic character which so disturbed Plato, but which has nonetheless survived as one of the happier legends of Western culture. With Dylan Thomas we have recovered much that we had believed lost, and I know that many Americans share with me the wonder that proceeds from the fact that in our time the voice that speaks to us most clearly comes—not from among skyscrapers or from the great plains or from the wide new cities of the West—but from a little village quite settled in its silence on the far shores of Wales."

When I had finished reading, Dylan said, as if he were quoting a newspaper headline: "Randy-dandy Curly-girly Poet Leaps into Sea from Overdose of Praise," and made as if to throw himself over the sea wall. "All there is for me to do now is disappear," he said. "I didn't know you thought I was *that* good." When Caitlin said she liked the piece, lunch ended in the first general good feeling since the beginning of our visit.

As Bill took his camera and was about to set off on a tour of the village, Dylan asked me if I would mind coming to the studio to hear some of his new poems. Taking two bottles of ale with us, we climbed through the brambled garden, walked along the upper wall from which we could see the great esses the tide left in the estuary, the "scummed, starfish sands/With their fishwife cross/Gulls, pipers, cockles, and sails," and went into the studio. He first read "In the White Giant's Thigh," then, "Poem for His Birthday." His reading in private, while naturally less loud, was fully as rich and dramatic as in public. His professional attitude toward each poem as a text to be communicated dissolved any feeling of embarrassment that might have touched so intimate a performance. Then he scrawled the inscription "To dear John from cheap Dylan, with love" across the bottom of a typewritten copy of a poem he was going to use as a prologue to the new English and American editions of his *Collected Poems,* and asked me to read it. But, first, he would have to point out the rhyme scheme, which he did not think anyone would notice without careful study. The first line of the first section rhymed with the last line of the second section—with one hundred other lines between; the second line of the first section with the second from the last line of the second section, and so on until lines fifty-one and fifty-two formed the only rhymed couplet in the poem. When I expressed amazement at the intricacy of this scheme, Dylan said, "As a matter of fact, the poem began as a letter to you." "What happened to the letter?" I asked. "I just kept the idea and some of the images and went on with the poem instead." I told him I was pleased, naturally, that the letter had proved such an inspiration, and suggested, a little caustically, that he write more often, if only as a means of finding his way into new poems.

He had finished another poem, still untitled, which he had written for his father who, he felt, had but little time to live. It began, "Do not go gentle into that good night." I asked him if he had shown the poem to his father. He had not, he said, but hoped he would have the courage to read it to him very soon. What he most wanted me to hear were fragments of a "kind of play for voices" he was thinking about. This would be called "Llareggub Hill" (the first word can be read backwards) and was to be a dramatic poem on the life of a Welsh village very much like Laugharne. It would have no conventional dramatic continuity, but would consist of an interweaving of many voices, with the strong central voice of a narrator to supply the unities of time, place and situation. He then read me the section that revealed Captain Cat speaking the dreams that take him back to a life at sea. This was one of the fragments that was to be expanded into his last work, "Under Milk Wood."

We began to speak of working methods. I had noticed that on many of his manuscripts Dylan would add a single word or a phrase, or a new punctuation, then recopy the whole poem in longhand. When another addition or revision was made, no matter how minor or major, he would then copy the whole poem again. When I asked him about this laborious repetition, he showed me his drafts of "Fern Hill." There were more than two hundred separate and distinct versions of the poem. It was, he explained, his way of "keeping the poem together," so that its process of growth was like that of an organism. He began almost every poem merely with some phrase he had carried about in his head. If this phrase was right, which is to say, if it were resonant or pregnant, it would suggest another phrase. In this way a poem would "accumulate." Once "given" a word (sometimes the prime movers of poems were the words of other poems or mere words of the dictionary that called out to be "set") or a phrase or a line (or whatever it is that is "given" when there is yet a poem to "prove") he could often envision it or "locate" it within a pattern of other words or phrases or lines that, not given, had yet to be discovered: so that sometimes it would be possible to surmise accurately that the "given" unit would occur near the end of the poem or near the beginning or near the middle or somewhere between.

He had picked up somewhere a notion that he liked: poems are hypothetical and theorematic. In this view the hypothesis of a poem would be the emotional experience, the instant of vision or insight, the source of radiance, the minute focal point of impulse and impression. While these make up what is commonly called inspiration, poetic logic should prove the validity of the ephemeral moments they describe. To look at a new poem, then, is to ask: How successfully does it demonstrate its hypothesis?

About the reading of poetry, he felt that only perusal of the printed page—or perhaps the interior or critical monologue, or private discussion—could give to each poem the full concentrated time that any poem is justified in asking for the assessment of its success or failure to demonstrate its own hypothesis. In public, only the poem itself can be presented, and there its effect depends upon the immediacy with which the hypothesis, the moment and motive of inspiration, can affect the reader through his ear. In other words, and as he was later fond of saying, the printed page is the place in which to examine the works of a poem, the platform the place in which to give the poem the works.

There was one line in "Fern Hill," he said, that embarrassed him. He felt he should not have allowed the poem to be published until the line had been excised in favor of a better one. But months of thinking how to change it had led nowhere. When I asked him what the offending line was, he gave me a copy of the poem and asked me to pick it out. I could not. Then he pointed to the passage,

> And honoured among foxes and pheasants by the gay house
> Under the new made clouds and happy as the heart was long,
> In the sun born over and over,
>   I ran my heedless ways, . . .

and said with a sneer, "'*ran* my *heed*less ways!'—that's bloody bad."

Our talk rambled, then, but I remember clearly Dylan's saying that now, finally, he was determined to write only "happy poems." But that was a great trouble—it was so very much more difficult to write a poem happy in sentiment rather than tragic and still manage to have it come out believable and good. He was absorbed in this notion, I could see, but also troubled. Implicitly, he was saying what many of his poems had already said: that his wisdom was the perception of joy—an insight so comprehensive and instantaneous that the meaning of joy is defined not as a relative state of human emotion but as another name for life itself. Yet there was little joy in his face as he thumbed hesitantly through a clutter of unfinished manuscripts, and little conviction in his voice as he spoke of his writing plans. At last, as if to conclude our visit, he said that his aim now was to produce "poems in praise of God's world by a man who doesn't believe in God."

. . . . .

1953: SEPTEMBER—NOVEMBER

When I sailed for home that night my thoughts were ambivalent: if I was sorry that Dylan had not heeded my judgment, I was pleased he had sought my encouragement, especially as it seemed that the decisions he had arrived at were likely to lead to a sweeping change in his financial circumstances; yet his irascible temper and the mental turbulence of which it was a sign, left me doubtful and uneasy because I knew that its underlying stresses would be removed neither by money, mobility, nor public acclaim, and certainly not by the scattering of his talent into purchasable fragments. Nevertheless we had made our commitments. As soon as I was home in Cambridge, I went to a travel agent to arrange passage for Dylan and Caitlin. From him, I learned that it would be impossible to obtain berths in tourist class accommodations for mid-October—still the "high" season for westward crossings—without delay and uncertainty. Since the first performance of *Under Milk Wood* was now scheduled to be the opening event of the Poetry Center season on October 24th, I had to make a quick decision. I cabled Dylan, asking if he would consider flying over alone, with Caitlin following by the first ship on which I might be able to book passage. He cabled back that he was coming alone. From the meager phrasing of this answer I could not tell whether Caitlin had altogether given up her intention of coming, or whether Dylan had simply recognized the expedience of his coming by air in order to meet his first engagement.

A plane ticket was forwarded to him by the travel agency; he was due to arrive in New York on the morning of October 14th. Liz was planning to meet him at Idlewild, but when she checked with the airline, Dylan's name was not on the passenger list. Three days went by without news of him. As we later learned, he was already in London and ready to depart when his ticket was just being delivered in Laugharne. On October 17th I received a cable:

PICKETT [SIC] ARRIVED COUPLE DAYS TOO LATE NOW CATCHING PLANE 7:30 MONDAY 19TH DESPERATELY SORRY DYLAN.

When he finally arrived, complaining of the heat yet wearing a prickly camel's-hair scarf and a rug-heavy suit, Liz was there to greet him. He wanted a drink "right off," but as they approached the airport bar they found it was being picketed for alleged nonunion practices. Dylan's thirst was so great that he was willing to put aside compunctions he would normally have considered binding. But if he was ready to cross the picket line, Liz was not. When he could see that she was adamant, he gave up. "All right," he said, "but only for you and the Rights of Man." As they got into the taxi for Manhattan, Dylan sank back with a tremendous sigh. His visit in London, he said, "was the worst week of my entire life." Caitlin had been with him, and now that his American trip had led to just the makeshift situation she had most wanted to avoid, mutual unhappiness and guilt had caused continual dissension. But he was curiously preoccupied by something that had happened on the flight: an Irish priest from New York, returning from a visit to his homeland, had boarded the plane roaring drunk at Shannon. When he continued to drink, and to the distress of other passengers, became garrulous and increasingly obstreperous, the stewardess had declared the bar closed to his orders. Without liquor, he soon had an attack of delirium tremens, and had finally to be bound and shut in the men's room. He was kept prisoner there until, at Gander, he was taken off the plane in the care of a physician. While Dylan made some grim comedy of his report of the incident, he was perhaps as shaken by it as he was amused.

At the Chelsea, he discovered that the reservations I had made for him had been canceled because of his three-day tardiness, and that, for several days at least, none of the large, bright rooms facing onto Twenty-third Street would be available. He was given a small room in the rear of the hotel. While he seldom seemed to pay the slightest attention to his living quarters anywhere, being put into a small dark room when he had become used to the best in the house upset him inordinately and made him sullen. But a drink with Liz at the Silver Rail on Seventh Avenue soon pulled him out of his sudden depression. After they had had a quiet dinner at a Spanish restaurant in the Village, he was in a sober and serious mood for a rehearsal of the newly revised and now fairly complete play-script. To the actors, who not only held him in warm affection as a person but who showed an almost awed respect for his ingenuity as a man of the theatre, his presence was magic. Under his direction, the new version of *Under Milk Wood* fairly leaped into shape. After the rehearsal, which had put him into the mellowest of humors, Dylan wanted to visit the White Horse; with Liz and a young poet friend of his he stayed there in quiet conversation until two.

On the next morning, as he and Liz were walking toward the Village from Twenty-third Street, he spotted a billboard poster advertising a new movie, *Houdini*. Dylan called Liz's attention to the sign, remarking that the great magician had always fascinated him, particularly for his fabulous escapes from the many ingenious traps that he had allowed to be devised for him. The worst horror in life, said Dylan, the horror beyond horrors, was the sense of being hopelessly trapped. It was a subject he was going to write about—in fact, he said, he was already well along into a prose-piece about an "escape artist." "Autobiographical?" asked Liz, and Dylan smiled and said, "You know me too well."

In the middle of the afternoon, after he had gone to have a few drinks by himself in Julius's, Liz rejoined him. But he said he was feeling unwell, that perhaps he had better return to the hotel to rest. Liz accompanied him, sat with him through the remainder of the afternoon, and later went out to a nearby delicatessen to get him a light supper. After he had eaten, he said he felt he could sleep, and she left him in the early evening. Before he closed his eyes, he turned to her and said with a weak smile: "It looks as though I'm putting you on as nurse awfully quickly . . . but no," his expression became thoughtfully sober and his voice remote, as if he were addressing only himself, "no, not my nurse, not my secretary—my friend, my *real* friend."

He slept late the next morning and was sober and professionally concentrated when the next rehearsal of *Under Milk Wood* took place in the afternoon. Later in the day, he went to a Yorkville bar with Liz and a British photographer, drank moderately, and shortly announced that he wanted to have a good meal. They taxied downtown to Herdt's, on Sixth Avenue near Fourteenth Street. There he ate an enormous dinner—a dinner which, in the course of events, was to be his last full meal. Continuing in the ingratiating sobriety he had shown through the day, he mentioned repeatedly, yet without explanation, his immense relief in having "escaped" from London.

Liz met him for lunch the next day at a sea-food restaurant near the Chelsea. But the food so displeased him that he went into a rage —a most unusual thing for him to do under any circumstances—and would not eat a bite. While he sulked and fumed after his outburst, it became obvious to Liz that Dylan was in an acute state of nervous agitation; she walked back with him to the hotel where, ostensibly, he was going to settle down to work further on his script.

Two or three hours later, she phoned him from her office. Dylan answered in a voice barely audible; apparently he had become stupefied with drink. Alarmed, Liz hurried to the hotel. There she found him with a group of people from Cinema 16 who had come to arrange for his appearance on a symposium they were sponsoring. Also in the room was an eminent literary critic whose work Dylan much admired, and who had simply dropped by to talk with him. But when Liz could see that the critic's visit had only led to heavier drinking, that Dylan was now completely intoxicated and quite out of connection with his company, she asked all of the visitors to leave. She persuaded Dylan to rest, then, and, within a few hours, he had returned to comparative sobriety, and was able to work on new scenes of the play. He dictated to Liz new passages which, in spite of his shaky condition, were composed on the instant. All of these remained as part of the finished work.

Early in the evening they went together to rehearsal, but by the time they had reached the auditorium, Dylan said he felt too ill to participate. Herb Hannum, an architect whose acquaintance Dylan had made more than a year before, and for whom he had since developed a deep affection, had come to the Poetry Center to go out with them afterwards. While Dylan remained in Herb's care, Liz went on stage to read his lines while he attempted to rest on a couch in the Green Room. When he had first walked into the auditorium that evening, Dylan had said that he found the place stifling hot; but within a few minutes he said that he was freezing, that he couldn't get warm enough. Herb covered him with overcoats borrowed from the dressing room, but Dylan said he was still shivering cold. When he dozed off for perhaps fifteen minutes, Herb went out to bring him food—clam chowder and crackers and coffee and, in the hope of making him warm, brandy and hot water-bottles. Dylan accepted these ministrations "like a baby," according to Herb, but could not fall asleep or be rid of his spasmodic restlessness. Sitting upright every few minutes, he would say, "What's going on? What part are they reading now?"

At a rehearsal-break, Liz came back to type up new sections of the script. Dylan told her that he would join the actors, to read "the new stuff," when the rehearsal was called. Doubtful, she asked him if he really felt capable of reading. Dylan answered yes, firmly, and went on stage to read with his company through the final twenty minutes of the play. When he returned to the Green Room he became nauseated and had to vomit, retching so violently that he lost his balance and fell to the floor. When Herb had helped him back onto his feet, Dylan, gasping, leaned against the wall. "I can't do anything any more," he said. "I'm too tired to do anything. I can't——, I can't eat, I can't drink—I'm even too tired to sleep." He lay down on the couch. "I have seen the gates of hell tonight," he said. "Oh, but I do want to go on—for another ten years anyway. But not as a bloody invalid—not as a bloody invalid." He groaned and turned his face to the wall. "I'm too sick too much of the time." After a few minutes of sleep, he opened his eyes and, calmly, sadly, said: "Tonight in my home the men have their arms around one another, and they are singing."

When Liz and Herb went back to the hotel with him he seemed exhausted, overwhelmed by miseries that had led him beyond despair into fear. Unwilling to leave him alone, they saw him to sleep and Liz stayed with him through the night. Dylan was sleeping soundly when, next morning, she left the Chelsea to go to her apartment.

Herb came to see Dylan later in the morning and they went out to breakfast at the Chelsea Chop House. Shaken by what he had experienced with Dylan the night before, Herb asked: "Dylan, how long have you been this way?" "Never this sick," said Dylan, "never this much before. After last night and now this morning, I've come to the melancholy conclusion that my health is totally gone. I can't drink at all. I always could, before . . . but now most of the time I can't even swallow beer without being sick. I tell myself that if I'd only lay off whisky and stick to beer I'd be all right . . . but I never do. I guess I just forgot to sleep and eat for too long. I'll have to give up something." "What do you mean, Dylan," asked Herb, "do you mean life?" "No," Dylan said soberly, "I don't know . . . I want to go on . . . but I don't know if I can. I don't feel able any more. Without my health I'm frightened. I can't explain it. It's something I don't know about. I never felt this way before and it scares me. When I was waiting for the plane this time in London, I found I was drinking in a mad hurry . . . like a fool, good God, one after another whisky and there was no hurry at all . . . I had all the time in the world to wait, but I was drinking as though there wasn't much time left for me . . . to drink or wait. I was shocked . . . I felt as though something in me wanted to explode, it was just as though I were going to burst. I got on the plane and watched my watch, got drunk and stayed frightened all the way here . . . really only a little booze on the plane but mostly frightened and sick with the thought of death. I felt as sick as death all the way over. I know I've had a lot of things wrong with my body lately, especially the past year or so. Since I was thirty-five I've felt myself getting harder to heal. I've been warned by doctors about me, but I could never really believe them . . . that I was ever sick seriously or in any real danger. I didn't know how to believe it . . . or maybe I did believe it, but couldn't accept it. I think I just felt that I might be getting older faster than I expected to, older than I should be at my age. But now I don't know. Maybe I've always been frightened but didn't know it until I couldn't drink when I wanted to."

When Herb suggested that it would be wise for him to see a doctor, a psychotherapist, Dylan seemed surprised. "Do you really think that could help me now?" he asked. "Certainly," said Herb. "But I don't know how to help myself any more," said Dylan; "how can anybody help someone who can't do that? I've always wanted to be my own psychiatrist, just as I've always wanted everybody to be their own doctor and father."

Liz, meanwhile, returning to the Chelsea, found a note from Dylan asking her to join him and Herb. When she did, Herb asked her help in persuading Dylan to see a doctor—not a psychotherapist, but a physician who might tender Dylan the immediate attention he needed. While Dylan at first resisted this idea—not vehemently, but with the routine antipathy he showed toward all efforts designed to convince him that he needed help—he was quite easily prevailed upon. Liz made a phone call that resulted in an appointment almost at once.

When they went for a consultation with Dr. Milton Feltenstein, Dylan was given an injection of ACTH (cortisone). The doctor, for whom Dylan felt a warm personal as well as professional regard, had months before warned him that only a rigorous and unbroken regimen would begin to relieve him of his physical torments. On this new occasion, he made clear to Dylan that the injection was but a temporary boost—a prop that would help him get through the next few days—and emphasized again the necessity of his agreeing to a long-range program of medical care.

As Liz and Dylan strolled up Third Avenue after their visit to the doctor, she asked him if he would tell her more of the nature of his illness. "I have such a feeling of dread," he told her, "a terrible pressure—as if there were an iron band around my skull." But even as he spoke, the injection of ACTH was taking positive effect. Dylan soon remarked that he was beginning to feel much better and, more physically alert than he had felt for days, seemed comparatively outgoing and relieved of self-concern. As they were passing an Army & Navy store, he said that he needed some handkerchiefs. They went in, and Dylan bought six big plain white ones, then wandered about the shop. He especially liked American working-men's clothes, he said—he had taken a number of shirts back to Wales in the previous spring, and wanted to take more of them this time—blue ones. Leaving the store, they took a taxi uptown for the final rehearsal of *Under Milk Wood,* which was to be publicly performed that evening.

My only personal contact with Dylan since he had come to New York was a welcoming call I had made from Cambridge on the day he arrived. Having heard nothing of the events of the past five days, I came to the Poetry Center that afternoon to find rehearsal going on in the darkened auditorium. When I discerned Dylan sitting in a front row from which he was supervising action on the stage, I took a seat directly beside him. When he recognized me, we exchanged a whispered greeting so as not to disturb the actors, then sat in silence for another ten minutes. When the house lights went up and I could see him, I was so shocked by his appearance I could barely stop myself from gasping aloud. His face was lime-white, his lips loose and twisted, his eyes dulled, gelid, and sunk in his head. He showed the countenance of a man who has been appalled by something beyond comprehension. Since there was still another scene to be run through on the stage, I left him, promising to join him and Liz at the nearby Irish bar within the hour. Backstage I sought out Liz. "What's the matter with Dylan, he looks terrible." She closed her eyes and slowly turned her head from side to side. "It's something very strange, John," she said, "something new and dreadful. I don't know what it means, I don't think Dylan does. . . ." And briefly she told me of Dylan's agonized talk the night before.

After an hour of desk chores in the Poetry Center office, I went to our Irish bar rendezvous, only to wait in vain for the appearance of Dylan and Liz. When I sought them in other likely places nearby and still could not locate them, I phoned the Chelsea. There was no response from Dylan's room. Puzzled, and downcast by this defection, I went back to my hotel.

With its original cast, and with final additions incorporated into the script, *Under Milk Wood* was given a third reading before a large audience that evening. While it was a good one, I felt it did not quite succeed in striking the fire of those performances I had seen in May. Conscious of the whiteness of Dylan's sick face as it showed through all the lights focused upon it, I could hear, above the music of his voice, "I have seen the gates of hell."

Rollie gave a party for the actors and their friends at her apartment after the performance. Most of the time, Dylan seemed rather muted in his talk and behavior. One of the guests later told me that during a conversation she had noticed that he refused the drinks offered him. When she had asked him why he was not drinking, he had answered casually, almost brightly, "It's just that I've seen the gates of hell, that's all." The words had already become something to say at a party. As a small group of us lingered on into the morning hours, Dylan grew expansive, talkative, laughed boisterously, much like his normal self, and my concern was for the moment alleviated—at least my alarm over the illness that could be read in his face. Still troubled by the feeling that I had been carelessly neglected by Dylan that afternoon, I had no way of knowing that his lapse of consideration was not, as I felt then, a failure of trust, but, as I soon learned, merely a confusion on both our parts of times and places.

He and Liz came next morning to see me at my hotel. There we had a strangely remote and disturbing talk about finances and the necessity of Dylan's having more money immediately. We spoke like strangers. The affectionate intimacy of our long discussions in Wales had entirely disappeared. The tone of our interview struck me as being like that of a business conference between someone who wanted money and someone who supposedly could be made to supply it if sufficient pressure were brought to bear. With a new shock of disillusion, I felt as though I had been used to good advantage over a long period, but that now my term of usefulness was over except perhaps in my ability to rake up immediate cash. Overwhelmed by this impasse in which disappointment and anger were equally at work, I was barely able to speak. If I had known then that Liz had also found affectionate communication with Dylan abruptly broken off, and that she too was bewildered by this development, I could have viewed the incident objectively. Ignorant of everything but what I had witnessed, I could only retreat.

We taxied to the Poetry Center auditorium, Liz and I silent for reasons of our own, Dylan suddenly chipper and as full of song as a lark. The matinee of *Under Milk Wood,* on Sunday, October 25th, the last in which Dylan was to participate, was by every report its greatest performance. A thousand people were left hushed by its lyrical harmonies and its grandeur, among them Robert Shaw, the eminent choral director, who came backstage and, moved to tears, expressed his admiration. Dylan himself said he had at last heard the performance he wanted to hear.

Unable to explain to myself the curious change in Dylan or to come upon any means of re-establishing a happier sense of ourselves, I spent the afternoon in withering depression. Meanwhile, suffering her own dilemma, Liz nevertheless accompanied him to a party on Sutton Place—a party which, we later learned from Dylan himself, had been "set up" by the particular friend whose claim for Dylan's attention was now largely his zeal as a procurer. While some of his recent offerings had been refused, he had on this occasion come up with a prize—a handsome refugee countess whose "sense of comic despair," according to Dylan, was the most attractive thing about her. She was hostess to the party, which had hardly gone on for an hour when Dylan broke his abstinence of days by gulping down one tumbler of Irish whisky after another; he then became boisterous and brawling, and shortly disappeared for hours with her into the upper regions of her large town house.

My own gloomy afternoon, spent with Rollie in her apartment, had made me so lugubrious a companion that she finally drew me out to tell her what was on my mind. When I did, she told me what I had not known—that on the previous afternoon, just when I had been searching for Dylan and Liz, they had been searching for me. When they had phoned Rollie in an attempt to locate me, she had learned that both Dylan and Liz felt I had been neglecting them, that my apparent lack of concern for Dylan had troubled him deeply, and that they were puzzled as to what to make of my behavior. When even this knowledge could not overcome my sense of disillusion to the point where I could act, Rollie firmly insisted that I not leave the city, as I was about to do, before seeking them out. Under her prodding, I came to realize that I could do nothing but find Dylan in order to confirm or be rid of the burdens of our inscrutable predicament.

When I got to the Sutton Place address, only nine or ten people were left, most of them seated on the floor having a lounging sort of supper around a low circular table. I spoke with Liz and greeted Dylan with a feint at cheerfulness. A few tense minutes later, I asked Liz if she and Dylan would join me where we might talk apart from the company. We went up a flight of stairs into a drawing room and sat down, Liz and Dylan on a couch, I on a chair facing them. The room was semidark, lighted only from the hallway and by checkered reflections of lights on the river.

Sick at heart, I began to say words I had rehearsed in the taxi ride down, only to find that, as I quickly came to tears, I need say nothing. Dylan began to weep, and Liz wept. Speaking half-articulate phrases, we learned that each of us had felt shut off, that each had sensed disillusion with the other, and that the clumsy silence into which we had retreated was the consequence of a sensitivity so acute and of a misunderstanding so vast that only now could we begin to comprehend it. Suddenly all the tensions surrounding the last two days seemed to be dissolving into thin air. Holding my face in my hands as I attempted to regain composure, I felt strong arms about me. Standing behind me as he held me very firmly, Dylan spoke the last words I was ever to hear him say directly to me: "John, you know, don't you? —this is forever."

Moments later, feeling absurd and foolishly dramatic as we wiped our tears and blew our noses in the semidark elegance of our surroundings, we knew that our paralyzing impasse had been broken, and that we had awakened into a new sense of one another as if from a dream in which we moved about like tight-lipped strangers. Free at a stroke from the tensions we had so silently brought upstairs, we went downstairs and joined the party. Liz and I sat on a couch, water-lights and the dim shrieks of tugboats moving on the river behind us. Dylan, having just been served a fresh tumbler of whisky, joined a group gathered around the mantelpiece across the room.

We spoke only of Dylan; not until days later did it occur to me that this was the only time she and I had conversed in intimate confidence about him. Now that the emotional pressures of the day had been lifted, and their causes dispersed, we felt bound by an understanding perhaps possible only to those to whom Dylan had been both a living delight and a living torment. He was, Liz said, without any question, the most lovable human being she had ever known. While she adored him, she knew also that he was a destroyer—that he had an instinct for drawing to him those most capable of being annihilated by him. In the short time in which she had known Dylan, the attentions he demanded, whether these were conscious or unconscious, had caused her to lose all sense of her own existence, and to be attuned only to his. Now, she felt she was at a breaking point. Tonight she was going to let him know that she could no longer be with him, and that she could no longer take care of him.

This first discussion of the consequences of our having known Dylan was a mutual revelation—our feelings were identical, and the bewilderment we shared was of the same nature and sprang from much the same experience. We both took his poetic genius for granted; and while we could accept—though not wholly comprehend—his genius as a human being, we could not avoid seeing ourselves in some ways as circumstantial victims of an enchantment Dylan inevitably put upon any one who came close to him. He knew by instinct who was, and who was not, susceptible to this enchantment. More than once, recognizing his power to exert it, and then to betray those who were subject to it, he had said to Liz that he felt "like a murderer." While he persisted in it, his Machiavellian role brought him neither pleasure nor security, but only further self-distrust and a deeper sense of self-degradation. The briefest review of Dylan's emotional life would suggest that no man was ever more adept in killing what he loved, or suffered more in the consequence. While this was an agonizing recognition to make, in meeting upon it, we had found a new bond of strength which, all too soon, would be all that we might trust in.

As the evening wore on, Dylan returned to unbashed dalliance with his hostess while, sprawling on the floor, he spilled liquor and ashes over himself, and seemed to have retreated into that state of loud drunkenness in which babyish self-indulgence overtook all of his lovable qualities and left him a figure of ridicule to strangers and a figure of despair to friends. Resigned to this development, and again almost as unhappy as we had been hours earlier, Liz and I decided to leave the party together. We were putting on our coats in the entrance hall when, like a child who fears he has been deserted, his eyes wide and rueful, his little briefcase clutched in his hand, behind us came Dylan. "Here I am," he said, and quickly put on his coat and came along with us.

Several others from the party got into our taxi, and I was dropped off at Grand Central where I was to catch a train for Boston. As the taxi proceeded downtown, Dylan asked Liz to come with him to the White Horse; she said no—she wanted now only to go home. When the taxi drew into her neighborhood, Dylan said, "I *used* to have a friend who lived near here." "You still do," said Liz, and left him. Dylan went on to the White Horse, stayed out most of the night, and returned to his hotel with a girl "loaned" to him by one of his drinking companions.

On the next morning, October 26th, Liz phoned him on matters related to the production of his play, then went to her office. Still determined to leave him, in personal torment from the circumstances into which she and Dylan had come, she was nevertheless fearful that, heedless of his doctor's advice, he would continue to go without food and to abuse himself with drink. In the middle of the afternoon she had a phone call from Dylan; he wanted to see her "terribly," he said, and begged her to meet him. When she went to join him at the Algonquin, she found him in conversation with a Dutch businessman whose acquaintance he had made just a few minutes before. Dylan, already drunk, ordered one whisky after another. When the conversation turned toward politics and war, without warning, he suddenly went into a raving fantasy. His talk, implying that he had been in actual wartime combat, that he had witnessed horrors involving his family, became disconnected, violent, maudlin and obscene. A waiter came to the table to quiet him, but Dylan, helplessly gripped by his fantasy, ranted on about blood and mutilation and burning and death. In an attempt to calm him, Liz held his hand; he broke into tears and began to sob. The Dutchman, more sympathetic than alarmed, indicated that he understood the irrational nature of Dylan's lapse, and left him in Liz's hands, saying, "He is a good man, take care of him."

When they left the Algonquin a few minutes later, Dylan continued in drunken behavior that seemed to be touched frighteningly with a streak of insanity. He made gargoyle faces at people passing by in the street, walked in a tottering and lunging parody of drunkenness, spoke four-letter words loudly with complete disregard for who might hear them. As they stopped for a traffic light, Dylan turned to her. "You really hate me, don't you?" he said. "No," said Liz, "but it's not for your lack of trying." He became less erratic then, and wanted to go to a movie. In one of the crowded Forty-second Street houses, they sat through a double feature, Dylan apparently recovered sufficiently not only to give attention to a Mickey Spillane thriller and to a western but to indicate that he was absorbed and delighted by both of them. When the movies were over, he was sober and wanted to go to Goody's, one of the bars of the Village where he and Liz had often spent quiet evenings together. Now they would go there, he said, in a spirit of "reunion." As they sat at the bar, Dylan, apparently overtaken by a new pang of anguish, began to speak of himself. "I'm really afraid I'm going mad," he said, "there's something terribly wrong with my mind. Perhaps it's sex, perhaps I'm not normal—perhaps the analysts could find it out." A while later, returning from the cigarette machine, he noticed a young couple in a booth, their heads amorously together. "How filthy!" he said to Liz. Amazed at such an unexpected remark, Liz told him that he spoke like a Puritan. "Yes," he said, as if for the first time he had understood something about himself, "I *am* a Puritan!" As he talked further of his mental confusion, Liz said quietly that he would have to find the answers, that if he were going to avoid despair he would have to find professional help. Dylan agreed, then abruptly ended the session at Goody's by saying that they must leave at once, that he could not stay there a minute longer. As they were stepping into a taxi, a young man approached. "Are you Dylan Thomas?" Dylan nodded, whereupon the young man launched into an explosive paean of hero-worship, and asked for an autograph. On a small piece of paper, leaning out of the taxi window, Dylan wrote (it was now after midnight) "Dylan Thomas, October 27. Birthday," and gave it to the boy saying that he was really only posing as Dylan Thomas. Liz accompanied him to the Horse, but Dylan was too distressed and ill to stay for more than a few minutes. When they returned to the hotel, she said good night to him with a promise to phone early in the morning.

His birthday began quietly enough, Liz returning to have breakfast with him before going to her office. When she went to meet him at the Horse at six in the evening, she found Howard Moss, who had come to buy Dylan a birthday drink. After toasts to the event, Howard left, and Liz, with Dylan and a group who had joined them, went on to the apartment of his friends, Rose and Dave Slivka, who had prepared a celebration in his honor. In a crowd of invited guests, Dylan was wretched and nervous, unable, after the first half-hour, to join conversation or to partake of the elaborate dinner that had been prepared. When he announced that he was sick and would have to return to the hotel immediately, his host drove him and Liz to the Chelsea.

Back in his room he fell upon the bed, saying, "What a filthy, undignified creature I am," and remarking upon the "awful" occasion of his "wretched age." Unwilling to let him sink any further into despair, Liz spoke to him firmly, begging him to do something to save himself, to fight against the terrors that were slowly overwhelming him. As she spoke—not gently this time, but out of the grief and impatience to which his alternating gestures of self-destruction and appeals for loving attention had brought her—he shouted for her to stop. Sharply hurt by his response, Liz rose and was about to leave the room when Dylan said, "That won't help my agony." He wept then, and as Liz tried to comfort him he spoke of Caitlin. "I know she's crying, too," he said.

In the late evening, I phoned from Cambridge to wish Dylan well on his birthday. From his mere whispers of response I sensed that he was either ill or had had too much to drink. I tried, ineffectively in the circumstance, to convey an affectionate greeting, but he seemed so far away and out of connection that I doubted he knew who was calling.

He read his poems at the City College of New York on the following day and spent hours drinking with new acquaintances he made there. When Liz went to see him at the hotel in the early evening, he was about to leave for the symposium on film art arranged by Cinema 16 with a delegation of people who had called for him. In his vague greeting to Liz, she had a disturbing feeling that he did not remember that they had agreed to meet. She went with him to the program, the panel of which was made up of Arthur Miller, Parker Tyler, Maya Deren, with Willard Maas as moderator. Dylan, apparently in fine fettle, was a frequent and serious participant in the discussion, expressing incomprehension and then alarm at some of the sophisticated notions proffered by Mr. Maas and Miss Deren, particularly when they spoke of "levels, conscious and unconscious," and offering his own simple feelings with the remark that, as far as he was concerned, he "just liked stories." The most "poetic" of films, he felt, were those of Charles Chaplin and the Marx Brothers. When, late in the discussion, Willard Maas remarked that no one had yet introduced a consideration of "love" as a factor in the art of the cinema, Dylan coyly turned to him. "O, *Willard,*" he said, "I didn't know you *cared.*" A group accompanied him and Liz to the White Horse afterwards, where Dylan, delighted by a series of caricatures Liz had made during the course of the evening, passed them about for everyone to see.

Swearing to Liz, and perhaps to himself, that he would drink nothing now but beer, Dylan headed into another busy day. He met his Sutton Place inamorata for lunch and, while he had intended to work on the cutting of *Under Milk Wood* for publication in *Mademoiselle,* dallied through most of the afternoon with her in her town house. In the evening, he and Liz went to dinner with Cyrilly Abels and her husband, Jerome Weinstein, whose other guests were the Indian writer, Santha Rama Rau and her husband. Happy in this company, Dylan participated warmly in a lengthy political discussion, and, later, told ghost stories in the narration of which he and Miss Rama Rau were chillingly proficient. For the hundredth time, Liz was struck by his ability to be easy and gracious in all the ways that the misery in his face belied.

On the next evening, when she met him at six o'clock to attend a dinner party at the home of Ruthven Todd, she found him with Herb

Hannum and his refugee countess, who, she had already learned from Dylan, had asked him to marry her. It was a difficult session for everyone. When she asked them all to come to dinner on Sutton Place, Dylan told her of their previous engagement and indicated that it was time now for them to go. He had, as it turned out, resolved that very day to see no more of her. Rebuffed, his lady suitor left and they went on to Ruthven's. Under his host's subtle and sympathetic insistence, Dylan drank only beer, and talked through the evening with fourteen or fifteen people, among them a young Negro novelist with whom he discussed at length technical points of fiction. When the party broke up, he asked Liz and Herb to come with him to the Horse for a night-cap.

On the morning of October 31st, Dylan had a phone call from a young woman, a close friend of Liz's, whom he had met when he stayed with her and her husband on one of his college visits. Delighted by the opportunity to see her again, Dylan made a date to take her and Liz to lunch. When they met, he said that he wanted their luncheon to be very special—they would have the "poshest" one they could possibly order and they would do this at Luchow's. While Dylan himself ate next to nothing, merely picking at the dishes he ordered, this turned out to be a pleasant, even merry occasion, and the party did not break up until it had been moved to Costello's on Third Avenue, one of Dylan's first American haunts. There he was later called for by Harvey Breit and taken off to a dinner party. Before leaving, he promised to rejoin Liz and her friend at eleven o'clock. After going separate ways, they returned to Costello's in the late evening, but Dylan did not show up.

When Liz spoke with him by phone on the following morning, he said he was in dreadful condition, that his hangover was "a real horror." Worse than that, he said, was the memory of something he had done: in the dimly recalled night before, he had taken a sudden dislike to a woman who was riding in a cab with him and had literally thrown her out into the street, simply because he could not for another moment bear the sight of her. He asked Liz to meet him and about noon they went to the Horse. A number of friends and acquaintances drifted by as Dylan drank beer and raw eggs—a diet which, for days now, had provided his only nourishment—and slowly began to recover equilibrium. Early in the evening, a group of people clustering around his table moved on to dinner at a Village restaurant, and later some of them went on to a small party in an apartment on Central Park West. While this was meant to be a quiet gathering,

Dylan became drunk, unstrung, messy in behavior, made obvious advances to a lady dancer whom he pursued about the apartment (while his pursuit was unsuccessful, it was so physically awkward that the young woman spent weeks afterwards under medical care for a concussion), and showed every sign that, ill or no, he could still muster the zest of his famous party behavior.

After midnight, Howard Moss invited a group from the party to come to his apartment for a nightcap. As they were making desultory conversation and listening to music there, Dylan said nervously: "I just saw a mouse. Did you see it?" He pointed to a door. "It went under there." Liz and the others did not see it, and sensed immediately that there was no real mouse to see. But Dylan was obviously so distraught that Liz said Yes, she had seen it, and he seemed relieved. Asked by Howard if he would read a poem or two, Dylan said he would like to very much. In a few minutes, leafing through the later poems of Yeats which, to Dylan, were the greatest of all modern poems and which had become increasingly the models of what he himself strove toward, he began the last reading he was ever to give. Among the pieces he chose were "Lapis Lazuli," "News for the Delphic Oracle," "Long-Legged Fly," "John Kinsella's Lament for Mrs. Mary Moore." Before he had finished his recital, he also read W. H. Auden's, "September 1, 1939."

It was a warm night. When the reading, which had lasted for more than an hour, was over, he went with Howard out onto the terrace of the apartment to look at a rose tree which now bore its last blossom of the summer. Approaching in darkness, Dylan went too close and scratched his eyeball on a thorny stem. He winced and cursed as he withdrew, but fortunately the sharpness of the pain lasted only for a moment. Shortly he was back in the apartment and had settled down to drink until the party broke up about five A.M.

When he awoke in his hotel after a few hours of sleep, the pain from his bruised eye and the throb of his hangover was so great that he was unable to leave his bed. Liz nursed him through a long painful day and by early evening he had returned to a semblance of normality. Against her advice, he decided that he should not give up a social engagement he had promised to meet that evening: an unveiling of a statue of Sir Thomas Lipton by the sculptor, Frank Dobson, taking place at the Wildenstein Galleries. After this ceremony was over, he and Liz went to the Colony for dinner as guests of Ben Sonnenberg, the publicist, who was in charge of the unveiling. In a soiled shirt, and an ill-fitting bargain suit an acquaintance had persuaded him to buy at a garment-district emporium, Dylan made polite, even enthusiastic, conversation in the opulence of the Colony, at ease with everyone except, perhaps, himself.

It was an elegant gathering, and while Dylan ate nothing, he did take advantage of the occasion to have his first drinks of the day. As he and Liz were about to leave the restaurant when the dinner party broke up, Dylan spotted William Faulkner and a lady companion at a nearby table. He went over to Faulkner, exchanged brief greetings with him, and returned with the remark to Liz that someday, he hoped he and Faulkner would really be able to talk.

Dylan wanted to go on to Costello's. As they sat in a booth there, Liz made drawings and caricatures. Delighted by these, Dylan asked for a whole series of eccentric figures, including one of "The drunkest man in the world." Liz attempted this but, try as she might, the features of the drunkest man in the world were impossible to get just right. Soon Dylan said he was hungry and that he wanted to go back to the Chelsea. At his insistence, they bought quantities of food at a delicatessen; but when the midnight supper was prepared, Dylan would have nothing but a bowl of soup.

On November 3rd, Election Day, Ruthven Todd and Herb Hannum came to the hotel early to visit with Dylan. Liz joined them in a late morning's talk, then said she would have to take leave of them in order to vote. Dylan took a satirical view of this, but could not dissuade her. When she and Ruthven returned from the polls, a young poet had come to join the group, and a new drinking session was soon well under way. To forestall, if she possibly could, the onset of another alcoholic day, Liz prevailed upon them to leave. Dylan slept then, to be awakened only by the arrival of the lecture agent whose offer, made in the previous summer, had been one of his main reasons for coming to America. After a brief conversation with the agent, Dylan signed a contract that would guarantee him one thousand dollars per week for his services. His connection with the agency would begin immediately, and there was a clause in the contract stating that he could withdraw at any time when his earnings did not reach that figure.

When he had handed back the signed contracts and said good-by to his new agent, he lay down on his bed. While he had made a late afternoon appointment to have cocktails with Santha Rama Rau and her husband, and Cheryl Crawford, the theatrical producer, he said now that he could not go anywhere. He seemed exhausted, self-preoccupied and morbidly depressed, but after a short nap he awoke saying that he would keep his cocktail date after all. Liz went with him to Miss Rama Rau's apartment, where he drank moderately, played with her little boy, and seemed quite his congenial self in conversation with Miss Crawford.

Afterwards they went to visit the sculptor, Frank Dobson, at his hotel. While they had planned to go with him and a theater party he had organized to see *Take a Giant Step,* Dylan felt that he was not up to it. When they had made their excuses to Dobson, they returned to the hotel. Dylan's exhaustion seemed as much mental as physical as, hardly able to speak, he fell asleep immediately. Liz sat with him through the evening. Fretfully turning on his bed, he awoke to speak, sometimes in tears, of his wife, of the misery of his existence, and of his wish to die. "I want to go to the Garden of Eden," he said, "to die . . . to be forever unconscious. . . ." And then, later, "You know, I adore my little boy. . . . I can't bear the thought that I'm not going to see him again. Poor little bugger, he doesn't deserve this." "Doesn't deserve what?" asked Liz. "He doesn't deserve my wanting to die. I truly want to die." Speaking of Caitlin, then, he said, "You have no idea how beautiful she is. There is an illumination about her . . . she shines." As Liz attempted to comfort him, telling him that he did not have to die, that he could get well, he began to weep uncontrollably.

In fitful sleep, broken only by disconnected and further agonized snatches of talk, he kept to his bed until two A.M. Then, suddenly, he reared up with a fierce look in his eyes. "I've got to have a drink," he said, "I've got to go out and have a drink. I'll come back in half an hour." Liz pleaded with him, but he ignored her entreaties and left her. Alone in the room, she waited as half an hour went by, then an hour, then an hour and a half. Dylan opened the door, walked to the center of the room and said laconically, "I've had eighteen straight whiskies. I think that's the record." He sank onto his knees, reached out his arms, and fell into her lap saying, "I love you . . . but I'm alone," and went to sleep.

When he awoke in midmorning, he said he was suffocating, that he had to get out into the air right away. Liz went with him for a walk that led, inevitably, to the White Horse where he had two glasses of beer, chatting meanwhile with a truck-driver acquaintance. But he was too sick to stay for long. When they returned to the hotel, and without allowing him opportunity to object, Liz said, "I'm going to call the doctor." Dylan resigned himself to this, and Dr. Feltenstein was summoned and arrived within the half-hour. The doctor gave him medication that would relieve his suffering, temporarily at least, and instructed Liz in procedures for taking care of him. Dylan slept, off and on, through the afternoon, and when he awoke with another severe attack of nausea and vomiting, Dr. Feltenstein was summoned again. With equivocation, he told Dylan he would have to begin immediately on a regimen of medical attention. In response, Dylan was evasive, pointing out that he had engagements to fulfill at Wheaton College, at M.I.T. and at Mt. Holyoke, and declared that he felt he would soon be all right. The doctor dismissed his arguments, gave him a shot of ACTH, and told him that the new regimen would begin at once. Restive, Dylan protested again, whereupon the doctor made a slight compromise: he would allow him to fulfill just one of his engagements, after which he would have to return to New York immediately for continuance of treatment. As Dylan, still reluctant, fretted and showed his impatience by groans and sighs, the doctor asked forcefully, "Do you want to go on being sick?" Quietly, firmly, Dylan said, "No." When the interview was over, Liz stepped into the hallway with the doctor. When she returned to the room, Dylan asked, "What did he say to you? Did he say I was going to die?" "No," said Liz. "He didn't say that. . . . He simply said that you will have to accept the fact that you're very ill and that you'll have to begin today to do something about it." "I will," said Dylan, "I'll do whatever you wish." "But," said Liz, "is that what *you* wish?" "Yes," said Dylan, "I truly, truly do."

After another vomiting spell—a consequence of his alcoholic gastritis—he became drowsy and fell asleep. Liz had meantime phoned me in Cambridge to say that plans for the week end—when Dylan was to spend a leisurely five days with me after his engagement at Wheaton College—would have to be canceled. In the late afternoon, she went out to buy supplies the doctor had recommended for Dylan's new diet. He slept for a couple of hours, awoke to vomit and, when this subsided, lay down again, but not to rest. As Liz almost instantly recognized, Dylan was beginning to go into delirium tremens. He indicated that he was "seeing" something, that it was "not animals . . . abstractions." As perspiration broke out on his face and he began to retch again, Liz phoned Dr. Feltenstein, who came to the hotel immediately. As Dylan raving now, begged to be "put out," the doctor gave him a sedative. Fearing that delirium tremens might make Dylan uncontrollable, the doctor advised Liz to call in some friend to stay with her, insisting that it be a man. After several attempts to locate friends of hers and Dylan's by phone, she was able to get the help of

Jack Heliker, the painter, who arrived within a few minutes. By this time Dylan had become a little more peaceful. As Heliker came into the room, Dylan held out his hand—"This is a hell of a way to greet a man, isn't it?"—and very soon fell into a restless sleep. Liz and Heliker sat by his bed as Dylan waked and dozed intermittently. "The horrors" were still there, he said—"abstractions, triangles and squares and circles." Once he said to Liz, "You told me you had a friend who had d.t.'s. What was it like?" "He saw white mice and roses," said Liz. "Roses plural?" asked Dylan, "or Rose's roses, with an apostrophe?" Then Liz said, "You know, Dylan, one thing about horrors—just remember, they go away, they do go away—" "Yes," said Dylan, "I believe you." As she sat beside him holding his hand in hers, she suddenly felt his grip stiffen. When she looked at Dylan his face was turning blue. A quick call to Dr. Feltenstein brought an ambulance that took Dylan to St. Vincent's Hospital.

At home in Cambridge, I was asleep when, at 2:30 in the morning, I was awakened by the insistent ringing of the phone. It was Liz, calling from New York. Her voice shrill, barely controlled, she told me that she was speaking from St. Vincent's Hospital, where Dylan had been received into the emergency ward. Quickly filling in details of the dreadful evening since her talk with me by phone in the late afternoon, she said that Dylan had passed into coma, that he had been given oxygen, that a spinal tap was being made to ascertain whether he had sustained a cerebral hemorrhage, and that his name was on the critical list. As she spoke quickly, disconnectedly, she broke down. I could hear her weeping, for a time unable to speak at all. And then, dismissing all details, she said with an anguished sob, "John, he may be dying . . . he may be dying," and implored me to come at once.

Three hours later, on the first plane available, I was flying over Long Island Sound in the pink and orange sun of a windless morning. In this numb suspension, I sat sick and chill, attempting to sort out thoughts and feelings that had gripped me since Liz's call. While my mind would not work, I knew that I was stunned—as if I were leaning against a well of apprehension that would give way if I moved so much as an inch. I had made the flight between Boston and New York hundreds of times, yet the memory of that one passage remains with me precise in every detail, from the moment I boarded the plane, until I left. It was as though my attention would fix on anything but the one fear that obsessed it.

Liz had asked me to phone her apartment on Charles Street—just a few steps from St. Vincent's—as soon as I reached New York. When I phoned from the airport, Jack Heliker answered. Liz was still at the hospital. Since she would have phoned him with news of any critical change, and since she had not, he assumed that Dylan's condition was at least no worse.

I took a taxi to the hospital, which is located on Eleventh Street at Seventh Avenue. As I hurried in by the front entrance, I could see Liz, comforted by Ruthven Todd, being led in the direction away from me down the corridor. I called out to them. By their dazed expressions, I believed at once that Dylan was dead. I put my arms around Liz, and she wept on my chest. Ruthven embraced both of us, saying, "No, we haven't lost him, John, he's still with us." We retired to a waiting room. Barely able to speak from the shock and grief of the night's events and her long vigil, Liz told me that Dylan's condition was so critical that any moment might bring word of his death. While the spinal tap had shown no evidence of the cerebral hemorrhage doctors had first suspected, there was some evidence that Dylan had sustained a diabetic shock, and this clue was being followed up. Minute by minute, as we sat in a ghastly apprehensive embrace in the dim waiting room, we watched for a word or sign from the Emergency Ward. As she tried to tell me of the events that had led to this moment, Liz faltered and had only breath enough to say, "Oh, John, why didn't I call the *police*?" No one calls the police, I told her, no one calls the police.

Within an hour, the swinging doors of the adjoining corridor were pushed open. Dylan, outstretched under sheets, was wheeled to an elevator and taken to the third floor, where he was put in a room in the St. Joseph's division of the Hospital. Doctors and nurses surrounded him as he was rolled past the waiting room; we could see only that he lay inert, his fact in an oxygen mask, his wild hair limp and wet, his face blotched with fever. We grasped at one small hope; since the physicians had allowed him to be removed from the Emergency Ward, he was at least not sinking.

Dr. Feltenstein came to us shortly and, in medical terms, impressed us anew with the minute-by-minute balance upon which Dylan's life depended. When he questioned us about any knowledge we might have had of a recent fall, and about the diabetic condition that the doctors now suspected, we had nothing to offer. In 1950, Dylan mentioned to me that he believed he had cirrhosis of the liver, but had never spoken of diabetes, or ever again of the suspected liver condition.

Within half an hour we were allowed to go upstairs to see him. He was breathing heavily through the oxygen mask, attended by doctors and nurses while a blood transfusion was being administered. Since there was nothing to do but look on helplessly, soon we returned to the waiting room. There we found Ruthven's wife, Joellen, and shortly came Rose and Dave Slivka, who were particularly close friends of Caitlin's. When Liz and I went to the third floor again, we were not allowed at Dylan's bedside. Activity around him continued without respite. Standing at the door of his room, we could observe only that he was still alive and that ceaseless effort was being made to save him.

Later in the morning, I made local and long-distance calls to people who were close to Dylan, and arranged to have Caitlin notified. Our vigil was soon joined by Herb Hannum, Rollie and Howard Moss. We spent the endless afternoon waiting, Liz and I conferring at intervals with Dr. Feltenstein and Dr. James McVeigh, the staff physician who had been put in charge of Dylan. When we learned that it was now established that Dylan had sustained "a severe insult to the brain," and that this was due to direct alcoholic poisoning of brain cells and brain tissue, we made arrangements with Dr. Feltenstein to call in a brain specialist for consultation. Dr. Leo Davidoff was our choice, since we had learned of his reputation as one of the world's leading specialists, and we set about securing his services.

By early evening we had to accept two seemingly contradictory statements: on the one hand, Dr. Feltenstein informed us, the longer Dylan remained in coma the less were his chances of recovery, since the long duration of the coma indicated the severity of injury to the brain. On the other hand, Dr. McVeigh pointed out, the longer Dylan remained alive, the more evidence did we have of his basic strength to endure and perhaps overcome the violence of the shock he had sustained. Physicians had spent the whole day attempting to restore basic somatic balances. By evening, this had been achieved. But there was no sign that the coma was any less deep than at the very beginning.

Just before midnight, at the request of the nurse who was attending him, Liz and I spoke to Dylan a number of times, saying the same words and phrases over and over again. At moments, we believed we saw flickers of response and the nurse encouraged us to continue. But to almost every observation Dylan remained wholly unconscious, only his eyes moving now and then, sightless and without focus. Half an hour later, when Rose Slivka and I were at the bedside, I tried again, saying softly to Dylan that he was not alone, that Caitlin was coming to him, that Liz and I would stay with him, and attempting otherwise to have him recognize me if only by my voice. While I spoke there was a sudden definite reaction. The rhythm of his breathing became slightly agitated, and he uttered a sound that seemed to indicate that his whole body was straining toward speech. This seemed a miracle, yet I doubted the evidence of what I saw and heard. A few minutes later, I spoke to him again, and again came the same response, an effort so agonized and instantaneous, and yet so inconclusive that I could hardly bear to watch. Whether Dylan had heard and somehow understood—or whether his reaction was but a muscular spasm was impossible to know. While I took hope in the thought that, whatever its nature, his response was immediate and unmistakable, doctors later told me that his coma was of such depth as to leave him utterly senseless to any influence.

Through the hospital dimness I could now discern new faces in the doorway. John Berryman, the poet and critic, had come from Princeton and, along with a number of people whom I did not know, David Lougée, one of Dylan's first American friends. Strangers came and went through the long night. One was an elegantly dressed young woman who simply appeared at the door of the room, stared at him for half an hour, and departed without speaking to anyone. Many others came only long enough to look in, or to speak to the nurses, and so confirm for themselves the rumor of Dylan's plight. About four A.M., Sister Consilio, who was in charge of the St. Joseph's Division, came to us and advised us to go home to bed. She assured us that Dylan's physical functioning had been restored, that his condition had become much less critical, and that he was now out of immediate danger. While most of us tended to accept the truth of this, we were still reluctant to leave the hospital. Gaunt, mesmerized by her unbroken vigil of more than twenty-four hours, Liz would not accept the nun's word or her advice. Sister Consilio then became adamant, changed her counsel into an order, and led us away from Dylan's room toward the main entrance of the hospital. Liz, as adamant as she, and too distraught now to comprehend the situation, refused to leave. But, finally prevailed upon, she was taken away from the hospital by friends who stayed with her through the night.

Back in the hospital just before eight o'clock, I found the only response I could elicit was "no change." The oxygen mask was still on

Dylan's face, his eyes, spasmodically turning, fluttering, were open, but their unseeing gaze only confirmed his unfathomable sleep. Liz returned shortly and we waited together through the morning, moving from Dylan's bedside to the waiting room in turns, retreating only when we felt our presence might be an annoyance to the doctors and nurses who continually came and went. In the early afternoon, we learned that Dr. Leo Davidoff would not be available, but that he had unqualifiedly recommended to us Dr. C. G. de Gutierrez-Mahoney, a brain specialist and brain surgeon. He arrived shortly, and Dr. Feltenstein escorted him to Dylan's bedside. When the two physicians returned after an hour's consultation, Liz and I were asked into an anteroom to speak with them. We found Dr. de Gutierrez-Mahoney to be an elegant, soft-spoken man who knew Dylan's work and understood its worth, and who seemed to understand by instinct not only every nuance of our concern but the circumstances that had given us the responsibility of providing for Dylan's care. Confirming the earlier diagnosis of "direct alcoholic toxicity in brain tissue and brain cells," he said that in the nature of the case there was no basis for undertaking surgery. Everything that could be done to make possible Dylan's survival had already been done, but it was likely that his condition was not reversible. He had been on the phone to London where friends of Dylan's, having read of his illness in the newspapers, had found a physician who offered facts pertinent to Dylan's previous physical condition. Among these were points of information we ourselves had never known: that Dylan had suffered "blackouts" on several recent occasions in Wales and in London, and that in a visit to his Swansea physician, he had been specifically warned that alcoholism had brought him to the threshold of an attack such as had overtaken him. Observing that Liz and I were unable to accept the notion that nothing further could be done, Dr. de Gutierrez-Mahoney asked if there were unresolved questions in our minds. I inquired whether Dylan's ability to have sustained the initial shock that led to coma (it was now more than forty hours in duration) might give us hope—whether he might already have shown unexpected reserves of physical strength that might point to some chance of his survival. The doctor's answer was that, somatically speaking, Dylan had been restored to comparative normal functioning; the "X" factor, and the crucial one, was the still indeterminable degree of "insult to the brain."

Our bedside vigil continued into the evening. By now the hospital staff, plagued with telephone calls by the hundreds, bewildered to find its waiting room continually overflowing with visitors bent on seeing Dylan or having direct news of him, had ordered that only Liz and I be allowed to visit Dylan. Passes to this effect had been given to us. About ten o'clock we could see, by the increased activity of doctors and nurses, that Dylan was undergoing a change. At three o'clock that afternoon we had conferred at length with Dr. McVeigh who had predicted a probable change, for better or for worse, within twelve hours. We knew now that the change had come, and had little hope that it would be for the better. For the first time, Liz and I were asked to leave the bedside and return to the waiting room. There we found a whole new group of people, a few of whom were our friends. In the appalling hospital silence of late evening, we sat without speaking. Just before midnight, Sister Consilio approached us, her face grave. "Mr. Thomas's condition is now highly critical," she said. "Would any of you care to come with me to the chapel to pray?" Three of the group accompanied her. Liz and I, with the others who stayed, shared a silence that was itself a prayer.

Yet this crisis passed. When we were allowed to make a brief visit to Dylan, we found that a tracheotomy had been performed. Mucus and other impedimenta had obstructed his breathing to the point of suffocation. Swift surgery had removed the obstructive matter; now there was a tube inserted into his nose and another in his throat. While he breathed more freely and with more regularity than earlier in the evening, his body now seemed hopelessly ravaged, as though he were not a man but some organism kept alive by invention. When we spoke to this pathetic body that now seemed to have given all of its will to the accouterments sustaining its life, I felt finally that I was no longer speaking to Dylan, and knew that the remote hope I had come upon the night before was gone.

When a cable containing a tender message to Dylan from Caitlin had been delivered in the afternoon, we had put it on his bedside table in the meager chance that it would be the first thing he would see should he come out of coma. But as we looked upon his expressionless face that lay mere inches away from her message, the distance between became immeasurable. Dylan was now beyond all love, even Caitlin's. When we spoke to him now, our words formed no question because we knew there could be no answer.

This was the longest night of all, when every clock stood still, and we sat in a desert of hopelessness. Still we made our alternating vigils, waiting for the only end we could now contemplate. Just before dawn, Sister Consilio came to us. Dylan's condition remained critical, she said, but she would like to have us accept her assurance that he was not likely to die within the next few hours. The tracheotomy had successfully relieved the crisis of the late evening; he had gained strength since then and was now breathing peacefully. We left, then, and I slept for two hours.

Again on Saturday morning the report was "no change"—and we knew by this simply that Dylan's enormous physical strength was continuing to resist the "insult" to his brain. But by early afternoon we could see that he was sinking. His breathing was troubled and irregular; his temperature rose and fell in sudden changes that left his face alternately red and perspiring, blue and pallid. Now we had to find strength to act upon a new development. We learned that in London efforts were being made to find a seat for Caitlin on a plane scheduled to take off for New York at three P.M. If, as seemed certain now, Dylan would die within the next few hours, her coming might be a compounded misery for herself and for others. While Dr. McVeigh confirmed our observation that he was now sinking rapidly, there was still the possibility that Dylan might continue to confound prognosis. If there was any chance that Caitlin might share Dylan's last hours of life, that chance would have to be made possible. Yet, should she arrive in New York too late, it would likely be worse than if she had never come at all.

A phone call was put through to London, where Caitlin, awaiting her plane, was being cared for by David Higham, Dylan's literary agent and long-time friend. The imminence of Dylan's death was impressed upon Higham with the expectation that he would convey the facts to Caitlin. Higham was uncertain about what she would do and felt it unlikely that she would be able to leave on the three o'clock plane, since it was now less than two hours from flight time, and no seat was yet available. In any case, Higham said, he would cable as soon as Caitlin had made up her mind.

While Dr. Feltenstein remained as attendant physician, Dr. de Gutierrez-Mahoney had now assumed complete supervision of Dylan, had subsequently called in other specialists, and had himself been a constant visitor to the bedside during the past two days. His failure to give us any sign that might feed a last flickering hope had slowly brought us to resignation. When we conferred with Dr. Feltenstein, we learned that Dylan's death was not only next to inevitable, but that it was now also to be desired: should he somehow manage to survive, the damage to his brain was so great that he would be a permanent invalid, physically as well as mentally. When we comprehended this, when we could grasp the idea of Dylan's mind brought into some half-articulate and crippled distortion of itself, we could only wish that death would come soon. While we had been assured from the first that he was conscious of no pain, it was impossible to look upon that struggling body as it fought for breath, its eyes roaming without rest, and not suffer the conviction that Dylan was embroiled in speechless agony.

E. E. Cummings and his wife came to the hospital that afternoon, and scores of strangers, some of whom were now in the habit of making daily visits. In our conversations with them, we became aware that, while out intimate knowledge of Dylan's worsening condition had led us to accept the reality of his death, others, completely unprepared to accept it, listened to us with faces showing skepticism or outright disbelief. On Friday morning, the *New York Times* had carried a brief report of his having been taken ill, but otherwise, except for rumors that had run about the city—one reporting that he had had a cerebral hemorrhage, one that he had fallen downstairs while intoxicated, another that he had been mugged by unknown assailants, still others too repulsive to mention—there had been no public report of his true condition.

Visits through the evening showed no change in Dylan's now high and constant fever that at times reached 105.5. Caitlin, meanwhile, had sent a cable saying that she had found a place on the three o'clock plane from London. Now that she was en route, the only thing to do was to pray that she would not come in vain, and to set about insuring that not a moment be lost between her landing at Idlewild and her arrival at St. Vincent's. I phoned first the British Consulate and then the headquarters of the British Delegation to the United Nations. The former was taken quite by surprise, having had no previous word of Dylan's illness; and the latter was all but closed up. I was promised assistance from both offices should the proper individuals in authority be reached; but since it was Saturday night, it would be difficult to locate those with power to act. In view of this, I phoned Washington and got a friend there to work directly through the British Embassy. He, in turn, phoned an attaché who promised to make arrangements through the Consulate in New York, and assured us that everything would be done to see that Caitlin would not be impeded by customs or other immigration formalities. The business of arranging this, with intermittent visits to Dylan in between, had taken more than three hours. Half-blind and useless from fatigue, I was taken away from the hospital at two A.M. by Howard Moss, who gave me sedatives and put me to bed. Against all advice, Liz remained at Dylan's side through the night.

When I awoke just after eight, I hurried back to St. Vincent's. Entering by the main door, I caught sight of Caitlin, escorted by Rose and Dave Slivka who had gone to Idlewild to meet her, coming in through the Emergency Ward corridor. We embraced, kissed, and she said, "Why didn't you write to me? Is the bloody man dead or alive?" I led her upstairs to Dylan's room, but a nurse asked that we wait for a few minutes before entering. As we stood outside while the nurse finished bathing Dylan, I could see Liz sitting alone at the far end of the corridor. Caitlin and I went in. Dylan was now in an oxygen tent, his breathing much less forceful and steady than it had been on the night before. Caitlin took his hand and spoke to him. I left her, and went to Liz. Within fifteen minutes, Caitlin came from the room. As I approached her, I could see that the reality of Dylan's condition had registered its whole truth. Silently, she circled about, her hands uplifted, as if she were under a spell; then she moved with a sudden lurch to a window and pounded her head against it in an attempt to smash it through. But the window, reinforced with a netting of wire-mesh, did not break. She became calmer then, and I escorted her back to the waiting room where Rose and Dave Slivka took her away to their apartment nearby. Returning to Liz then, I found her calm, resigned to a circumstance too complex to unravel and, as she had determined days before, ready now to remove herself from a scene where, by all official and conventional canons, she had no place.

When Liz left the hospital, I was alone for the first time in four days. In the magnified stillness of Sunday morning, the waiting room was empty. When I went upstairs to see Dylan, wintry-bright sun streamed into his room and made a prism of the transparent oxygen tent covering the upper part of him. He breathed easily, quietly, his eyes closed, his face calm. I sensed the resignation of each of his faculties, the composition of all of his will. The dark night of his soul was over, and the long day of his dying. At his own pace, in his own time, Dylan was approaching his own good night. When I spoke to him, I knew I spoke only to myself.

Back in the empty waiting room, I sat down in a misery of recognition so piercing that it was as if I had just that moment come upon the scene I witnessed. Until then I had never really believed, in spite of the evidence of the doctors and of my own eyes, that Dylan was doomed. When, at last, I knew—not with my mind, since it would accept only what had happened and still stubbornly resisted what might, but with all of my being—that Dylan would die, I wept away the disbelief that had somehow held me together since the moment of Liz's call to Cambridge. There had never been a lonelier hour of my life, but by the time grief had run its term and found the limits of the expression I could give it, I had come upon new strength.

In our responsibility for Dylan which, in the absence of any other authority, Liz and I had had to assume, we had naturally proceeded with no caution for expenses, either in regard to hospital fees or to those of physicians. Had we known that St. Vincent's Hospital would eventually cancel all costs for Dylan's care, the problem of money would not have forced itself upon us as acutely as it then did. But now, we felt, the time had come to prepare for medical fees quite beyond our private means, to provide ready money for expenses that would come at Dylan's death, and to raise funds for Caitlin and her three children. After I had spent two hours in making phone calls, first to James Laughlin, Dylan's publisher, who said he would fly in from his home in Connecticut immediately, and then to other individuals who I thought might give money to take care of immediate expenses, Caitlin returned in the company of Dave and Rose Slivka.

She was wearing a striking, close-fitting black wool dress; her tawny yellow hair was loosely done up; she looked radiantly beautiful, and she had had too much to drink. Before we went upstairs, she embraced me, a bit unsteadily, and held me to her for fully a minute. She stayed at Dylan's bedside for about twenty minutes, and then she was asked to leave the room by distraught nurses who could not keep her from lighting cigarettes in the danger zone of the oxygen tent, or from pressing herself upon Dylan in such a way as to obstruct his breathing. When she was led to an adjoining room—which the nuns had made available to her as a private waiting room—I joined her there with Rose, David Lougée and Rollie. Someone had brought whisky at Caitlin's request. She drank from the bottle and was very soon in a state of distraction in which, suddenly berserk, she wildly assaulted me and then turned fiercely on those who tried to pull her away. As she still fought and wrestled with the others through the length of the room, I went dazedly into the corridor and tried to come upon some perspective through which to view a development that now threatened to overwhelm us all. Entering Dylan's room, I stood in the dim blue light of his bedside and watched his sleep for perhaps ten minutes. As I stepped back out into the corridor and was about to return to Caitlin, the sister in charge of the floor approached me in great agitation. Caitlin's behavior, she reported, had become uncontrollable. She had torn a crucifix from a wall and smashed it, demolished some pots containing plants set on a wall-shelf, and splintered to bits a statue of the Virgin. Fighting off nuns and nurses, as well as the friends who tried to calm her, she was now in a state of hysteria. Rollie, who had witnessed all of this, came to me and suggested that a physician be called, since Caitlin was now impervious to any entreaty. The nun in charge sent for one of the doctors on duty in the Emergency Ward. Within a few minutes, he had come with an attendant and a wheel chair. Caitlin was led from the anteroom; her face was flushed, but she was momentarily docile. She refused the wheel chair with a burst of profanity, and was escorted into the elevator and down to the Emergency Ward. There she flared up again, biting an orderly on the hand, attacking the doctors attending her, and tearing the habit of a nun. When I went downstairs a few minutes later, I learned that she had finally been restrained in a strait jacket.

Shortly I was called to an office where a staff physician asked me to answer a number of questions about Caitlin. Having seen her violence and the dismay it had caused among the nurses and doctors attempting to control her, his manner was angry and impatient as he filled in a large yellow form with details I supplied. The Slivkas joined me in the course of this interrogation, and were able to offer several points of information I did not possess. The doctor filled up the form swiftly, but with such obvious irritation with us and the situation that we became distrustful. His reactions to the information we gave him were rancorous, almost malicious. When we asked him the purpose of the form he was so angrily filling in, he replied that it was a necessary document in preparation for having Caitlin admitted to Bellevue, the municipal psychiatric hospital. This was deporable news and we expressed our reaction to him in tones that were as rancorous as his. While he had sufficient data for his form, he still would have to have a signature before Caitlin could be committed. Not one of us would sign. Furious at our refusal, he said that, in any case, Caitlin would not be allowed to remain at St. Vincent's, and spitefully detailed to us her violence toward orderlies and nuns, and her profanity toward those who attempted to take care of her. He seemed far more concerned for the sensibilities of the nuns than for the wretched state into which events had brought Caitlin. We could recognize the reasons for his impatience, but his disregard of the circumstances that had led Caitlin to her present plight seemed unprofessional, bigoted, and in sharp contrast to the great kindness of other members of the hospital staff. Would he, we asked, give us an hour's time within which we might confer with Dr. Feltenstein? Grudgingly, yet of necessity, since he could act no further without a signature, he agreed to wait for one hour.

We phoned Dr. Feltenstein, who said he would come immediately. Meanwhile, James Laughlin had arrived. Liz, who had come back to the hospital for this purpose, went out with him and me so that we might present our ideas for the establishment of a fund to take care of Dylan's expenses now and in the future. When we returned, Dr. Feltenstein was just coming from an interview with Caitlin, who was being kept in a room adjoining the Emergency Ward. He impressed us with the extremity of her hysteria, warned us that she was a menace not only to herself but to others, and told us that on no account could she be released. When we made clear our refusal to be party to any action that would commit Caitlin to Bellevue, he offered to bring in a psychiatrist. This man, Dr. Adolf Zeckel, came within half an hour, examined Caitlin, then conferred with Dr. Feltenstein, Rose Slivka, and myself. This was the dilemma: since Caitlin was not rational and would have to be cared for, and St. Vincent's refused to keep her, the only recourse would be to have her sent to a private hospital. He recommended that we authorize him to send her to Rivercrest, an institution in Astoria, Long Island, just across the river from Manhattan. When he could see that we were still hesitant and unhappy, Dr. Zeckel pointed out our only two other alternatives—either to commit Caitlin to Bellevue, or to assume personal responsibility for her care. After all we had witnessed, we had to admit—even against the press of a circumstance that might cause anyone to take leave of his senses—that Caitlin's need was not the ministrations of well-intentioned friends but of professionals. An ambulance was arranged for. Dr. Feltenstein took two hundred dollars from his pocket to be used as a deposit at Rivercrest. With Rose, and Ruthven Todd, attending her, Caitlin was taken away to the Long Island institution. When the ambulance arrived there, I learned later, she had become calm and rational enough to assess her situation, and to commit herself.

When James Laughlin returned with his friend, Philip Wittenberg, the well-known literary and theatrical attorney, the three of us sat down to a brief conference during which we devised initial steps for putting the machinery of a fund into operation. This would be named the Dylan Thomas Memorial Fund. The first letters of the appeal, containing the names of literary sponsors who would be approached by telephone that very evening, were to be ready for mailing on the following day. Philip Wittenberg would serve as Treasurer, and checks would be received at his mid-town office. Our talk was brief and to the point, no one now indulging in any sentimental hope that a memorial fund would prove premature.

All through that day and on until after midnight, as he slept, far from the grotesque violence and grief that surrounded him, Dylan had shown little change. But on Monday morning, November 9th, my first glance told me that, somewhere in the night, he had gone into his final phase. His fever had subsided; his breathing had become so slight as to be almost inaudible, and now and then there would be little gasps and long breathless intervals that threatened to last forever. His face was wan and expressionless, his eyes half-opening for moments at a time, his body inert.

When I phoned Rivercrest in the hope that I might speak with Caitlin, I was told that she had spent a quiet night, but that no one could yet speak with her or come to visit her. When I inquired into the possibility of her being released, I was told that this would not be considered until Dr. Zeckel came to see her on Monday evening. This seemed an intolerably long time for her to be alone, no matter what professional assistance might be available to her. I then phoned Dr. Zeckel and obtained his permission for an afternoon visit by her closest friends, Rose and Dave Slivka. As to the possibility of her being released, the psychiatrist felt that we would have to accept the likelihood that she would be confined for at least two or three days.

Dylan's life simply ebbed away, without any further sign of struggle, through the long morning. With Liz, who had returned to the hospital late the night before, I made frequent visits; we sometimes took his hands in ours, sometimes spoke softly to him in the last hope that some small word of love and comfort might penetrate the limbo in which he lay.

When a British physician who was visiting in New York recommended to Ruthven Todd that Dr. James Smith of Bellevue, an alcoholic specialist, be called in Liz and I went to see Dr. de Gutierrez-Mahoney in order to secure clearance for his consultation. While Dylan's doctor welcomed this development, we could sense that, while he carefully said nothing that might deepen the despair we felt, he regarded Dylan's condition as terminal. When we returned to inform Dr. McVeigh that Dr. Smith would be coming to see Dylan in the early afternoon, he advised us to phone Dr. Smith and urge that he come at once. We did this, and he arrived at the hospital within fifteen minutes. After his examination of Dylan and his report to the physicians, he conferred with Liz and me. He told us that he had made certain recommendations, that these were "purely a matter of chemistry," and that it appeared to him that Dylan's condition was not reversible. Now there was suddenly increased activity at the bedside, with an anesthetist constantly in attendance.

A few minutes after one o'clock in the afternoon, Liz and I sat with a group of people—some of whom we had never seen before—in the shuffling dimness of the waiting room. When someone asked Liz to come out for a cup of coffee, I urged her to go along. Before she left I said I wanted to go upstairs to Dylan just one more time. Liz said that she would wait until I had come down. As I stepped from the waiting room into the corridor, I saw John Berryman rushing toward me. "He's dead! He's dead! Where were you?" I could not believe him but I did. "When?" "A few minutes ago. I just came from the room." I turned and walked slowly back through a group of strangers toward Liz, took both of her hands in mine, and nodded. She rose instantly, her hands fiercely gripping mine, and we rushed to the elevator.

In Dylan's room nurses were dimantling the oxygen tent and clearing away other instruments. He had stopped breathing, one of them told us, while she was bathing him. As she was about to turn him over on his right side she had heard him utter a slight gasp, and then he had become silent. When the nurses left us alone, Liz sat down in the chair in which she had watched all the nights of his dying. Dylan was pale and blue, his eyes no longer blindly searching but calm, shut, and ineffably at peace. When I took his feet in my hands all warmth was gone; it was as if I could feel the little distance between his life and death. Liz whispered to him and kissed him on the forehead. We stood then at the foot of his bed for a few very long minutes, and did not weep or speak. Now, as always, where Dylan was, there were no tears at all.

from *Leftover Life to Kill*

CAITLIN THOMAS

IV

Dylan was always about three jumps ahead of me, and had already put the argument backwards, inside out, and upside down, by the time I had got it eventually standing up straight. And this trick of always demolishing, with the invaluable aid of ridicule, a perfectly adequate work, or, just as soon, a masterpiece, then rebuilding it in his own freakish fashion, used to make me hopping cross; presumably because I was out of my depths. And he insisted, though I never agreed, that women have *no* sense of fun: verbal fun I think he meant; and were a spewing mass of generalizations and clicks (as our high-brow poetess in Laugharne calls clichés), only fit for the bed and the kitchen.

When I wake in the morning, when it is still dark, before even the bells or hullabaloo below has started, with the tears streaming, uncalled for, down my face, and Colm sleeping so small and reminiscently against me; and remember who I am, and where I am, and think of Dylan: Dylan in Laugharne, Dylan in this island, and Dylan wherever I am; and pine, as keenly as a sick cow for its calf just removed, for the feel of him, the smell of him; and go on daftly half waiting for him to come back, when I know he cannot; but it is not a bit of good for reason to tell me that, it cannot stop the wanting so badly, reasonable or not; and where can I put it, what can I do with it? It is not a chasm, it is an enormous fruit cake, of wanting: I am invaded with a stream of incessant babbling jingly, jangling; oh, why can't it stop for a minute? yesterdays. And the tomorrows stretch in somno-

From *Leftover Life to Kill* by Caitlin Thomas (Boston: Atlantic–Little, Brown & Co., 1957), pp. 51–66.

lent torpor, paying no attention to my gnawing and prodding behind the shutters.

I go to the glass, look into the pin-pointed, criss-crossed holes which contain, a thousand fathoms back, my ensnared reproachful eyes; and think, 'This is not the Rock Caitlin that Dylan loved: this damp, bedraggled string of seaweed.' And he would flood me with a contempt of words; there is no fury like the weak, against the weak; and he knew how to use words insultingly, as well as poetically. But because of his own Welsh hypochondrias he hated to see any sign of them in others and had no patience with any nervous ailments or manifestations in his children, because they came from him; though prepared to nurse his own, or preferably be nursed if that were forthcoming, with loving care, and wealth of descriptive detail.

He was never his proper self till there was something wrong with him; and, if ever there was a danger of him becoming 'whole,' which was very remote, he would crack another of his chicken bones, without delay, and wander happily round in his sling, piling up plates with cucumber, pickled onions, tins of cod's roe, boiled sweets; to push into his mouth with an unseeing hand, as they came, while he went on solidly reading his trash. His passion for lies was congenital: more a practice in invention than a lie. He would tell quite unnecessary ones, which did not in any way improve his situation: such as, when he had been to one cinema, saying it was another, and making up the film that was on: and the obvious ones, that only his mother pretended not to see through, like being carted off the bus into his home, and saying he had been having coffee, in a café, with a friend.

The reason we got along so well in the house was because of our mutually organic—meaning the organs were functioning but not much else—natures when off parade. The home was to Dylan, more especially, a private sanctum, where for once he was not compelled, by himself admittedly, to put on an act, to be amusing, to perpetuate the myth of the *Enfant Terrible:* one of the most damaging myths, and a curse to grow out of. We lived almost separate lives, though physically close, and passed each other with a detached phrase on strictly practical matters; as though we were no more than familiar landmarks, in the furniture of our minds. Excluding the times, more frequent at night, when the house rattled, and banged, and thudded, and groaned with our murder of each other.

But these fights, which were an essential part of our everyday life, and became fiercer and more deadly at each onslaught, so that you could have sworn no two people reviled each other more; and could never, under any fabulous change of circumstances, come together again: were almost worth-while because, when the reconcillation did take place, according to how long we could stick it out, it was so doubly, trebly, quadruply sweet, and we could never have ventured to conceive of such a thing happening again.

As far as the waiting game was concerned, I was the millimetre of an inch more adept than Dylan: owing to more false pride, and, as I sadly see now, more time to play around, so that it was he who nearly always made the first move back to normality, while I was reluctantly persuaded. And thinking back now, I see he was in a great hurry to fit in so many things; and could not be bothered with the extra spade work that to most people is compulsory. And many afternoons he wanted me to go to bed with him and I would not because of some ridiculous Upright principle that I chose to presume guided me. (God has some queer twists up His sleeve and, by whatever means you try to outwit or anticipate Him, He will nip you just where you least expect it.)

Jesus, he even kept saying he would die before me: would never reach forty: and I would be a flighty widow dancing on his grave. And I laughed, completely unmoved; for all the impression it made on me, he might as well have been talking to an elephant. And other things, to my discredit, come back to me: how he used to pursue me with the latest version of a poem in progress; and only ask me to stand still and let him read it to me; and how I would wriggle, do everything in my power to escape, block my ears (I hope without showing it), till in the end, he could not but notice my surly unwillingness, and swore never to read to me again, but always did. And this behaviour I find plain unforgivable, no two ways about it, and I can't account for my reaction, because I always had faith in Dylan as a poet: and even helped over choosing alternative words and on small points of preference; and he had a touching belief in my judgment. Putting it on the kindest level, I can say, I must have subconsciously felt I had something of my own worth preserving, and did not want to be influenced by Dylan's highly disturbing stuff. On the unkindest: that I was spitefully jealous, and resented, like any typical, man-swallowing woman, such a powerful rival to myself. But this I will not, and do not believe, even now. And I did all I could to make him work, at his own special work, and not public money-making work. And it was only with our kind of purely vegetable background, which entailed months on end of isolated, stodgy dullness and drudgery for me, that he was flattened out enough to be able to concentrate.

One of the most remarkable things about him, to me, was his singular gift for adapting himself to every kind of different, basically opposed, person and place. With no visible transition, he would settle down among the new set, as though he had been there all his life. And with equal ease cut off the old like dead leaves: though retaining surprising loyalties to old buddies, and motherly bodies overlapping and spilling with fistfuls of fat: one of our favourite kill-times in Laugharne was to sit in the window of the Brown's and imagine these Colossi (with which Laugharne was well stocked) walking, ten abreast, up the street, stark naked. And calculate how much money we would give to see such an impressive sight: nearly all we had.

So he was much better than me at contenting himself with the very simple, I might justly say moronic, life. Because, there is no other possible explanation, he lived in a world of his own: 'out of this world', as they so succinctly put it in America. Thus: the best part of the morning in the kitchen of this same high class establishment, putting bets on horses, listening, yes, actually listening for once, open mouthed, to local gossip and scandal, while drinking slow consecutive pints of disgustingly flat, cold-tea, bitter beer. Muzzily back to late lunch, of one of our rich fatty brews, always eaten alone, apart from the children: and I can't blame him for that, as there is nothing worse than brawling children's meals. He went so far, like a respectable Victorian father, as not travelling in the same carriage with them, though it was not often we went anywhere *en masse*, and I cannot blame him for that either. Then, blown up with muck and somnolence, up to his humble shed, nestling high above the estuary; and bang into intensive scribbling, muttering, whispering, intoning, bellowing and juggling of words; till seven o'clock prompt.

Then straight back to one of the alternative dumps; we had long discussions as to which was the deadliest; to spend the rest of the evening in 'brilliant repartee.' That was a sample day with all the innards and lights taken out.

VI

I am not, to my unlimited sorrow, a spontaneous person; not since my halcyon Isadora Duncan days, when I chose to fancy myself as flowing with melody, movement, and everything but the kitchen sink, including Grecian draperies, and Mercurian sandals, no half measures for me. It did not occur to me that all that flows is not, of necessity, gold; was it not *me* who was flowing? As a matter of fact it was not;

being me, I was tying myself in knots, and refusing to respond to the music, though I could hear, quite distinctly, what it was saying to me; and one hitch of the brain too late, would spring into action. Whenever I did come, triumphantly one with the music: I am not using the expression 'come' loosely, I mean in the loving sense; no loving come ever gave such prolonged ecstasy. And I did, comparatively often when I was alone, but as soon as I spotted the 'glance' of an audience, I was finished: the brain on the alert, all suspicion again, put the pincers on, and the capricious flow stopped abruptly. I was as lost as a sleepwalker, tapped unawares into wakefulness on the edge of a roof, and had no more idea where I was or what to do next: the music was a meaningless noise offending my ears, and obstructing my thinking.

This was one reason, now I come to think of it, why Dylan found it so annoying: it is the direct opposite of words, and talk; and, in a greater, and deeper degree, of poetry. It may be one of the substances that poetry is made out of; that words are formed from; but its elemental—right back, through the encumbering ages, to the creation, the planets, the floods, the dinosaurs; the skeletons and protoplasms—force is, above any other point of supremacy, *wordless.* So that to pin it on to poetry, as an accompaniment, is not only an absurdity, but an insult to both. How Dylan would have loathed this style of abstract ranting, as he would have called it, of mine; but I should never have dared put it down if he was going to see it.

He had the same dislike, amounting to superstitious horror, of philosophy, psychology, analysis, criticism; all these vaguely termed ponderous tomes; but most of all, of the gentle art of discussing poetry; not that I was likely to do that. We had a mutual agreement to keep off that touchy subject; and, if well-meaning friends started an abstruse, intense interpretation of some of Dylan's most obscure lines, which he had long ago forgotten the meaning of himself, it was not long before Dylan was on the floor wrapped up in the carpet, scratching himself, like a flea-bitten hyena, in paroxysms of acute boredom, ending, happily for him, in snoring amnesia. Not that such a delicate hint deterred the everlasting friend, who had now, by devious, unrelenting routes, introduced his own verse; and a dash of existentialism as well; while I was left politely nodding over the soup, planning all the hells I would put Dylan through for this, and wishing I had not been so well brought up; never to speed the parting guest; who, it was evident, had no intention of departing.

This very pronounced attitude of Dylan's against every type of flowery excursion into intellectualism made all the more surprising his extreme patience and tolerance in America, when confronted with the full blast of their adulation. There is, it appears, no limit to the quantity of flattery that one person is prepared to take about themselves; and, from whatever source, and, however far-fetched, they show a remarkable indulgence on this, their pet topic. I am perfectly alive, from my own vain experience, to the large part vanity plays in the least suspected lives: quite apart from our shameless flamboyancy. But Dylan always seemed to me to stand right outside this poetical junketing, this clannish backbiting, these teaspoon-tongued, little-finger-extended, oh so too too, Societies for the Prevention of Cruelty to Poets; if for the only reason that he had no need to swim in those shallow babbling waters. So that when he succumbed, like a mesmerized bait, only in this case a short-legged one, to the multitudinous, scavenging, spawn of America, I knew, though was too falsely proud to let myself know, it was the end of me; and, not long after, the fatal end of him.

It is easy to understand that, when the unflagging, disarming American charm met Dylan's professional charm, it caused a general melting fudge of a sticky, syrupy, irresistible fluid, impossible for such as us: raw from the harsh Welsh backward blacknesses, starved of any public attention; accustomed to the half-said, half-swallowed greeting; the ever-present fear of a taint of effusion; both incapable of saying *No* to any invitation, in case we missed something: to extricate ourselves from, intact. Because it got me, at second hand, as a thankless extension of Dylan, and even then, from that comparatively safe distance, barbed and horned as I was, it was too much for me, and I was left a soulless lump of inanimate meat. So what can Dylan have felt like, in spite of his incredible resistance, and amazingly quick recovery powers? One moment he was flat out, in utter self-abandonment, coughing and heaving up his heart, down to the soles of his boots; the next, dolled up, like a puppy's supper, dapper and spruce, or as near as he could get to it. But there was always a grotesque flaw in the tailor's dummy, which, if I mentioned, I was slaughtered; and if I did not I was blamed for not being interested. Jocularly joking, as though that other prostrate negation, parody of a romantic poet in tubercular convulsions, had no connection in the narrow world, with him. Then nervously twitching, and acrimoniously nagging me, about tiny petty things, which neither of us took seriously; but which outsiders were alarmed into thinking was at least the breaking up of our marriage. But our marriage was not a cobweb house drifting on sand; and we enjoyed the back chat, if nobody else did.

So, with the last burning question: 'Was he better with a hat on or off?' to which I always answered: on; but that did not please him either, because he thought I meant there would be less of him to see. The momentous decision between a bow tie and a long one, with the spotted bow a certain winner; and between two equally dirty, scrofulous pairs of trousers, that had stood, all night, in concertina'd neatness, at the foot of the bed; he was off to the Killer, poetry reading.

Dylan used to read to me in bed, in our first, know-nothing, lamb-sappy days; to be more exact, Dylan may have been a skinny, springy lambkin, but I was more like its buxom mother then, and distinctly recollect carrying him across streams under one arm; till the roles were reversed, and he blew out, and I caved in, through the pressure of family life, and the advent of holy-fire destroying babies. He read interminable Dickens novels, to which he was loyally devoted, and when Dylan was loyally devoted, no sentimental verbosities could change him, though he did bog down somewhere in *Little Dorrit*. He categorically refused to look at Proust, Jane Austen, Tolstoy, Dostoevski, and a lot of the obvious classics, though I furiously asked him, how could he know he wouldn't like them, without bothering to look; but there is no doubt he knew all right. He probably knew, more than anybody, what he liked, and what he didn't like, and what he wanted, and what he didn't want; without, like most people, having to find out. Once again that fiendish element of his days being numbered, comes into it; and all that sickly, stinking stuff about: It had to be, there was no other way; the illogical, poets must die young, ruthless reasoning that made him follow, nobly and foolishly, that exorable pattern. And it was not necessary at all, not without that baby-snatching seduction: there was no hope, after that; to America.

In case my opinions reek of fanaticism, I should like to make clear two things: one, that had I been in Dylan's place, I should have reacted far worse, had my head, not only turned, but swivelling in a thousand fascinating rotating directions, my roots waving riotously overhead; wheras Dylan was, even at his worst, Dylan; and there was one part of him that nobody could get at, that was impregnable, untouchable, not of his own making, but handed down from generations of close-tied, puritanical, family tradition. Handed down from his father, that most unhappy of all men I have ever met; who did all the spade work of casting off the humble beginnings, bettering himself, assiduously cultivating the arts; and finished up a miserable finicky failure: while passing on to Dylan, on a heaped up plate, the fruits of all his years of unrewarding labour. To an outsider his step up the social ladder might not seem so impressive: the transition from farmhouse and railwaymen standards, to schoolmaster in a semi-detached suburban matchbox. But it made the leaping change from lavish rough comforts to pinched penny-pricing gentility; to the taxing position of being looked up to by the neighbours, therefore having to keep up the most trussed-in, belted, camouflaged and gloved system of appearances; instead of being so low you had not got to bother, and could wear and say what you liked, make as much noise, and enjoy yourself, without being stigmatized. No blue-blooded gentleman was a quarter as gentlemanly as Dylan's father. And, though Dylan imagined himself to be completely emancipated from his family background, there was a very strong puritanical streak in him, that his friends never suspected; but of which I got the disapproving benefit.

Those who only saw his bar-leaning on, and on, and on story, with no detectable end, telling; would never credit that other punctilious pettifogging niggler for detail, making such a fuss over the correct dress for me to wear for the Carmarthen market, I mean it, right down to gloves, stockings, shoes; and he would have preferred a hat, but knew that was too much, even for him, to ask of me. His ideal dress for a woman: black from head to foot, relieved with a touch of white, as a concession, a neat starched collar and impeccable cuffs: and the shoes not *too* high, nor *too* low: flaps, sandals, or boots, the most offensive; inconspicuous the key word, and tidily laced, with a prim bow. The final production the direct opposite of me: a politician's perfect secretary. And dandleable.

The other thing, in case there is any misapprehension of my attitude: the American people. To us, of the frozen north, as I always think of our chilblained island, it is very hard at first not to suspect such a basketful of warmth, generosity, and hospitality; but whether it springs pristine from the heart, or is a cultivated college art, it is equally pleasant; and should be taken at face value: appreciated, and responded to; not carped at, as some nasty people do. I am a great believer in whatever you say and do often enough, becoming true; on a lesser scale, but the same line of thought, as the Catholic religion. And the individuals, when you learn to distinguish them: but that is nonsense on my part, they are easily distinguishable: have all the initial, too-good-to-be-trueness, and, as though that weren't enough, they add intelligence: and I don't mean just bright wiffs, but an all around, thorough, comprehensive education; and have not only read, but made theses on, all the books we should have, but never quite did, read. And this remarkable combination they cap with a boyish open enthusiasm; and, what surely is the height of friendliness and tact, which the crustiest crank is not proof against, the genuine desire, or as near as it is possible to get to it, to hear *your* opinion; and a simply stupendous hearing—dripping with sympathy, listening ability. And very soon, in spite of your stubbornest self, you will imperceptibly start softening down into a cushiony pulp, airtight and hermetically corked, under the neutralizing influence.

This is known as the American breaking-in process, which has slaughtered the health and spirit of many a gallant adventurer. But where, I asked myself, is the fly, the itch, the scabies of contention that makes these people fly in all directions, on frivolous errands, and never be still: that makes them put such untiring energy, though not, I think, deep pleasure in the Latin sense, into their amusements, and their zealous touching quest for culture? Perhaps it is just that ant of dissatisfaction that crawls insidiously under the skin, that drives them on to such lengths of munificence, magnificence, grandiloquence. That glosses over poverty, gives the lie to suffering, and makes even of death a grandguignol travesty.

For Dylan, more than anybody, this was a poisonous atmosphere: he needed opposition, gentle, but firm, constant curbing, and a steady dull, homely bed of straw to breed his fantasies in. Nobody ever needed encouragement less, and he was drowned in it. He gave to those wide-open-beaked readings the concentrated artillery of his flesh and blood, and, above all, his breath. I used to come in late and hear, through the mikes, the breath-staining panting: making too much wind for an actor, which he liked to fancy he was, but admitted he hammed unrestrainedly; booming blue thunder into the teen-agers' delighted bras and briefs. And I thought, Jesus, why doesn't he pipe down; they would be just as pleased with a bacon-rind of that rich tinker's spoils, sizzling over the flames.

Then the clustering round for autographs; the students' apple-polished, shining faces, with creaseless wonder: I should have been grateful for a pucker of consternation on those too smooth brows.

But this negligible element was swept aside by the sea of the matriarchs, surging glorious-plumed, perfumed, jewelled; chanting, exclaiming, declaiming; indomitably avalanching to drain the reflex twitches, faint spasms, from the exhausted corpse.

To the best, most patient, understanding wife, my position was not an easy one; but to me, stiff with rancour, my own teeming passions fermenting angrily inside me, it was a hanging execution of my all-important pride. I, deliberately antagonized, said, almost inaudibly, the thing that hurt in the place that hurt; as though I was a rip-roaring delinquent, starved of love and light. When, as far as I can remember, what we suffered from most, was too much freedom, running wild; and the consequent inability to discipline ourselves or join, with any aptitude, a regulated social group. Whether I was loved or not never occurred to me: children do not know that they need love, and only later feel the lack of it. And I am one of the renegades who think grown-ups need it more: that the older they get, and the less love they get, the more they need it: the more they are willing to sell their nothing for it.

I did not for a second resent Dylan's success, except that it took him away from me; I wanted him to have everything that was good for him, made him happy. But an essential condition of that happiness must be me: I had to be the thing that made him happiest. So when he started taking notice of other women: they had never bothered him before seriously; I cannot pretend I was serenely sweet-tongued. In America, they hunted singly, in pairs, and more often in packs, and as soon as one pack was downed and wiped out, from those limitless wide open spaces came fresh hordes, massing numberless, in the tracks of the old. They had never heard of that out-of-date claptrap that a woman should at least make a dissimulation of waiting for the man to make the first move. Not them, they were candidly, if not prepossessingly, spreadeagled, from the first tomtomed rumour of a famous name. They conducted their courting with the ferocity and tenacity of caged amazons; and nothing less than the evaporation of their prey would make them let go.

These thieves of my love, which I was so presumptuously sure was mine only, I bitterly, jealously resented, with all the primitive catfish instincts that I didn't even know were there, and the vile, sinking, retching lurch, that jealousy engenders.

Dylan felt as badly as me, in this respect, at the inconceivability to him of me even distantly contemplating anybody else; and he reacted more abominably than me; no cruelty or physical mutilation was too much, for such an unpardonable crime. It seems extraordinary to me now that we did not kill each other outright, we certainly got dangerously near to it, on those bloodthirsty vengeances.

I wish to God somebody would analyse out of me all the theories, kinks, and bed sores I am guilty of; it would be unadulterated heaven and peace to be without them, but not me. But who, may I ask, in their right senses, would want to stay me, not me, I am sure of that. And what do I know of heaven or peace? I only know they are the opposite of everything I am, and therefore must be good; that there should be nothing I am not prepared to see, hear and feel; that there are *no* certain things that are better kept out of sight; from a skinned rabbit to a Belsen camp. The drooling, spoon-fed imbeciles; the truncated, kindly, refinedly preserved, to save their feelings; it would not be ours, would it? from embarrassing attention: the half men, with brains awhirl, and no hands, the war heroes. And the caged, the barred, from animals to man made animal. However much I rail against my wrongs, I have that much sense left to know that my prison does not compare with the official prison: no sun, no water, no air. And, have I got to say this too, Dylan basely humiliated with the disgusting things he dreaded most; not one organ in his body working in its own right, without mechanical assistance: intravenal feeding, tubes attached blatantly to each vulnerable shy orifice; the head encased in a transparent tent, pumping oxygen into him; the eyes turned up, bulging, unseeing; the breath roaring like a winded horse pounding up a slope; and no Dylan there, no contact. Only the limp hands lying, separate, speaking to me. And everybody knowing it was hopeless and all over; that this was a farcical artificial prolongation of what had already gone.

. . . . .

So now we must be dragged, though not much dragging was needed with Dylan and me, to the inevitable party, after the reading. I do not know what I expected, or wanted, from a party, but ever since I was a child I thought, and still cannot rid myself of the idea, that the gates of some exotic scintillating world would open, diametrically disconnected with my own. So when they turned out to be more stolidly plebeian, humdrumly golden-hearted, in spite of the gallons of frozen fire water that were being consistently poured down, than any stability, security, continuity I had ever known, I had a sense of astonished anti-climax. I was always waiting for something stupendous to happen, to change the whole course of my life; at the back of my mind this stupendous happening was me rising to my feet and electrifying the company with a masterpiece of inspired dance, the like of which had never been seen before. But before I could get myself into the state of not caring what I did, of being bold enough to let myself go, without stint or concern for the ill-fitting dignity of my wifely position, or the repercussing hereafter; I had to wolf down so many fast drinks, that by the time I was ready to take the floor, I could only turn in blind circles, with my skirt over my head. Not very edifying.

When Dylan was the lion, he sat, as though to the manner born, and, as though he had never sat otherwise, couched immovably in the guest-of-honour chair, with his disciples, mostly female, squatting at his feet, agogedly eager: anyone who has seen a spaniel waiting the call of the gun will know what I mean; to devour his next words; which came stumbling, haltingly, one on top of the other, in a broken, stuttering rush. While I, pinioned as far away as possible, was being politely sought out by kind, pitying, neither one thing nor the other, friends; and asked all about my children, their ages, and sexes, etc.; to which I answered in surly monosyllables, I wanted so much to be gracious; and could put on a first class Queen Mother act, on demand; that was the silly contradiction of it; but not with Dylan, not with him monopolizing every ear in the room.

He had the same dislike of me receiving any attention or limelight, not that this happened so frequently. Was this entirely due to a husband and wife relationship, or were we worse than most? It is a sobering thought, and not an inducement to life-long shackles of tyrant habits and accumulating, threadbare-curtained detestation, when under the pressure of too long quilted intimacies, the dears and darlings become *dears* and *darlings:* 'Would you mind moving up, my *dear,* and giving me a little room in the bed.' This never happened to us, but we were nipped early.

But every now and then, through the indistinguishable waves of gush, came a clear cut human being, as dear and familiar as a moth-eaten aunt, who had lain too long at the bottom of a trunk in the attic. No words were needed, the 'understanding' was immediate and mutual; we instinctively held together: a tiny oddly-assorted oasis, in a city of planes, and blocks and sinister sky-scrapers, harbouring millions of hiding lives; each with its separate fascinating drama to be unravelled. And these misfit friends of mine, yes, really mine as well, were not stereotyped, or made to measure: they were the artists, the pariah dogs, and, though I hate to have to say it, the much maligned bohemians. But the bohemians in America are not, by a very long well-creased leg, the same as that original romantic Parisian article, starving in a garret, in an atmosphere, reeking in equal proportions of beards, misunderstood genius, and plain filth.

Dylan and I fell between the two extremes; and though we both had a great loathing for poverty and squalor and did all we could, which was mostly talk, to get out of it, and achieve that ideal state of bourgeois respectability and armchair comfort we both craved; or to be exact, Dylan did; to me there was nothing between the barn and the Salon; we never quite, though we got pretty near, achieved it. It was the same with money: we spent hours planning all the sensible, civilized things we would do with it; eking it out on *moderate* enjoyment, like proper people; vowing and swearing before our Holy Maker, never again to indulge in those racketing wastes that wrought such havoc in us; and in which a good half of our lives was spent. But the valuable quality of moderation was totally lacking in both of us; in one was bad enough, but in both it was fatal. So when the eventual lump came: as far back as I can remember, we were living on hopes of a usually mythical lump coming to solve all our troubles, past and future; the feel of a couple of crinklers was so foreign, and so intoxicating to us, that an immediate celebration, and a riot of spending on all the things we had wanted so long, and a lot more we had not, but just could not resist; was one of those things that the best people simply *had* to do, and it never seriously occurred to us not to, in spite of the messes we got ourselves into. So the back debts went on pressing, only harder, getting steadily more voracious; and the future was laden with threats and wrangling tortures: all the belittling intricacies of money worries. Poor nervous Dylan, who had inherited, besides his father's hypochondria, his acid pessimism for always anticipating the worst, suffered sleepless nights more than me. I had developed, through never having any, and my mother's lofty teaching, that it is vulgar to speak of money, a happy detachment from it, and, though nobody enjoyed the spending of it more, it was a solemn duty with me, yet I could never make myself feel it really mattered, or appreciate the value of it. And of course it was Dylan had the job of making it.

A First Word

ALASTAIR REID

When I was at school in Edinburgh as a boy, I bought for no reason a copy of *Eighteen Poems*, and carried it everywhere until I had pawed the cover off. For no reason, because I was not then faintly interested in poetry as poetry, I read the book with awe, in a pure literary innocence. It was an astonishment that nowhere fitted into the world as I knew it then. Walking home across the park, I would say single lines to myself over and over again. The words seemed to me as absolute and inevitable as air, and I could not conceive of them as ever having been written by anyone. Even now, through the clutter of literary know-how that accumulates round our reading, I think the poems insist on a similar innocence from anyone who wishes to read them well.

The matter of all the scattered fragments of conversation I had, here, there, and everywhere with Dylan Thomas was most of the time words themselves; or if we talked of things of things outside them, the words chosen took more than their customary share of attention. He often suspended talk to roll the last words, his own or anyone else's, round his head. Sometimes, in the middle of someone's sentence, he would hear a word he wanted and would save it, saying it over once or twice to make sure it was still there. He would talk to anyone about anything, listening intently to their words, because it always seemed incredible to him that there could be a word for things. I remember both his delight over sub-titling himself for an advertising man, "The Ugly Suckling," and his astonishment when we found once on a menu that the word "live" backwards spelt "evil." It was the same astonishment that he would fix suddenly on a man rolling barrels in the street, or a face, or an egg.

From the *Yale Literary Magazine*, November, 1954, p. 20. Reprinted with special permission of the *Yale Literary Magazine*.

He was, I think, very shy of the unspoken; when he met people, he would always wait, outside of them, until they had spoken for a time. Once in New York, not long before he died, he was talking about writing. "When I experience anything," he said, "I experience it as a thing and a word at the same time, both equally amazing." He told me once that writing the "Ballad of the Long Legged Bait" had been like carrying a huge armful of words to a table he thought was upstairs, and wondering if he could reach it in time, or if it would still be there.

The relation between a poet and his poetry, like that between husbands and wives, is often very far below the surface, unexpected, confusing, perhaps impossible to find. With Dylan Thomas, it was clean and clear. When he was busy with them, existence and language were to him twin miracles. His poetry was trying always to make them simultaneously dawn, as they dawned on him. It seems to me that his poetry, whatever its literary fate, covers prior to anything the miracle of the first speaking creation, the wonder of words bringing about the wonder beyond them.* And sometimes, in the middle of talk, one saw in the same way the man who praised existence because it would have been inconceivable to him not to, who wrote with a grateful amazement that such a thing as poetry was possible at all.

* It is not so much poetry about a world which exists in time and place; it is poetry which is continually bringing a world into existence, as for the first time.

Recollections of Dylan Thomas

GEOFFREY GRIGSON

Ditch, Dirty Dylan, the Changeling, the Ugly Suckling, the Disembodied Gland—these early private names were still not invented. The rumour which was to increase to the legend of the purest genius had scarcely begun, at this moment, in the Thirties, when, in a tea-room, an awkward *Mr* Thomas faced an awkward, also an unconvinced, *Mr* Myself across a corner table. The tea-room was in a courtyard between the dull quiet of the Temple and the dull mumble of Fleet Street.

Young *Mr* Thomas was up from Cwmdonkin Drive, Swansea, in big London, where poets existed. He was uncertain of his part. He might, sitting there in the corner below the grey panes, have been acting a new Rimbaud. In features, still unpoached at this time, he looked rather like the Rimbaud portrayed in a group by Fantin Latour. But he had not heard of Rimbaud, in Swansea; he wore a different poetic uniform, imitated, I rather think, from a frontispiece of Rossetti when young. Curls thatched his head, a Bohemian poetry tie flowed down and out below his soft collar. He talked poetry, his biographers might be surprised to learn. Young but not quite so young *Mr* Myself suspiciously regarded this tie, and suspiciously heard a proffer of names he had not expected. Rossetti was one of them, Francis Thompson was another, James Thomson (B. V.) was a third. Stephen Spender, though was a fourth.

Names, as I say, were proffered: were held out, withdrawn, held out again, much as one might offer bits of food to a beast of uncertain nature and temper with whom one found onself unexpectedly but ineluctably roomed or cabined or boxed.

Our presence with each other was Stephen Spender's indirect doing.

From *The London Magazine,* September, 1957, pp.39–45. Reprinted by permission of the author.

Odd poems above the name Dylan Thomas had appeared in the *Sunday Referee*, in the Poets' Corner conducted by the odd Victor Neuberg, a little man who for a while had been changed and enlarged into a camel, so it was rumoured, by the satanist Aleister Crowley. I think Stephen Spender must have been one of the first unloony persons to remark on these poems and to enquire about their author, so fixing a label to him as 'someone to be watched.' I recall Spender assuring me at any rate that I ought to ask Dylan Thomas for contributions to *New Verse*. He may have given me Dylan's address. Letters had gone to Wales, letters and poems in pale blue ink in that slow, leftward-sloping, pre-adolescent, unpersuasive hand from which Dylan never freed himself, had returned from 5 Cwmdonkin Drive and perhaps another Swansea address; and at this encounter we now *mistered* each other and investigated each other and *mistered* each other again, in the grey tea-room.

Dylan had not yet succeeded enough, or sloughed off enough of lowest-middle-class Swansea, to resemble the painting of him by John. He was not so cocky. He needed assurance, with which he was never generously and liberatingly supplied. But London quickly intimidated him less, and was entered by him more frequently. Art-adulating zanies in Parton Street, near Red Lion Square, frequenting a café on one side and a bookshop on the other, eyed him first like schoolboy butterfly-collectors eyeing a Camberwell Beauty on the wing. They were persons of a kind needing shots of the notion of art as others need shots of insulin; of a kind put on heat by contact with artists of any degree. If Mr. John Malcolm Brinnin's America is fantastically full of such people, whom Dylan Thomas learnt rapidly to use and kept on using till they lapped around his death in a New York hospital, the London supply of them is never to be despised.

Modernism's higher command, whether it might be Wyndham Lewis hidden in Notting Hill Gate or T. S. Eliot cocooned in his publishing office in Russell Square, was not impressed; Eliot at least was offered and considered—and then refused—a collection of his poems. Nor, although Stephen Spender helped to float him, at least by talk, was Dylan Thomas then sure enough of himself to approach the Inner Command of the Thirties. (I use this image of a 'command', in either case, approximately, or as a metaphor.) If the zanies of all levels bored him, at first, if others repelled him or scared him, he found friends in London who were independent of the Commands. One was the poet Norman Cameron, now dead, who was linked to

Robert Graves rather than to Eliot. Another was Bernard Spencer, linked only to himself. I was a third, Ruthven Todd, the universal friend newly down from Edinburgh, became a fourth.

We caused him less trepidation, kept him less on edge. Our appetites, our laziness or easygoingness, our scepticism, were less forbidding. He could enjoy with us verbal jokes and myths and inventions which committed him to no decision, no ideal of mental or spiritual conduct. He could trust himself to clown, to swear, to talk of women, or sex; he could borrow our beds, our underclothes and our cash, be washed, be on occasion mended and dry-cleaned by our wives; and he could learn from us co-ordinating signs and landmarks of a Thirties London. If I was Doc, the Doctor, Doc Terry or Terry to him, Norman Cameron, that aloof and blunt and uncommonsensible poet, who said to his first wife after the consummatory act of their marriage *Thanks very much* and turned over to sleep, was rapidly christened Normal by Dylan Thomas—much as a large man in the RAF is christened Tiny.

Serial jokes and myths—word jokes and word myths—ran through our association as they run in families; especially a serial myth of advertisements for *night custard,* a Thomas invention and patent, an alchemical liquid almost, which satisfied, with every obscene twist, that 'night starvation' already postulated, with Cameron's help (since he was a copywriter), in the advertisements for one of those beverages you drink hot before going to bed. We could make fun-figures out of critics, prigs, editors, poets, holy lady poets whom we did not like; we could give them names and play with them.

Also we could advance our curious elf in the way of reputation, and in the way at least of making drink money, if not a living. In one character I could publish poems by him in *New Verse,* in another I could give him books to review on the *Morning Post.*

Which books? Thrillers; of which week by week he devoured half-a-dozen or more, reviewed them or, as the writers would have thought, misreviewed them, with a gay improbable wordage, and then sold them. Between ourselves, and the zanies, and Swansea, Dylan Thomas now appeared, disappeared, appeared again—usually without money.

Rossetti and the waterfall tie had vanished. Dylan Thomas found that London preferred to aesthetic debauch, or its uniform, the Toughish Boy, the Boy with a Load of Beer, in and out, so boringly, of the pubs. The part was more congenial and more genuine, with a scope for virtuosity. It was defensive, already—defence, release, escape. And by this time I suspect that Dylan had been reading Hart Crane, and *The Bridge*.

Here, then, for us, certainly for me, was Ditch, here was Dirty Dylan—since we retaliated with our own names. Generally he was the Toughish Boy elsewhere; he reappeared from zanies, from sluts (often combined), from drunkenness, he needed washing, so did his shirts, he needed a little regularity, a little sobriety; and accepted them all, for short whiles. In fears of disease, he had to be taken to doctors. I found him one day in the bath in my flat in Keats Grove, pitying himself and mocking himself in verbal antics because a pink rash beautifully enflamed him back and front. Hauled down by bus to the neighbourhood of the British Museum, to an Irish doctor, Dylan stripped to his meagre body. The doctor assured him he had no need to worry, after all; laughed at him, and pulled down a coloured chart, still more lividly pink than Dylan himself, to give an accurate warning of what the symptoms *might* be, another time. For a minor illness he did retire before long to Wales and to its more comfortable familiar things, begging me by letter that retreat and illness should not be mentioned in London, for fear of curtailing his activities when he recovered and returned.

I agree to Dylan's companionableness, to his clowning, fooling, mocking talent, to, best of all, a certain primal quality, rooted far behind our backs in suburban Swansea, in chock-a-block Welsh cemeteries, in the hilly viridian farms between Laugharne and Llanstephan or in the Gower; but he was also the snotty troll, *to himself enough*, when it suited him, he was also the changeling who had been lifted from under the foxgloves and set in the proper and decent calvinistic bed. He was also cartilaginous, out of humanity, the Disembodied Gland, which was my coinage, Ditch, which was Norman Cameron's, the Ugly Suckling, which was Bernard Spencer's, indicating a wilful and at times nasty babyishness. When he disappeared, it was a relief; when he reappeared, a pleasure.

Adaptation or adjustment continued. One heard less from Dylan about James Thomson (B. V.), who had satisfied in him both a morbidity and a leaning to grandiloquence, less about Francis Thompson (for whose effect on Dylan Thomas the inquisitive should turn to the *Ode to the Setting Sun*, in which stuffy insufferable poem they will find the pattern of Dylan Thomas lines, questions, verbs and other tricks—

It is the falling star that trails the night—

Who scarfed her with the morning?—

Who lit the furnace of the mammoth's heart?
Who shagged him like Pilatus' ribbed flanks?—

Who girt dissolved lightnings in the grape?
Summered the opal with an Irised flush?

—as well as the *fons et origo* of the Thomas attitude of birth-copulation-death:

For birth hath in itself the germ of death,
But death hath in itself the germ of birth.
It is the falling acorn buds the tree,
The falling rain that bears the greenery,
The fern-plants moulder when the ferns arise,
For there is nothing lives but something dies,
And there is nothing dies but something lives.)

It would be exaggeration to say that he substituted much other reading. He seldom opened books in these days, unless they were thrillers or dreadfuls. Having introduced himself as a poet, he ceased to talk of at any rate dead poets. He was innocent of learning or intellectualism or intellectual appetite, so much, so obviously, that one now felt sure a development, even a continuance, would be impossible beyond a point which must quite soon be reached. Dylan might seem a hole in the ground up through which life or a biological and mortal essence was sulphureously boiling, bubbling, troubling, confusing; but he was not worshipful (we should have worshipped him readily if he had been); he was adding nothing viable to the automatic acceptances and accumulations of childhood, which were not inexhaustible. He might only have more explication to do. It seemed to me also (it still does) that a keener sense in his appreciators and magnifiers would have recognized how much decayed romanticism there is in his phrases and rhythms, much of it twisted arse-versily and new-applied, as if Sir William Watson, in the *Times*, had taken to a symbolism of up wanton up. I published poems by Dylan doubting (as I still do) whether they had not a softer inside below a soft outside.

Dylan, though, was also something other than his poems, other than the oblong grubby scraps off a lined pad on which they appeared or from which they were amalgamated. He had enough magnetism, though one leg of the magnet might exert repulsion, to cause worry by his upsets or difficulties. We may not have detected every symptom or joined up the ones we did detect, we may not entirely have seen (it was clearer afterwards) how Dylan was being compelled to live beyond his spiritual or intellectual income—or capital; a compulsion which explained some of his defensive clowning and a good deal of his load of beer. (So far as I know the first of the genius-parties at which Dylan defended himself, or saved or tried to save his face, by being drunk, was given for him by Cyril Connolly in the King's Road in Chelsea, a reluctant, beery Dylan having been despatched, late, by Norman Cameron from a bar in the Fulham Road: he told the celebrities—whose dinner had been spoiled—dirty chestnuts they had all heard in their childhood.) Occasionally, though, he hinted at TB, and spitting blood; he drank too much, he was too frequently ill or out of sorts. It was after some such hints, after drinking too much had sobered him and frightened him a little, after the beginning of the genius-hunting parties, that Dylan and I went off for some weeks, in a summer before the war, to Donegal.

There was a valley above the Atlantic entered by no road, not even a well-defined path, over a ridge of rock, peat and heather. In this valley of Glen Lough between Ardara and Killybegs, I knew a solitary farmer and his wife. A year or two before, the place had been discovered by the American artist Rockwell Kent, who liked its wilderness and loneliness between mountains, or mountains and lakes, and the sea. He had concreted a donkey-shed into a sleeping-room and studio, and had abandoned it. It was in that shed, on the edge of a small stream from the lakes, that Dylan and I lived for a while, building turf fires to dry ourselves out and keeping a quart bottle of potheen—illegal, colourless whisky—hidden in a potato patch outside, below a lushness of chickweed. If indeed he had been in danger of TB, I daresay he ought not to have been in the dampness and softness of Ireland; but here he was drinking less potheen, at any rate, than he had drunk of beer and spirits in London, and less porter than milk and buttermilk.

The Swansea Changeling, who might at any time go back to his people, waded through mixed flames of loosestrife and corn marigold which floored the valley. From the cliffs he watched gannets drop and fleck the Atlantic; or climbing steeply to the lakes at the back of the farm and the converted stable, we shouted up to the surrounding, ringing mountains *We are the Dead*, for the multiple echo to reply in sequence *We are the Dead, the Dead, the Dead, the Dead.* We shouted to these mountains above the lake one evening till we frightened ourselves, stumbling down afterwards through heather and fern and sog to the comfort of the cottage, where Dylan stretched stained white feet, Swansea feet, to the warm turf, alongside the brown, huge feet of the farmer Dan Ward. At times we sneaked down the enormous cliffs to a cold soul-tightening ocean, and sang the *Ram of Derbyshire* to black seals. There was no sand, no gravel, below these cliffs, only white pebbles shaped like eggs or heads by Brancusi. We drew faces on them with black crayon, we named them, set them against rock, and cracked them, with fling after fling of other huge white pebbles, into literary nothingness—since the faces were of authors—and literary oblivion. Several faces were those of people who were to find Dylan, to Dylan's dangerous surprise, a vessel of holiness.

I do not know how much, if at all, Dylan was moved by this peculiar valley in which man was camping as he camps so small in the cruel wilderness of Hercules Seghers. It is again, though, my feeling that he received only what was given to him by childhood's environment of place, person, and literature.

> Stroke and a stress that stars and storms deliver,
> That guilt is hushed by, hearts are flushed by and melt—

He, in a way, knew that energizing, quietening, flushing and melting influence, that preamble to a deeper poetry; but, in Hopkins's added words, what did Dylan Thomas *fable*, what central reality did he then miss, what reality *riding time like a river?*

After about a fortnight I had to go home, Dylan staying in the glen for several more weeks, looked after by Dan Ward and Rose Ward, who felt his magnetism—to their cost, because he left suddenly one day, walking over the mountains towards Wales or London without paying them (though he had ample money) a penny of the agreed sum for all his food and his lodging.

Certainly out of memory I could fish other details, it might be meetings of Dylan Thomas and George Orwell, in a Hampstead bookshop in which Orwell worked, then less known than Dylan himself, it might be the nature of drawings in coloured chalks, inept, powdery, lurid, like horror-film images, or horror-comic images, green and pink essays of an amateur expressionism, which Dylan left with me and which were destroyed in the war. '*Only from the work the biography acquires significance*'—so it has been declared of one of the great committed poets of mankind (and I happen to be writing this in his town, which is Tübingen, above his cool reflective river). '*No life'*—no detail of life—*'concerns us that has not found adequate expression and shape.'*

Ask then whether the work, in this case—the answer must be your affair—contradicts the life. Or was there with Dylan Thomas too atrocious a war between what was given and what so temptingly was dangled and accepted?

A Memoir

PAMELA HANSFORD JOHNSON

I wrote to Dylan Thomas in September, 1933, admiring a poem of his printed in *The Sunday Referee.* He replied at once, and we corresponded steadily until the spring of 1934, when he came to stay with my family. He was nineteen, I was twenty-one. He arrived very late on a dull grey evening in spring, and he was nervous, as I was. 'It's nice to meet you after all those letters. Have you seen the Gauguins?' (He told me later that he had been preparing the remark about the Gauguins all the way from Swansea, and having made it, felt that his responsibility towards a cultural atmosphere was discharged.)

He was very small and light. Under a raincoat with bulging pockets, one of which contained a quartern bottle of brandy, another a crumpled mass of poems and stories, he wore a grey, polo-necked sweater, and a pair of very small trousers that still looked much too big for him. He had the body of a boy of fourteen. When he took off the pork-pie hat (which, he also told me later, was what he had decided poets wore) he revealed a large and remarkable head, not shaggy—for he was visiting—but heavy with hair the dull gold of threepenny bits springing in deep waves and curls from a precise middle parting. His brow was very broad, not very high: his eyes, the colour and opacity of caramels when he was solemn, the colour and transparency of sherry when he was lively, were large and fine, the lower rims rather heavily pigmented. His nose was a blob; his thick lips had a chapped appearance; a fleck of cigarette paper was stuck to the lower one. His chin was small, and the disparity between the breadth of the lower and upper parts of his face gave an impression at the same time comic and beautiful. He looked like a brilliant, audacious child, and at once my family loved and fussed over him as if he were one.

From *Adam International Review,* No. 238, 1953.

He stayed with us for a week or so on that occasion, for six weeks on the second, and for varying periods over a year or more. Gauguin wore off quickly. We walked over the Common on summer evenings to a little pub in Clapbham Old Town, sometimes we took the bus to Chelsea—which seemed to us a cultural Mecca—and sat in the garden of the Six Bells, watching the little fountain drip on to its muddy stones, the men playing on the bowling green, which was still there in those days. I read his poems, and criticized them with a kind of bold reverence; he read mine, and criticized them by ridicule which was hilariously funny and also perfectly just. Sometimes we wrote doggerel poems together, in alternate lines.

At home, he liked my mother to type his stories from his dictation. Sometimes there were stories of inconceivable impropriety by anybody's standards. My mother (abandoning the keys): 'Dylan, you *cannot* say that.' Dylan, with a wave of the hand: 'Put it in, Mrs. Johnson, just put it in. It's all right—I assure you, it's *perfectly* all right.'

In our quiet, middle-class neighborhood he not infrequently caused a stir; he meant to. I remember the disquiet of my aunt, one cold and foggy autumn morning, when she came downstairs to find Dylan about to go out into the busy main road wearing a blue and violet paisley dressing-gown that had once belonged to my six-foot uncle, and his own new, black, poetic felt hat. 'Dylan! What *do* you think you're doing?' Dylan (cowed, but with a look of unutterable appeal): 'Only going for cigarettes.' My aunt: 'Dylan, you can't go out like that! Come in at once!' Dylan (raising his hat in respect and acquiescence): 'Yes, Miss Howson. If you like. There may be something in what you say.'

I lost touch with him at the beginning of the war. I only knew him as a boy. He is that to me still.

A Visit to Laugharne

BILL READ

I met Dylan Thomas during the course of his first American visit when, among hundreds of others, I had been one of those who were called upon to help keep him entertained, housed, fed and on schedule as he went from one reading engagement to another. When, in July, 1951, I was in London and had the chance to be his guest for a long weekend at his home in Laugharne, Wales, I was delighted to accept the invitation.

The train trip through Wales to Carmarthen was one of startling contrasts. After Cardiff with its monumental piles of Victorian baroque architecture came the intense wet green hills alternating with the black slag piles of the mining country and, every now and then, cheerless towns of grimy stone. Among so much industrial blight, I thought somewhat wistfully of what Wales must have been like when King Arthur rode here, and suddenly I knew: the train curved alongside a small stream and there in the distance was a castle crowning a hill. With swirling white clouds for a background, the scene was like a manuscript illumination from the twelfth century. Soon the train pulled into Carmarthen. When I stepped off onto the platform, there was Dylan Thomas, round, bundled, and fiercely smoking a small cigar. We climbed into a big old car he had rented and set off.

It was twilight now, and the vague landscapes through which we passed seemed idyllic compared with all the blackened towns and the miles of hideously ugly hills withered by furnace fumes. We stopped to have a bitter—a pint of beer—in several pubs on our way. Dylan, grandly dressed in a new tweed suit and a colorful ascot, was eager to hear about mutual friends in America and we chatted kindly and unkindly of them as we made our interrupted journey toward Laugh-

A revised transcript of a radio broadcast over Boston University's station WBUR, October, 1957. Reprinted by permission of Bill Read.

arne. This is the town where Dylan had lived on and off since 1936 and which was soon to become famous as the original of "Llareggub," the town of *Under Milk Wood.* The dominating feature of Laugharne is the twelfth century castle in ruins that stands on the edge of the sea, covered with vines, crumbling to the ground. Around the castle on higher land away from the shore are whitewashed two-storey houses. Tightly built and medieval, they seem to huddle together for protection. Nearly all of the houses are built on the same plan: broad, two-storey, with a chimney in the gable at each end. A wide central hall goes through to the back door; one can look straight from the front door into the garden behind. The outside stone walls are coated with centuries of paint so that all the joints have disappeared and only an undulating, adobe-like, surface shows. We drove through the main street, past the town hall with its bell-topped tower, past the castle, and down to the edge of the sea where we stopped at "Phil's pub," officially known as the Cross Keys. There I could see that the town was not without pride in the success of its local boy: prominently displayed on the wall of the pub was a large framed photograph of Dylan at the age of seventeen or so—a childish oval face, large round eyes under a mass of uncombed ringlets. This delicate creature in a homespun sweater was an image of freshness and innocence. Dylan himself, now thirty-seven, had the same shining eyes as he stood beside it, even more tousled hair, and a vastly more mature and heavy face. We were drinking our first bitter when Caitlin, his wife, (whom he called "Cat") came in and joined us. She was tall, athletic, much more beautiful than I had imagined. Taller and slimmer than Dylan, she had variegated blonde hair casually brushed back, and a strikingly fair and glowing complexion. Her blue eyes were full of curiosity—they seldom looked directly at you and there was a kind of glaze over them which suggested a caution or perhaps a characteristic reserve. The pub was crowded, everyone seemed to know everyone else, and along with round upon round of drinks someone passed to us a jar of tiny pickled cockles. Mid-evening we left and, since it was low tide, chose to follow the uneven shore line toward the Thomas house. As we stalked off through the tall grasses in an afterglow of sea-light, the ivy-covered parapets of the castle threw long shadows down. Dylan strolled behind with a friend while Caitlin and I blazed a trail through the marshy grass and around the fishing boats sitting heavily in the soft sand. Now and then we had to leap rivulets and when we came to a particularly marshy section, I carried Caitlin piggy-back, slipping and sliding, and dropping my glasses which were quickly washed out to sea. The bay was very shallow, and the ebb tide exposed acres of sand flats in the dwindling light. After picking our way for half a mile or so, we passed through a gate in a stone wall and arrived at the pink three-storey Boat House hanging to a cliffside at the water's edge. Like other houses of the village, it had a stark beauty—a doorway in the middle, chimneys at each end, an unadorned facade. Its situation becomes particularly dramatic at high tide—the water comes in and laps around the retaining wall of the terrace so that, if you wanted to, you could dive off the living room balcony into the sea. Because of the precipitous bluff to which the house clings like a barnacle, the lower floor, with the kitchen and dining room, has a ground level entrance off the terrace; the second floor with the living room has a ground floor entrance on the front; and the third floor bedrooms are actually *below* the level of the entrance road which runs along above the house.

After dinner and more talk we retired—I to the room of young Llewelyn who was away on holiday. Now an economics student at Harvard, Llewelyn eight years ago had his room covered with pictures of cars and boats and planes. In the morning I met the two younger children. Aeron, a girl about seven, was shy, only making her presence known by squeals when her mother combed and braided her long flaxen hair. The darling of the family was obviously cherubic, little three-year old Colm (pronounced "colum"). His hair was soft as corn silk, the color of white gold, and massed in ringlets over his head. With his button nose and gleaming eyes he was a miniature of Dylan in his "angelic" period—a tiny Harpo Marx.

Dylan helped to prepare the breakfast of kippers and eggs on toast, and, as usual, we ate our meal out on the lower terrace beside the bay. Should there be any bread left over, I was told, it should be put in a wall basket reserved for "swan food." Later in the day wild swans would fly in at high tide to be fed their daily rations. Dylan proposed that we make a trip to the westernmost point in Wales, St. David's Head, and mid-morning we set out in a hired, vintage Buick with Billy Williams, the brother-in-law of the inn-keeper, as our driver. We went along the southern coast of Wales with low, rounded, well-defined hills to our right most of the time and shingly beaches to our left. We had taken swimming suits but the grey and misty wind coming in off the ocean made the water uninviting. Caitlin, however, was eager to plunge in and did, although she was alone in her chilly dip. Dylan seemed happy in his role as sight-seeing guide, and we stopped in an old village, Haverford West, for lunch in a pub and to buy fish for the next day.

The visible landscape is curiously irregular at the far end of Wales because all of the roads are lined with dense hedges which, most of the time, prevent one from seeing anything else. Then, suddenly, as one tops a hill, a whole checkerboard scene comes into view—fields of grass divided by hedgerows into a quilt pattern, dark green lines imposed on light green squares. Our goal was the ancient and tottering Cathedral of St. David. Connected with the church is a monastery in even greater ruin, with only fragments of walls still standing. When the sun came out faintly through the clouds of mist, we took snapshots among which was the beautiful one which was used as the cover on the October, 1955, issue of the *Atlantic Monthly.*

Next morning, Dylan asked me if I would like to see the "shack" where he worked. From the Boat House we climbed up a precipitous path and walked a hundred paces or so to the little one-room building that had the look of a gardener's tool house. About nine feet square, it had a stove and a work-table in front of a large window looking east out over the estuary. Another window on the south looked toward the village, the castle, and in the distance Sir John's Hill. The floor was littered with discarded versions of poems. There were dozens of scrappy revisions of poems everywhere, and Dylan began to talk about the poem he was working on—"Poem on His Birthday." Before he began the poem at all, he had the plan all worked out: it was to be about a poet who realizes he has arrived at "half his bible span." He means both to celebrate and spurn his birthday in a house high among trees, overlooking the sea. Birds and fishes move under and round him on their dying ways, and he, a craftsman in words, toils "towards his own wounds which are waiting in ambush for him." The poet "sings in the direction of his pain." Birds fly after the hawks that will kill them. Fishes swim towards the otters which will eat them. He sees herons walking in their shrouds, which is the water they fish in; and he, who is progressing, afraid, to his own fiery end, in the cloud of an atomic explosion, knows that, out at sea, sea-animals, who attack and eat other sea-animals, are tasting the flesh of their own death. Now exactly half of his three score and ten years have gone. He looks back at his times: his loves, his hates, all he has seen, and sees the logical progress of death in every thing he has been and done. His death lurks for him, and for all, in the next lunatic war. And, still singing, still praising the radiant earth, still loving, though remotely, the animal creation also gladly pursuing their inevitable and grievous ends, he goes towards his. Why should he praise God and the beauty of the world, as he moves to horrible death? He does not like the deep zero dark, and the nearer he gets to it, the louder he sings, the higher the salmon leap, the shriller the birds carol.

The extent of his study of the theme and the sublimation of many of its more obvious features can be seen by comparing this early plan with the final poem in the volume *In Country Sleep.* A manuscript of the poem shows how radically the wording of the poem was to be changed even after the metrical scheme had been established. In stanza three, for example, at least eight different adjectives were considered for the phrase "of the drowned streets": foaming, fuming, bearing, whelping, hymning, weaving, teeming, racking. When the final choice was made, it was not the adjective but the noun that was changed; and the line finally reads "of drowned ship towns." As an ultimate example of the lengths to which he carried revision, two versions of stanza nine are revealing. At an early stage it read as follows:

> Who is the light of straight
> And gulling Heaven where souls grow wild
> As windflowers in the woods:
> Oh, may this birthday man by the shrined
> And aloof heron's vows
> Grieve until the night pelts down and then
> Count his blessings aloud!
> May he make, in his thirty-fifth death,
> His last sweet will and shroud.

In its final version the syllabic count and rhythmic beat is carefully retained, but only one line survives unchanged:

> Who is the light of old
> And air shaped Heaven where souls grow wild
> As horses in the foam:
> Oh, let me midlife mourn by the shrined
> And druid heron's vows
> The voyage to ruin I must run,
> Dawn ships clouted aground,
> Yet, though I cry with tumbledown tongue,
> Count my blessings aloud:

Over the work-table in the Shack was a large, striking photograph of Walt Whitman and under this was a smaller picture of William Blake. The walls were covered with pictures clipped from magazines and with reproductions of paintings: a portrait of Edward

Thomas, one of Frank Harris, a youthful Edith Sitwell, Marianne Moore. The prints included a Chinese painting, a Cartier-Bresson photograph of Mexicans crowned with thorns (this partially covered another print, a handsome French renaissance treatment of *le beau tétin*), an Italian primitive, a photo of huge Indian street dolls, a Rouault, and many others.

On the following morning I went with Dylan to visit his parents in their house in town, "The Pelican." Mrs. Thomas was a lively little white-haired lady with black-rimmed glasses who seemed delighted to have callers. We soon went out to the kitchen garden where Mr. Thomas and I gathered beans and lettuce and potatoes. Dylan's schoolmaster father who was convalescing from a recent illness, was a small man, very gentle in manner, and very carefully dressed. Dylan, during his father's illness, had written a villanelle which began, "Do not go gentle into that good night." Dylan said that he thought he would not publish it while his father was alive.

On the way back we stopped at Brown's Hotel to have a bitter in the kitchen of Dylan's friend, Mrs. Ivy Williams, a charming, motherly person who, I learned, was especially good to know because one could always be sure of a bitter on her premises, whether or not closing hours were in effect.

At lunchtime we ate around the old wooden table on the Boat House terrace, watching the movements of sea birds on the sand flats. One odd inky black bird stood upright with both wings stretched out for minutes at a time perfectly motionless. The herons fished for eels; there were many strange bird calls; and the fishes made loud plunks as they leaped out of the water. During our conversation, Caitlin embarrassed Dylan when she quoted him as saying one should never use "like" or "as" in a poem, and he tried to deny that he had ever said it.

His critical opinions, it seemed to me, were often contradictory—usually based on the announced principle that he preferred to judge poetry on the quality of the poet as a man, not merely on what he produced. But even this opinion was inconsistently held, too. Later I heard him make strong statements of his admiration for Louis MacNeice, yet at this moment he said that the most over-rated poets in England were Louis MacNeice and Stephen Spender, and, in America, Archibald MacLeish and Robert Frost. He was full of amusing stories, such as the one about his poet friend Norman Cameron who, he said, had bought up and burned many copies of George Barker's first book because he didn't want anyone to read such bad poems. Mostly

Dylan preferred to talk about people and not about poetry, least of all about criticism. Once when a critical piece, flattering to him, was read aloud he went off into a mock-heroic rhapsody about how the curly-headed poet overcome with hyacinthine praise threw himself to the swans in the sea.

In the afternoon I wandered off alone through the town and up Sir John's Hill. The road had characteristically high-walled sides—earth embankments about four or five feet high topped with hedge fences—that made walking up the hill like going through a roofless tunnel or an eighteenth century maze. Finally, high on top, I leaped a fence into a meadow where there was a panoramic view of the countryside, the town, and the Bay. On the way home I passed through St. Martin's Churchyard where Dylan now is buried. On the old stones were rough-made verses like this one from 1705:

> Mortality behold and fear
> What a change of flesh is here.

My four days with the Thomases were about to come to an end, and when we had said goodbye on the next morning. I walked along the cliff path above the house with a new sense of Dylan and the remoteness and quietude of his creative life. In spite of many evidences of domestic discord that no one attempted to keep from the eyes of a visitor, Dylan had been a gracious host, a warm paterfamilias, and even a Welshman proud of his native countryside. As Billy Williams drove me to Carmarthen to catch the train, I could not help feeling how vastly different was his life at home from the boisterous public behavior that had been the cause of so much comment in America. Then, as if to supply an explanation I had unconsciously been searching for, the little castle loomed into sight, riding its elevation as though it still guarded a special and very peaceful corner of the world.

The Death, and Some Dominions of It

WINFIELD TOWNLEY SCOTT

What colour is glory? death's feather? . . .

Why do people *like* to have a poet die?

I am asking a question more complex than I can answer, though I am sure there are several answers which, if they could be synthesized, would combine to a profound answer. Among surviving poets there are certain to be some, when so famously successful a poet as Dylan Thomas dies, who find increased satisfaction with a world bereft of a talent too obviously bigger than their own: they are like those kings—in a line of Elizabeth Barrett Browning's—who after the fall of Napoleon "creep out to feel the sun." (The event really avails such poets nothing; but I am not arguing that any of the assumed advantages in the event are sane—they are merely human.) Mediocrity usually hates genius, yet there are still others of the lesser tribe who find some contentment in association with the celebrated, and so in his death a larger and more manipulative reflected glory.

Still, the satisfaction runs far beyond this or that small literary crowd. There has been this past year a widespread excitement. People have read obituaries, have read memorial articles, have heard of memorial meetings, have listened to broadcasts of Thomas' recordings of his prose and verse—people who heretofore have known nothing of Dylan Thomas; and they are impressed with Thomas and pleased with themselves. Why?

Well, they are illustrating the old saw that a dead poet is a great

From the *Yale Literary Magazine*, November, 1954, pp. 13–14. Reprinted with special permission of the *Yale Literary Magazine*.

man whereas the fellow who lives next door and writes poetry is obviously a damned fool: they are acquainted with this one—how therefore can he be important or immortal? But there is a deeper psychology than this. I think people know, even when they know little about poetry and care less, that a poet serves Truth. Truth is an unpredictable, a dangerous thing; avoided by most people. A poet is a rebuke, a higher and more responsible consciousness in our midst. He is, while alive, more alive than most people.

The most people do not, of course, so phrase these things at all: they express them, rather, in at least an impatience with or at most a resentment of the impraticable, lifelong preoccupation of a poet. His very responsibility indeed is translated commonly as irresponsibility. Nevertheless, history assigns an "importance" to the great, the safely great, poets of the past. Now when a Dylan Thomas enters that past, people have him where they can use him, where they can control him, where they want him. And with a heightened satisfaction when their skepticisms are borne out, when as in Thomas' case the death seems wilful and his children require (of course!) the benefits of a Fund. This way, they can have a poet and eat him too. Yes, all the world loves a dead poet.

Death is the greatest dramatist: it gives final meaning to any life and objectifies it so all who will may see. And this is, as to Thomas, a time for regrets and laments and elegies. It should not be a time for lies. For how shall we give him the honor of understanding if we do not try fully to understand his life and his work? If we do not see that his poems are all parts of a single poem, and some but not all magnificent, if we do not define his limitations, we shall not define him; nor ourselves. And it is that ultimate definition for which poets exist.

While for his family and others who personally loved him Thomas' death is tragic loss, there are signs it was not tragic for him or for literature. The expense of energy on lesser things than his poems, the marked decrease of poetic production in his last decade, the forced and sometimes Yeats—or Thomas—derivative not of what he did produce: all this may mean he was spared a long Swinburnian death-in-life. The talents, after all, were similar; like Swinburne, Thomas was an intoxicant of words and with a few young things to say.

His potent nostalgias were two: back to childhood and forward to oblivion. Edith Sitwell thinks Thomas "knew that he must die young." Must, in what sense? He speaks in his 35th-birthday poem of "midlife" in a way which seems not to mean "amidst life" but, literally, "half-way to threescore and ten":

Oh, let me midlife mourn by the shrined
And druid heron's vows
The voyage to ruin I must run, . . .

No, I think (though I did not know him) he did not feel he was fated to die young. But the evidence shows that he pursued self-destruction and accomplished it: he wanted to die. Why?

The question would seem easy if asked about a poet who had suffered neglect, had no influence, felt either mistaken or ignored. On the contrary Thomas, supremely in my generation, received every kind of exterior reward. But the real sense of failure is as private as despair, and no man knows what another conception of it may be. That stress between childhood and death admitted little of adult life into his poetry. Did the genes which made possible "Fern Hill" and "Poem in October" seed also a fatal drive? We have yet to discover and decide. Did Thomas, like an athlete, feel that he had had his triumph? Well, he has it; and after the curious repercussions of his death are gone—the confused mourning of it, the leeching upon it, the goddamned gratifications out of it—a few of his pages, fixed among the English poets', will carry that triumph still.

Dylan Thomas and Company

AUGUSTUS JOHN

It was at the Fitzroy Tavern that I first met Dylan Thomas. William Empson was also present. It was a crowded evening with Nina Hamnett well to the fore. Dylan and I became fast friends and later met frequently in London, Hampshire and Laugharne. In fact it was in the latter place that Dylan met Caitlin Macnamara, an old friend of mine, and instantly fell in love with her as indeed she did with him. At this time Dylan was a cherubic young fellow with a shock of auburn hair: full of fun and high spirits, he had an extensive repertoire of Welsh stories, and though he didn't speak Welsh, was proficient in the Welsh-English dialect of the region. His mother and father however were both Welsh speakers. As a Pembrokeshire man myself, I was in no linguistic difficulties for my native country in general and Laugharne in particular is English speaking and permeated with Flemish blood from Haverford West downwards, though the latter town before the coming of the Flemings had been a Scandinavian stronghold, from which occupation not a few words still survive to remind us of the Vikings. Dylan Thomas was Carmarthenshire born, and that is not surprising, for though preponderantly Welsh-speaking, this country is justly famous for the beauty of its English, unequalled, I should say, in the whole Kingdom. Those who have heard the golden sonorous voice of Dylan either in intimacy or recorded from a public platform, here or in the U.S.A. must surely have recognized the authentic accents of poetic genius and of one who in defiance of syntax or propriety alternates between an exquisite sensibility and reckless humour.

Dylan was a good companion and though apt to be pugnacious, we never came to blows. He had not thought for the morrow and in-

As reprinted here, this is a revised version of an article which first appeared in the *Sunday Times* (London), September, 1958.

deed seemed to be oblivious of time. Eating bored him but his appetite for beer was unbounded. No *whisky* for him in those innocent pre-American days! We both played shove ha'penny, at which game we were about equal. He borrowed freely of his richer acquaintances but, on principal, never repaid them. I got him to sit for his portrait twice. When provided with a bottle of beer, he sat like an angel and rather looked like one too. After the marriage, Dylan and Caitlin (pronounced Kathleen), took a house at Laugharne which I had coveted myself. Tall, narrow and detached, like a house in a play, it was slightly sinister. Dylan had a number of admirers in that part of the world, some of whom would sometimes pay him a call. When I was staying there one of these pilgrims arrived. We passed the evening of course at Brown's Hotel, the only pub in Laugharne except for another less distinguished one in the "Lower Town" which is entirely inhabited by Flemish cockle gatherers, Laugharne's only industry. Next morning Caitlin told me that during the night, on hearing strange sounds in the guest-chamber, she had entered it, to find the visitor kneeling stark naked on the floor and in an attitude of prayer. Retiring cautiously, she left him to his devotions. I understood this young man was also a poet. As for me, I stayed frequently at Richard Hughes' house where I was allowed to roam at will and sometimes took Dylan and his wife with me who, making themselves more than comfortable in the back of the car, left me to concentrate on the steering wheel.

It is beyond my powers to estimate the work of Dylan Thomas. Some of his poems or parts of his poems have pleased me immensely but I have never memorized one and I do not pretend to have read all of them by any means. I did not care for his play, "Under Milk Wood," which to me seemed false and sentimental. A distinguished and highly literary friend of mine used the word, "poppycock," bluntly, but another grudgingly admitted that Dylan "had something." But our neighbour and literary critic, Lord David Cecil, was impressed by Dylan's style and personality and was generously appreciative of his poetic gifts.

At one time Dylan told me he joined the Communist Party but on being ordered to make his writing a medium of propaganda, at once detached himself from the Party. He was never a student of sociology but simply felt in sympathy with the underdog. Wasn't he a young underdog himself? A kind of King of the Kennel. Like other monarchs in history, his relations with the bourgeoisie were chiefly monetary and always precarious: yet he made some good friends among them. Criminology was a cult of his and he had acquired a formidable library of "romans policiers." I rather think he wrote one or two himself.

from Dylan Thomas: Memories and Appreciations

I. DANIEL JONES

Our first meeting, nearly thirty years ago, is described in *Portrait of the Artist as a Young Dog*. I forget how the fight began. Dylan was slight, with curly hair, large soft eyes and full lips; he looked almost effeminate, but he was very tough. My own appearance was much the same, and I wore spectacles as well. Each of us seemed an easy victim, but as soon as the fight started contempt changed to respect and we became friends. This meant almost daily meetings between us for the next ten years, at his house, at my house, or, during school hours, in Cwmdonkin Park. We read aloud to one another, usually our own poems, and exchanged criticism; and some part of the time was always spent in writing, either separately or in collaboration. Music was not forgotten; I played my compositions to Dylan, and we extemporised together on the piano in four-handed duets, or on strange instruments of our own devising.

Five, Cwmdonkin Drive, and Warmley, the two houses, were very different in atmosphere. At Dylan's we had a gas fire that spluttered, an asthmatic sheep that coughed in the field opposite, and always a few owls hooting from the woods. I remember one terrifying night when we stared at one another in the gathering darkness until our heads became griffin and wyvern heads.

Warmley was not so mysterious, but it was more popular for several reasons; there were, for example, the Broadcasting Station and the Cricket Pitch. The Cricket Pitch in the back garden was about twelve feet long; every fine evening we played there without subtlety, hurling or driving the ball with the utmost force at one another, while old Harding, the neighbour, leaned on the wall smoking his pipe,

From *Encounter* (London), January, 1954, pp. 9–10, 12–13, 13–16.

sometimes calling out with perfect solemnity "Well played, sir!" and finally asking, with a certain wistfulness, "Will you be playing again tomorrow evening?"

Through the W.B.S. system, which consisted of two loudspeakers connected to the pickup of a radiogram, we were able to broadcast from the upstairs to the downstairs rooms. I still have some of the programmes: "The Rev. Percy will play three piano pieces, Buzzards at Dinner, Salute to Admiral Beattie, and Badgers Beneath My Vest"; "Rebecca Mn will give a recital on the Rebmetpes"; "Locomotive Bowen, the one-eyed cow-hand, will give a talk on the Rocking Horse and Varnishing Industry"; "Zoilredb Pogoho will read his poem Fiffokorp." These broadcasters became real people to us, and we collaborated in a biography of the greatest of them, Percy. Here is a description of one of the trying experiences we inflicted on Percy's old mother: "Near the outskirts of Panama the crippled negress was bitten severely and time upon time, invariably upon the nape, by a white hat-shaped bird."

In prose collaboration we had to consult together all the time; the alternate sentence method proved unsuccessful. In poetry collaboration, however, we always wrote alternate lines; I had the odd-numbered lines and Dylan the even-numbered, and we made it a rule that neither of us should suggest an alteration in the other's work. These poems, of which I still have about two hundred, are a different matter from the W.B.S. fooling. It is still play, but it is what I would call serious play. The poetic style of Walter Bram, as we called ourselves, is bafflingly inconsistent; it is fragile, furious, laconic, massive, delicate, incantatory, cool, flinty, violent, Chinese, Greek, and shocking. One poem may begin "You will be surprised when I remain obdurate," and the next, "I lay under the currant trees and told the beady berries about Jesus." Some of the poems are very, very beautiful; very. Especially those that tell of singularly gentle and godlike action by the third person plural.

They had come from the place high on
the coral hills
Where the light from the white sea fills
the soil with ascending grace.
And the sound of their power makes
motion as steep as the sky,
And the fruits of the great ground lie
like leaves from a vertical flower.
They had come from the place; they

had come and had gone again
In a season of delicate rain, in a smooth
ascension of grace.

We had word obsessions: everything at one time was "little" or "white"; and sometimes an adjective became irresistibly funny in almost any connection: "innumerable bananas," "wilful moccasin," "a certain Mrs. Prothero." These word games, and even the most facetious of our collaborations, had a serious experimental purpose, and there is no doubt that they played an important part in Dylan's early poetic development.

His own poetry passed in ten years from simple lyricism, reminiscent of W. H. Davies or de la Mare, to the violent imagery of the poems that first appeared in Victor Neuberg's corner of the *Sunday Referee:* on the way he came more or less under the influence of early Yeats, Aldington, Sacheverell Sitwell, Lawrence, and Hopkins, in that order; but of course there were many others.

Apart from purely literary influences Dylan was at this time self-sufficient. At the school, where his father was Senior English Master, everything offered to him was rejected. It is true that he edited the school magazine and wrote nearly all of it; that he acted in the dreary Drinkwater plays with which we were afflicted; and even argued in the debating society, if a triumphant use of the illogical can be called arguing; but school subjects were treated by him with disdain.

This was consistent; at that time, and throughout his life, Dylan hated the academic. But in those early years his antipathy had less discrimination; it was directed not only against the fossils but against much that was significantly alive as well, if he happened to find for it an academic association. For this reason, perhaps, his enthusiasm was limited almost wholly to contemporary verse; poets of the school text-book were suspect, and for the time being he kept them at arm's length. Passionately absorbed in language, he had no interest in languages, preferring to take whatever might trickle through the translator's sieve. For him, the impact of literature could only be weakened, and its vitality robbed, by study; even the word "literature" itself was suspect in its associations. The conventions of prosody came under the ban; Dylan was aware of them, but he contemptuously reserved them for humorous verse or parodies. For his serious poetry he preferred then, and afterwards, a convention of his own, the syllabic number of the line; this convention, while giving characteristic limitation to a poem, could never be formulated for poetry; its life could co-extend only with the life of one poem.

This early stand against the academic was very valuable to Dylan; he would have needed twice the time to accomplish all that he did accomplish if he had not discerned clearly and from the beginning the things that were of no use to him, or if he had not steadily ignored them. In these early years, words occupied Dylan's mind to the exclusion even of the things with which they have some connection: to him, the cushat and the ring-dove were as different as the ostrich and the humming-bird. Later, there was a change. He passed through the narrow gate of words and found a world more spacious than the world he had left, filled with the same things, but magically transformed.

III. LOUIS MAC NEICE

Yeats described the poet as one who knows "that Hamlet and Lear are gay." No poet of our time was a better example of this than Dylan Thomas. When his first work appeared it was astonishingly new and yet went back to the oldest of our roots—roots which had long been ignored, written off, or simply forgotten. He was not just a poet among poets; he was, as has often been remarked, a bard, with the three great bardic virtues of faith, joy, and craftsmanship—and, one could add, of charity. Many of his poems are concerned with death or the darker forces, yet they all have the joy of life in them. And many of his poems are obscure but it is never the obscurity of carelessness; though I, for one, assumed it might be when I first read his early work in the 1930's. Lastly, all the poems (a rare things in this age of doubt) are suffused both with a sense of value, a faith in something that is simultaneously physical and spiritual, and with (what is equally rare in an age of carping) a great breath of generosity, goodwill not only towards men but towards all created things.

The next few years will obviously see a spate of writing about Thomas—his vision, imagery, technique, etc.—and the writers will be beset by two distinct and opposite dangers—the danger of trying to equip him too exactly with a literary pedigree and the danger of isolating him as a sport, a Villon figure, a wild man who threw up works of genius without knowing what he was doing. The former mistake has been made for years by various academic critics, often Americans, who have dwelt at length on Thomas's relations to ancient Welsh poetry or to Rimbaud; though he has something in common with both (and though Wales in general and Swansea in particular were the most important factors in his make-up), it should be remembered that he had never read Rimbaud and could not read Welsh. As for the "wild man" conception, immediately after Thomas's death it was exploited in its most disgusting and imbecile form by certain of our daily papers. Of course Thomas liked pints of beer (so what? he also liked watching cricket) but he did not write his poems "with a pint in one hand"; no writer of our time approached his art in a more reverent spirit or gave it more devoted attention. One glance at a Thomas manuscript will show the almost incredible trouble he took over those elaborate arabesques that could yet emerge as fresh as any of the "wood-notes wild" expected from the born lyric poet. In fact, he *was* a born lyric poet but it was a birthright he worked and worked to secure.

His lyrical gift, though the most important, was only one of several gifts. He had a roaring sense of comedy, as shown in many of his prose works. He had a natural sense of theatre, as was shown not only in his everyday conversation but in those readings of poetry (and his taste, by the way, was catholic) which earned him such applause both here and in the U.S. He was moreover a subtle and versatile actor, as he proved repeatedly in radio performances. *And* he "took production." Though his special leaning (as was natural, given his astonishing voice) was to the sonorous and emotional, he enjoyed playing character parts, especially comic or grotesque ones, such as a friendly Raven which he played for me once in a dramatised Norwegian folk-tale. He could even "throw away" if required to. And in all these sidelines—as in all his verse and prose—there appeared the same characteristic blend of delight in what he was doing and care as to how he did it.

This does not seem to me the moment for analysing Dylan Thomas. He is assured of a place, and a unique one, in the history of English poetry. But, when such a personality dies, his friends are not much in the mood for literary criticism. What we remember is not a literary figure to be classified in the text-book but something quite unclassifiable, a wind that bloweth where it listeth, a wind with a chuckle in its voice and news from the end of the world. It is too easy to call him unconventional—which is either an understatement or a red herring. It is too easy to call him Bohemian—a word which implies affectations which were quite alien to Thomas. It is too easy even to call him anarchist—a better word but too self-conscious an attitude. Thomas was an actor—and would that more poets were—but he was not an attitudiniser. He eschewed politics but he had a sense of justice; that he once visited Prague proves nothing as to his leftness or rightness; it is merely one more proof that he thought men everywhere were human. Both in his life and his work he remained honest to the end. This, combined with his talents, made him a genius.

IV. MARJORIE ADIX

The following is an account of a conference held by Dylan Thomas with students at the University of Utah in 1952.

I met Dylan Thomas yesterday—that doesn't mean that I rushed up and told him how wonderful he was; it means that I sat three feet away from him in the Union lounge while Professor Brewster Ghiselin and his following questioned him for an hour and a half. Throughout it all you could feel the relationship between Dylan Thomas and Ghiselin—tremendous respect on both sides, and yet too great a distance ever to be close. Both of them shy men, really, who have hung their souls out on the line, yet kept firmly established egos: Ghiselin, the scholar-poet and host, never quite sure that his man wouldn't get up and leave through the open window; and Thomas, out of place, uneasy at being exposed on all sides, yet on his best behaviour, sticking it out.

Ghiselin led off with a brief introduction and then asked why a poet went around on a reading tour. Thomas, looking down at the table, facing no one, said softly: "My God, that's a hard question. I'm afraid I shall have to answer it straight: it's a way of seeing the country and I haven't any money. It's a matter of ego as well."

GHISELIN. But why is the poetry read aloud? Does it aid understanding?

THOMAS. People come to have a look at me. Here's a little fat man come to make a fool of himself, they think, and since they don't listen to what I read, it doesn't matter whether I make sense or not. . . . But that isn't quite fair of me—I am enjoying myself.

GHISELIN. You read much on the B.B.C. Do you feel that poetry must be read aloud before it is complete? Does it bring you closer to the meaning?

THOMAS. Yes—perhaps it helps in the interpretation or emphasis. It brings you closer to the poet.

QUESTION FROM A STUDENT. Do you listen to the sound of your own words? Is that as important to you as the rhyme and metre?"

THOMAS. Oh, God, that's a hard one too. Yes—you can struggle with rhyme and metre and style and still not have a poem. I'm sorry I'm not answering the way you would like.

STUDENT: But why do you read your own poetry?

THOMAS. For the noise it makes. And for the memory of the experience of writing it. But it has already said everything it had to say.

STUDENT. Do you say the words aloud as you write them?

THOMAS. Yes. That's why I live in a hut on a cliff.

ANOTHER STUDENT. Is it necessary for a poem to have an outcome? Robert Frost says that a poem should be resolved. It should not be too obscure to be understood. I have difficulty in understanding you, especially your early sonnets.

THOMAS. Then you should read Robert Frost. . . . But you are right: to the poet, at least, there is always an outcome. Those sonnets are only the writings of a boily boy in love with shapes and shadows on his pillow.

GHISELIN. I've wondered about the sonnets. I could never see anything very deep in them. It's good to know I need search no further.

THOMAS. Well, they would be of interest to another boily boy. Or a boily girl. [*Long pause.*] Boily-girly.

Here Thomas laughed to himself and seemed lost in very amusing word combinations—while everyone sat petrified, until somebody brought him back to us:

Is it ever fair deliberately to confuse the reader?

THOMAS. I thought someone would take me up on that. No—it is a deliberate avowal of your own inefficiency. It is impossible to be too clear. You can state too bluntly all you know, or put down very clearly what you intend, which may be very narrow and even cruel. But we don't know about anything. Especially people, nobody knows. There are scientific terms, but—why doesn't the water fly out of the ocean when the earth whirls? Because it is a ball of magic. It is impossible to be too clear. I am trying for more clarity now. At first I thought it enough to leave an impression of sound and feeling and let the meaning seep in later, but since I've been giving these broadcasts and reading other men's poetry as well as my own, I find it better to have more meaning at first reading.

GHISELIN. But, on the other hand, isn't it possible to narrow and fix a meaning to the exclusion of richer levels of meaning?

THOMAS. Oh God, isn't an education wonderful!

GHISELIN. I shall be silent from now on.

THOMAS. No, I mean it as a compliment. You say things so well, and I'm ashamed to be flippant and go down the side alleys. . . .

STUDENT. Do you find it necessary to study other things in order to find increasing satisfaction in your own poetry?"

THOMAS. There is never any satisfaction—that's why I write another poem. Do I study other things? Yes, people. . . . [*Long pause, the questioner nodding thoughtfully, then*] Me!

ANOTHER STUDENT: Why do you write poetry, Mr. Thomas?

THOMAS. Because I have the time. Because I have to live too; [*mumbled*] I don't know why. . . . It is very slow work, however. Only five poems published in the last six years. It is slow, but sometimes there is just nothing better to do. Sometimes it feels very good to have a blank piece of paper in front of you, and you put down the first line. Then you look at all the paper and think, Now I've got to rhyme this. And it's work! Oh God, it's awful! . . . I write some very bad poems.

STUDENT. What happens to them?

THOMAS. I keep them—too much of an egoist to throw them away. But neither do I do as Rossetti did, who buried them with his wife and had to dig them up later. I keep them in a drawer.

STUDENT. What do you do with them?

THOMAS. Nothing. When it's written it's finished.

GHISELIN. Perhaps you don't read your old poems over because there is a chance you might become infatuated with them and continue to write the same poem over and over. Some poets do.

THOMAS. Jove! I never thought of that! I wonder what's in the drawer. [*Pantomime.*] This isn't so bad after all! Delightful! [*He was gone again.*]

STUDENT. Who decides whether your poems are good or bad?

THOMAS. I do. Nobody reads the bad ones.

STUDENT. Then you don't ask a publisher for an opinion?

THOMAS. Oh, no. If he didn't like one that I thought was good, it would be too terrible.

STUDENT. If your own poetry gives you no satisfaction, is there any which does?

THOMAS. That's easy: Shakespeare!

STUDENT. Who is the best of the moderns?

THOMAS. The nice thing about poetry is that it isn't a competitive field. There isn't any *best;* but I do like Thomas Hardy, D. H. Lawrence, W. H. Auden and——— [*Here, Dr.———on my left squealed in surprise, and I missed the fourth name.*]

STUDENT. How do you tell whether a poem is good or not?"

THOMAS. If I like it.

STUDENT. But what do you go by?

THOMAS. I like one because it is better than the others. [*Silence.*] Before I find a poem I like I have to pass over a great many that I don't like. When I find one I like, I read it. I don't know why. The big problem is to find the poem, then read it—hang by your ears from the chandeliers, or however you read poetry—and enjoy it.

GHISELIN. Perhaps we should do as you suggest and like a poem because we think it better than others, but students have to pull it apart and analyse why they like it and write it all down for a professor.

THOMAS. People who think they know T. S. Eliot find it unbelievable that he enjoys Kipling, that rowdy rhymester. That is, the people who think they know Kipling too. Some of his poetry is excellent.

[*Very long pause. Dylan Thomas sips at his glass of water like a kitten bobbing its nose in a saucer. The glass is still full at the end of the session after at least a dozen embarrassed sips.*]

STUDENT. Do you address your noise only to yourself?

THOMAS. Oh no. No. Yes—well, I *am* lots of people. I think I am lots of people at any rate. Of course, I know, and the birds know, I'm only a fat little fool ranting on a cliff, but it seems that I am lots of people.

YOUNG LADY. Has your style changed?

THOMAS. Style? Yes. No—I'm still after the same things if that's what you mean.

GHISELIN. Your poetry seems to open little doors in quite ordinary and common events, sometimes by only shifting an image slightly to one side to let in the new idea.

THOMAS. How nicely you say it! That is exactly what I would like my poetry to do some day.

LADY. Do you revise?

THOMAS. No, I work it out a phrase at a time. It is very slow, but when it is once finished, all the revision has been done, and I don't change it.

LADY. Then it may take several days?

THOMAS. Months. Years. It might never be finished. But I am a patient man.

GHISELIN. You always seem to put in your poetry just what you are seeing at the moment—the heron, and the birds near the estuary, for instance?

THOMAS. Yes—yes. I wanted to write about the cliff, and there was a crow flying above it, and that seemed a good place to begin, so I wrote about the crow. Yes, if I see a bird, I put it in whether it belongs or not.

GHISELIN. Do you leave it there?

THOMAS. If it is happy and at home in the poetry I do. But really I should get a blind for my window.

STUDENT. But you do have some idea of what you are going to say?

THOMAS. Sometimes. You don't just sit and wait for the little doors to open. Twenty years ago I would have said 'inspiration.' It's hard work. But sometimes the mood is enough. Say a poet is gay and he wants to write a gay poem—about anything. It is spring, or he has a new pair of shoes, or his wife has left him. Everything is gaiety. But then, suddenly, in the middle of the poem, he might miss his wife. It would be a very sad poem. You can't always follow your original plan.

ANOTHER STUDENT. Do you pay any attention to critics,———, for instance?

THOMAS. Yes. Sometimes I wake up in the night and wonder about them. I don't know what they have against me. As far as ——— goes, it is a personal matter I'm sure. He just can't abide me. He can't stand to read me at all. I don't know why. I pay attention to the praise too—it's easier to take, although it isn't any truer and I don't believe it any more than the other. I mean, I can't be bought with a few sentences. I don't think they will change me. I know what kind of man I am. [*Quietly.*] Thirty-seven years with the same head. . . .

And so it went on, until Ghiselin asked Thomas to read one of his poems. He arose for the first time, gathered up his five books and stuffed them in his briefcase. I thought he was offended, but he finished stowing them away, kept one out, and turned back to us:

"I brought all these books in case I would be too frightened to answer your questions. I haven't answered them, but I wasn't frightened. Thank you for asking me."

He smiled and sat down again, and began to talk in a soft voice about his father, who, he said, had been a militant atheist, whose atheism had nothing to do with whether there was a god or not, but was a violent and personal dislike for God. He would glare out of the window and growl: "It's raining, blast Him!" or, "The sun is shining—Lord, what foolishness!" He went blind and was very ill before he died. He was in his eighties, and he grew soft and gentle at the last. Thomas hadn't wanted him to change. . . .

And all at once the little poet began to read, and his voice raged and surged with power and anger and a terrible desolation. He read "Do not go gentle into that good night." It was slow and rhythmic and deep. His eyes were bent down on the book, but he was not reading, for they would remain fixed for a long time and then wander over both pages for a moment and then freeze again. I can't express how startling the change was in him, from the shy, humble, apologetic, patiently eager man, to this tidal wave of humanity. I was uneasy at first because I felt that in either one position or the other he was only acting, but I could find no trace of insincerity ever. I suppose he knows best. He is lots of people.

Dylan Thomas

HOWARD MOSS

The word "human" is the one most commonly used when people try to define the qualities of Dylan Thomas' personality. And it is a sad commentary on what the rest of us are that the word should be used as a mark of distinction. Hackneyed as it is as a description, it is not without its truth. For Dylan Thomas was human in a way most people are not. The adulation and derogation he suffered were the symptoms of his being himself. Sober or drunk, he was more awake than most people ever are or become.

His importance to the many people he knew during his lifetime was a token of both a real and a spurious distinction: Thomas by being himself appeared to his audience to be a rebel. And it is a notorious fact that rebellion, unaccompanied by either talent or genius, is dangerous and sometimes fatal. Thomas's genius made him a safe symbol for other people's instincts for rebellion. To put it simply, everyone was secretly glad that *some*one was being himself and getting away with it.

Being oneself exacts a price most people cannot afford to pay. Thomas paid it. To say that he did not take his life into his own hands would be untrue. He seemed to want to be what he was; whether that was a free choice or not, no one can say. But to see him as a martyr, as many people do, is to distort the truth. Thomas enjoyed, or seemed to, his role; he let himself open to the kind of "story" he was to become; and if he was used by others in the pursuit of such gain, it is only fair to say that he used others, too.

Thomas left no one untouched who met him. For there was another side to him that accounts, in part, for the enormous pull of his personality. If he was a rebel, he was also a child. And his friends paid

Transcript of a radio broadcast over station WBAI, New York, November, 1958. Reprinted by permission of Howard Moss.

for their symbol by having to take care of it. The great howl that arose upon his death might be genuinely explained by the fact that a fine poet had died at the age of thirty-nine. Surely that is a matter for grief. But there was another reason for the general uproar: no one wanted to believe that there is a price to pay for romantic indulgence, or put another way, a profligate sickness, and it was hard for many of his followers to understand that a lifetime of drinking can result in death from alcohol. Thomas, who had a fondness for Third Avenue bars, could believe it. He was not a romantic symbol to himself.

That he saw himself as he was only made him the more illusory to people who insisted on his being an illusion. That Thomas's misbehavior, so-called, was more than a wanton flouting of convention is obvious. It was the nature of his "misbehavior" that made him irresistible to so many people.

He was not afraid to ask for what he wanted. When he was bored with literature and wanted life, he asked for that, too. And it was from the exercise of simple rights that Thomas started to become a legend. For who among us dares to ask for what he wants, dares to say what he means, dares to live a life that is interesting to him rather than to a thousand other people?

None of this alone would explain Thomas's aura. He was singular in his gifts for life as well as poetry. He was a spellbinding story teller, an inexhaustible fountain of verbal invention, and a marvelous mimic and actor. He had no respect for sham and pretension, even when they were masked as humility, and he was rarely boring. Being genuinely kind and loving, he seemed unique to those people who believe that kindness and love are moral qualities.

I think it would also be true to say that it was partly his adolescence that made him attractive to adolescents. That he was a highly civilized and sophisticated one merely confused the unwary who cannot believe that so many attributes can be combined in one person. To hide the fact that Thomas was often a chore and a burden to those who loved him the most would be a lie. And it should be obvious that they did not love him because he was a chore and a burden. He was, as most of us are not, a person. He was funny, enchanting, and alive.

That he hurt people is axiomatic. Whether it was worth it to them is their business. That they hurt him is axiomatic, too. It has been a long time since such a phenomenon made an appearance. But the phenomenon seems more special in that we are, most of us, so pedestrian. And it is—and will increasingly become so—only of interest to those who actually knew him as a person whether he was a victim of himself, or of the world that victimizes everyone. The truth is that he was a poet who left us magnificent poems. For that, we should be grateful.

Appendices

Bibliography

PRIMARY SOURCES

(Works by Dylan Thomas)

Adventures in the Skin Trade. (Norfolk, Conn.: New Directions, 1955).
A Child's Christmas in Wales. (Norfolk, Conn.: New Directions, 1955).
Collected Poems 1934–1952. (Norfolk, Conn.: New Directions, 1953).
Deaths and Entrances. (London: J. M. Dent & Sons, Ltd., 1946).
The Doctor and the Devils. (Norfolk, Conn.: New Directions, 1953).
18 Poems. (London: The Sunday Referee and The Parton Bookshop, 1934).
In Country Sleep. (New York: New Directions, 1952).
The Map of Love. (London: J. M. Dent & Sons, Ltd., 1939).
New Poems. (Norfolk, Conn.: New Directions, 1934).
"On Poetry: A Discussion" with James Stephens and Gerald Bullett. *Encounter,* November, 1954.
Portrait of the Artist as a Young Dog. (Norfolk, Conn.: New Directions, 1940).
A Prospect of the Sea. Edited by Daniel Jones. (London: J. M. Dent & Sons, Ltd., 1955).
Quite Early One Morning. (Norfolk, Conn.: New Directions, 1954).
Selected Writings. (New York: New Directions, 1946).
"Seven Letters to Oscar Williams (1945–1953)." *New World Writing,* 7th Mentor Selection, 1955.
Twenty-Five Poems. (London: J. M. Dent & Sons, Ltd., 1936).
Twenty-Six Poems. (London: J. M. Dent & Sons, Ltd., 1950).
Under Milk Wood. (Norfolk, Conn.: New Directions, 1954).
The World I Breathe. (Norfolk, Conn.: New Directions, 1939).

SECONDARY SOURCES

Books

ARNHEIM, RUDOLF, *et al. Poets at Work.* (New York: Harcourt, Brace & Company, Inc., 1948).

ASTRE, GEORGES-ALBERT. *Anthologie de la poésie anglaise contemporaine.* (Paris: L'Arche, 1949).

BERRYMAN, JOHN. "The Loud Hill of Wales," in John Crowe Ransom (ed.), *The Kenyon Critics.* (Cleveland: The World Publishing Company, 1951).

BOLTY, C. L. *Crown to Mend.* (London: Hamish Hamilton Ltd., 1945).

BRINNIN, JOHN MALCOLM. *Dylan Thomas in America.* (Boston: Atlantic-Little, Brown & Co., 1955). Available also in the paperback Compass Book Edition (New York: The Viking Press, Inc., 1957).

BULLOUGH, GEOFFREY. *The Trend of Modern Poetry.* (London: Oliver & Boyd, Ltd., 1949).

DAICHES, DAVID, and WILLIAM CHARVAT (eds.). *Poems in English, 1530–1940.* (New York: The Ronald Press Company, 1950).

DAY LEWIS, CECIL. *The Poetic Image.* (London: Jonathan Cape, Ltd., 1947).

DEUTSCH, BABETTE. *Poetry in Our Time.* (New York: Henry Holt & Company, Inc., 1952).

DREW, ELIZABETH, and JOHN L. SWEENEY. *Directions in Modern Poetry.* (New York: W. W. Norton & Company, Inc., 1940).

DURRELL, LAWRENCE. *Key to Modern Poetry.* (London: Peter Nevill, Ltd., 1952).

FRANKENBERG, LLOYD. *Pleasure Dome: On Reading Modern Poetry.* (Boston: Houghton Mifflin Company, 1949).

FRASER, G. S. *Dylan Thomas.* (Writers and Their Work, No. 90.) (London: Longmans, Green & Co., Ltd., 1957).

———. *The Modern Writer and His World.* (London: Derek Verschoyle, Ltd., 1953).

———. *Vision and Rhetoric.* (London: Faber & Faber, Ltd., 1959).

FRIAR, KIMON, and JOHN MALCOLM BRINNIN (eds.). *Modern Poetry: American and British.* (New York: Appleton-Century-Crofts, Inc., 1951).

GRAVES, ROBERT. *The Crowning Privilege.* (London: Cassell & Company, Ltd., 1955).

GRIGSON, GEOFFREY. *The Harp of Aeolus and Other Essays on Art, Literature and Nature.* (London: George Routledge & Sons, Ltd., 1948).

HENDRY, J. F. *The New Apocalypse.* (London: Fortune Press, 1940).

HIGHET, GILBERT. *Talents and Geniuses.* (New York: Oxford University Press, 1957).

HOFFMAN, FREDERICK. *Freudianism and the Literary Mind.* (Baton Rouge, La.: Louisiana State University Press, 1945).

HOLROYD, STUART. *Emergence from Chaos.* (Boston: Houghton Mifflin Company, 1957).

IZZO, CARLO. *Poesia inglese contemporanea da Thomas Hardy agli Apocalittici.* (Modena, Italy: Guanda U., 1950).

KUNITZ, STANLEY J. *Twentieth Century Authors.* (New York: H. W. Wilson Company, 1955).

LONGAKER, MARK, and EDWIN C. BOLLES (eds.). *Contemporary English Literature.* (New York: Appleton-Century-Crofts, Inc., 1953).

MARITAIN, JACQUES. *Creative Intuition in Art and Poetry.* (Bollingen Series, Vol. XXXV, No. 1.) (New York: Pantheon Books, Inc., 1953).

MILES, JOSEPHINE. *The Primary Language of Poetry in the 1940's.* (University of California Publications in English, Vol. XIX, No. 3.) (Berkeley and Los Angeles: University of California Press, 1951).

MUIR, EDWIN. *The Present Age from 1914.* (Introductions to Literature, Vol. V.) (London: The Cresset Press, Ltd., 1939).

OLSON, ELDER. *The Poetry of Dylan Thomas.* (Chicago: University of Chicago Press, 1954).

READ, HERBERT. *The True Voice of Feeling.* (London: Faber & Faber, Ltd., 1953).

REXROTH, KENNETH (ed.). *The New British Poets.* (Norfolk, Conn.: New Directions, 1949).

RHYS, KEIDRYCH. "Contemporary Welsh Literature," in *British Annual of Literature.* (London: British Authors' Press, Ltd., 1946).

ROLPH, J. ALEXANDER. *Dylan Thomas: A Bibliography.* Foreword by Dame Edith Sitwell. (New York: New Directions, 1956).

SAVAGE, D. S. *Little Reviews Anthology 1947–48.* (London: Eyre & Spottiswoode, Ltd., 1948).

SCARFE, FRANCIS. *Auden and After: The Liberation of Poetry, 1940–1941.* (London: George Routledge & Sons, Ltd., 1942).

SITWELL, EDITH. "Foreword: The Young Dylan Thomas," in *Dylan Thomas: A Bibliography,* by J. Alexander Rolph. (London: J. M. Dent & Sons, Ltd., and New York: New Directions, 1956).

———. (ed.). *The Atlantic Book of British and American Poetry.* (Boston: Atlantic-Little, Brown & Co., 1958).

STANFORD, DEREK. *Dylan Thomas.* (New York: Citadel Press, 1954).

SPENDER, STEPHEN. *Poetry Since 1939.* (New York: Longmans, Green & Co., Inc., 1946).

STEARNS, MARSHALL W. "A Critic Interprets a Poem," in S. Schemanski and H. Treece (eds.), *Transformation 3.* (London: Lindsay Drummond, Ltd., 1945). Also in Henry Treece *Dylan Thomas,* Appendix III. (London: Lindsay Drummond, Ltd., 1949).

SWEENEY, JOHN L. (ed.). *Selected Writings of Dylan Thomas.* (New York: New Directions, 1946).

SYMONS, JULIAN. "Of Crisis and Dismay: A Study of Writing in the Thirties," in B. Rajan and Andres Pearse (eds.), *Focus One.* (London: Denis Dobson, 1945).

THOMAS, CAITLIN. *Leftover Life to Kill.* (Boston: Atlantic-Little, Brown & Co., 1957). Also available in the paperback Evergreen edition (New York: Grove Press, 1959).

TINDALL, WILLIAM YORK. *Forces in Modern British Literature. 1885–1946.* (New York: Alfred A. Knopf, Inc., 1947).

TREECE, HENRY. *Dylan Thomas: "Dog Among the Fairies."* (London: Lindsay Drummond, Ltd., 1949).

UNTERMEYER, LOUIS. *Modern British Poetry.* (New York: Harcourt, Brace & Company, Inc., 1950).

WAIN, JOHN. *Preliminary Essays.* (London: Macmillan & Company, Ltd., and New York: St. Martin's Press, 1957).

WATKINS, VERNON. *Dylan Thomas Letters to Vernon Watkins.* (London: J. M. Dent & Sons, Ltd., and Faber & Faber, Ltd., 1957).

WILDER, AMOS N. *Modern Poetry and the Christian Tradition.* (New York: Charles Scribner's Sons, 1952).

WOODCOCK, GEORGE. *British Poetry Today.* (Lecture Series, No. 7.) (Vancouver, Canada: University of British Columbia, 1950).

Articles, Reviews, Memoirs

ABERPENNAR, DAVIES. "The Map of Love," *Wales,* 11 (Winter, 1939–40). (Review of *The Map of Love.*)

ADAMS, PHOEBE. "Symbols and Metaphors," *Atlantic,* 191 (May, 1953). (Review of *Collected Poems.*)

ADAMS, R. M. "Taste and Bad Taste in Metaphysical Poetry: Richard Crashaw and Dylan Thomas," *Hudson Review,* 8 (Spring, 1955).

ADIX, MARJORIE. "Dylan Thomas," *Explorations,* 4 (1955).

———. "Dylan Thomas: Memories and Appreciations," *Encounter,* 2 (January, 1954).

AGEE, JAMES. "A Dylan Thomas Screen Play," *New York Times Book Review,* December 6, 1953. (Review of *The Doctor and the Devils.*)

AIKEN, CONRAD. "The New Euphuism," *New Republic,* 110 (January 3, 1944).

———. "A Rocking Alphabet," *Poetry,* 56 (June, 1940). (Review of *The World I Breathe.*)

AIVAZ, DAVID. "The Poetry of Dylan Thomas," *Hudson Review,* 3 (Autumn, 1950).

AMIS, KINGSLEY. "An Evening with Dylan Thomas," *Spectator,* 199 (November 29, 1957).

ANDERSEN, KARL O. "Dylan Thomas," *Dialog,* 3 (1950).

ANONYMOUS. *Booklist,* 43 (February 1, 1947). (Review of *Selected Writings.*)

———. *Booklist,* 48 (May 15, 1952). (Review of *In Country Sleep.*)

———. *Booklist,* 49 (May 15, 1953). (Review of *Collected Poems.*)

———. *Booklist,* 50 (November 15, 1953). (Review of *The Doctor and the Devils.*)

———. *Bookmark,* 12 (January, 1953). (Review of *In Country Sleep.*)
———. *Chicago Sunday Tribune Magazine of Books* (April 13, 1952). (Review of *In Country Sleep.*)
———. "Dylan Thomas in Vancouver," *Contemporary Verse,* 31 (Spring, 1950).
———. "Editorial Note: The Second Phase of Neo-Romanticism," *Poetry and Poverty,* 4 (1953).
———. *English Studies,* 28 (June, 1947). (Review of *Deaths and Entrances.*)
———. "Film-script," *Times (London) Literary Supplement,* (May 29, 1953). (Review of *The Doctor and the Devils.*)
———. "In the White Giant's Thigh," *Atlantic,* 188 (November, 1951).
———. *Kirkus,* 21 (March 1, 1953). (Review of *Collected Poems.*)
———. "The Legend of Dylan Thomas," *Time,* 65 (May 30, 1955).
———. "A Lesson in Anatomy," *Time,* 62 (October 5, 1953). (Review of *The Doctor and the Devils.*)
———. *The Listener,* 22 (October 19, 1939). (Review of *The Map of Love.*)
———. *Manchester Guardian* (June 16, 1953). (Review of *The Doctor and the Devils.*)
———. "Mr. Dylan Thomas: Innovation and Tradition," *Times* (London) (November 10, 1953).
———. "Modernism in Poetry Yes and No; Readers' Free-for-All," *Poetry Review,* 44 (October–November, 1953).
———. *Nation,* 151 (November 23, 1940). (Review of *Portrait of the Artist as a Young Dog.*)
———. *Nation,* 157 (September 18, 1943). (Review of *New Poems.*)
———. *New Republic,* 115 (December 2, 1946). (Review of *Selected Writings.*)
———. *New Statesman and Nation,* 45 (June 27, 1953). (Review of *The Doctor and the Devils.*)
———. *New Verse,* 13 (February, 1935). (Review of *18 Poems.*)
———. *New Yorker,* 16 (October 26, 1940). (Review of *Portrait of the Artist as a Young Dog.*)
———. *New Yorker,* 22 (December 21, 1946). (Review of *Selected Writings.*)
———. "Obituary," *Illustrated London News,* 223 (November 21, 1953).
———. "Obituary," *New York Times* (November 10, 1953).
———. "Obituary," *Time,* 62 (November 16, 1953).
———. "Obituary," *Wilson Library Bulletin,* 28 (January, 1954).
———. "Passionate Pilgrim," *Time,* 48 (December 2, 1946). (Review of *Selected Writings.*)

———. "Poetry and Protest," *Poetry and Poverty*, 4 (1953). (Review of *Collected Poems.*)
———. Programme of the Group Theatre Presentation of Poetry, Drama, and Music in Homage to Dylan Thomas at the Globe Theatre, London, on Sunday, January 24, 1954.
———. "Romantics and Others," *Poetry Review* (May–June, 1943).
———. "Salute to a Poet," *Times (London) Literary Supplement* (November 28, 1952). (Review of *Collected Poems.*)
———. "The Script of a Screen play," *New York Herald Tribune Books* (November 29, 1953). (Review of *The Doctor and the Devils.*)
———. *Times (London) Literary Supplement* (September 19, 1936). (Review of *Twenty-Five Poems.*)
———. *Times (London) Literary Suppplement* (April 6, 1940). (Review of *Portrait of the Artist as a Young Dog.*)
———. *Times (London) Literary Supplement* (August 26, 1939). (Review of *The Map of Love.*)
———. *Weekly Book Review* (December 15, 1946). (Review of *Selected Writings.*)
———. "Welsh Rare One," *Time*, 61 (April 6, 1953). (Review of *Collected Poems.*)
———. *Wind and the Rain*, 3 (Autumn, 1946). (Review of *Deaths and Entrances.*)
ARLOTT, JOHN. "Dylan Thomas," *Spectator*, 191 (November 13–27, 1953).
ARNOLD, LILIAN. *John O'London's Weekly*, 43 (April 19, 1940).
ARROWSMITH, WILLIAM. "The Wisdom of Poetry," *Hudson Review*, 6 (Winter, 1954). (Review of *Collected Poems.*)
ASSELINEAU, ROGER. "Dylan Thomas," *Études Anglaises* (January, 1954).
ASTRE, GEORGES-ALBERT. "Un jeune et grand poète anglais," *Critique*, 4 (January, 1948).
AUDEN, WYSTAN H., *et al.* "Dylan Thomas Fund," *Saturday Review*, 36 (December 5, 1953).
AVISON, MARGARET. *Canadian Forum*, 23 (September, 1943). (Review of *New Poems.*)
BARKER, GEORGE. "Dylan Thomas: Memories and Appreciations," *Encounter*, 2 (January, 1954).
BARO, GENE. "Orator of Llareggub," *Poetry*, 87 (November, 1955).
BARRETT, MARY E. "Luncheon with Dylan Thomas," *Reporter*, 10 (April 27, 1954).
BARTLETT, PHYLLIS. "Thomas' 'Among Those Killed in the Dawn Raid Was a Man Aged One Hundred,' *Explicator*, 12 (1953).
BENÉT, WILLIAM ROSE. *Saturday Review*, 26 (October 16, 1943). (Review of *New Poems.*)

BERESFORD, J. D. *Manchester Guardian* (April 15, 1940). (Review of *Portrait of the Artist as a Young Dog.*)

BLISSETT, WILLIAM. "Dylan Thomas: A Reader in Search of a Poet," *Queen's Quarterly*, 63 (1956).

BOGAN, LOUISE. *New Yorker*, 28 (August 2, 1952). (Review of *In Country Sleep.*)

———. *New Yorker*, 15 (January 27, 1940). (Review of *The World I Breathe.*)

BOTTERILL, D. "Among the Younger Poets," *Life and Letters*, 51 (November, 1946).

BOWDEN, R. H. *Poetry Quarterly*, 14 (Winter, 1952–53). (Review of *Collected Poems.*)

BOZMAN, E. "Dylan Thomas," *Books* (December, 1953).

BREIT, HARVEY. "Farewell and Hail," *New York Times Book Review* (November 22, 1953).

———. "Haunting Drama of Dylan Thomas," *New York Times Magazine* (October 6, 1957).

———. "Talk With Dylan Thomas," *New York Times Book Review* (May 14, 1950).

BRINNIN, JOHN MALCOLM. "Dylan Thomas and His Village," *Mademoiselle*, 38 (February, 1954).

———. "Dylan Thomas in America," *Vassar Alumnae Magazine*, 37 (December, 1951).

———. *New York Times Book Review* (December 8, 1946). (Review of *Selected Writings.*)

——— ."Talent of Genius," *New Republic*, 130 (January 25, 1954).

BROOKS, ELMER L. "Thomas' 'Among Those Killed in the Dawn Raid Was a Man Aged One Hundred'," *Explicator*, 12 (1954).

BROSSARD, CHANDLER. "The Magic of Dylan Thomas," *Commonweal*, 62 (June 10, 1955).

BYRNE, BARRY. *Commonweal*, 33 (January 10, 1941). (Review of *Portrait of the Artist as a Young Dog.*)

CAMBON, GLAUCO. "Two Crazy Boats: Dylan Thomas and Rimbaud," *English Miscellany*, 7 (1956).

CAMPBELL, ROY. "Memories of Dylan Thomas at the B.B.C." *Poetry*, 87 (November, 1955).

CANE, MELVILLE. "Are Poets Returning to Lyricism?" *Saturday Review*, 37 (January 16, 1954).

CARLSON, HELEN. "The Overwrought Urn," *Folio*, 23 (1958).

CASSILL, V. R. "The Trial of Two Poets," *Western Review*, 20 (Spring, 1956).

CIARDI, JOHN. "The Real Thomas," *Saturday Review*, 41 (March 1, 1958).

———. "Six Hours of Dylan Thomas," *Saturday Review*, 41 (November 15, 1958).

CLANCY, J. P. "Dylan Thomas: Promise Clipped," *America*, 90 (December 12, 1953).

COFFMAN, STANLEY K., JR. *Books Abroad*, 27 (Autumn, 1953). (Review of *Collected Poems.*)

CONDON, RICHARD A. "Thomas' 'Ballad of the Long-Legged Bait'," *Explicator*, 16 (1958).

CONNOLLY, CYRIL. *New Statesman and Nation*, 18 (September 16, 1939). (Review of *The Map of Love.*)

CONNOLLY, THOMAS E. "Thomas' 'And Death Shall Have No Dominion,'" *Explicator*, 14 (1956).

CORMAN, CID. "Rhetorician in Mid-Career," *Accent*, 13 (Winter, 1953). (Review of *Collected Poems.*)

COX, R. G. "The Cult of Dylan Thomas," *Scrutiny*, 16 (September, 1949).

CULLIS, MICHAEL F. "Mr. Thomas and Mr. Auden," *Purpose*, 9 (April–June, 1937).

DAICHES, DAVID. "Contemporary Poetry in Britain," *Poetry*, 62 (June, 1943).

———. "The Poetry of Dylan Thomas," *College English*, 16 (1954).

DAVENPORT, JOHN. "Dylan Thomas," *Twentieth Century*, 153 (February, 1953).

DAVIE, DONALD. "Correspondence," *London Magazine*, 1 (March, 1954).

DAVIES, ANEIRIN TALFAN. "The Golden Echo," *Dock Leaves*, 5 (Spring, 1954).

DAVIES, RHYS. *Life and Letters Today*, 24 (March, 1940). (Review of *Portrait of the Artist as a Young Dog.*)

DEUTSCH, BABETTE. *New York Herald Tribune Books* (March 23, 1952). (Review of *In Country Sleep.*)

———. "Orient Wheat," *Virginia Quarterly Review*, 27 (April, 1951).

DOBRÉE, BONAMY. "Two Experiments," *Spectator*, 190 (June 12, 1953).

DUCHENE, L. F. *Manchester Guardian* (November 14, 1952). (Review of *Collected Poems.*)

DUPEE, F. W. *New Republic*, 103 (December 30, 1940). (Review of *Portrait of the Artist as a Young Dog.*)

DURRELL, LAWRENCE. "The Shades of Dylan Thomas," *Encounter*, 9 (1947).

DYMENT, CLIFFORD. *Time and Tide*, 20 (October 7, 1939). (Review of *The Map of Love.*)

EBERHART, RICHARD. "Some Memories of Dylan Thomas," *Yale Literary Magazine*, 122 (1954).

EDMAN, IRWIN. "The Spoken Word," *Saturday Review*, 35 (November 29, 1952).

EMPSON, WILLIAM. "How to Understand a Modern Poem," *Strand* (March, 1947).

———. *New Statesman and Nation* 48 (May 15, 1954). (Review of *Collected Poems* and *Under Milk Wood.*)

ENGLE, PAUL. "An Authentic Voice of Mid-Century: Dylan Thomas' Exciting, Baffling Poetry," *Chicago Sunday Tribune Magazine of Books* (April 5, 1953). (Review of *Collected Poems.*)

ESSIG, ERHARDT H. "Thomas' 'Sonnet I' ('Altarwise by Owl-Light')," *Explicator*, 16 (1958).

EVANS, OLIVER. "The Making of a Poem: Dylan Thomas' 'Do not go gentle into that good night'," *English Miscellany*, 6 (1955).

———. "The Making of a Poem (II): Dylan Thomas' 'Lament'," *English Miscellany*, 7 (1956).

FERLING, LAWRENCE. *San Francisco Chronicle* (April 12, 1953). (Review of *Collected Poems.*)

———. *San Francisco Chronicle* (March 9, 1952). (Review of *In Country Sleep.*)

FIEDLER, LESLIE. "The Latest Dylan Thomas," *Western Review*, 11 (Winter, 1947).

FITTS, DUDLEY. *Saturday Review*, 26 (August 28, 1943). (Review of *New Poems.*)

F[ITTS]., D[UDLEY]. *Saturday Review*, 22 (May 11, 1940). (Review of *The World I Breathe.*)

FOWLIE, WALLACE. "On the Death of Dylan Thomas," *Yale Literary Magazine*, 122 (1954).

FRANKENBERG, LLOYD. "Controlled Abandon," *New York Times Book Review* (April 6, 1952). (Review of *In Country Sleep.*)

FRASER, G. S. "The Artist as a Young Dog," *New Statesman and Nation*, 49 (June 11, 1955).

———. *New Statesman and Nation*, 44 (November 29, 1952). (Review of *Collected Poems.*)

FREMANTLE, ANNE. "Death of a Poet," *Commonweal*, 59 (December 18, 1953).

FRIAR, KIMON. "Dylan Thomas and the Poetic Drama," *Yale Literary Magazine*, 122 (1954).

GARDINER, H. C. "Welsh Chanter's Spell," *America*, 92 (January 1, 1955).

GARLICK, RAYMOND. "Editorial," *Dock Leaves*, 5 (Spring, 1954).

———. "The Endless Breviary," *The Month* (March, 1954).

GARRIGUE, JEAN. "Dark Is a Way and Light Is a Place," *Poetry*, 94 (May, 1959).

GHISELIN, BREWSTER. "Use of a Mango," *Rocky Mountain Review*, 8 (Spring, 1944).

GIBSON, HENRY. "A Comment," *The Critic*, 1 (Autumn, 1947).

GIOVANINNI, G. "Thomas' 'The force that through the green fuse'," *Explicator*, 8 (June, 1950).

GOÑI, ANÍBAL C. "El poeta de Fern Hill: Dylan Thomas," *Sur,* 253 (1958).

GOODFELLOW, DOROTHY W. "Dylan Thomas, 'The Boy of Summer'," *Lectures on Some Modern Poets* (Carnegie Series in English No. 2) (1955).

GRADDON, JOHN. "The Interior Life," *Poetry Review,* 44 (April–June, 1953). (Review of *Collected Poems.*)

GREENHUT, MORRIS. "Opinion," *Beloit Poetry Journal,* 2 (Summer, 1952).

GREGORY, HORACE. *New York Times Book Review* (July 25, 1943). (Review of *New Poems.*)

———. "Romantic Heritage in the Writings of Dylan Thomas," *Poetry,* 69 (March, 1947).

GRENANDER, M. E. "Sonnet V from Dylan Thomas' *Altarwise by Owl-Light* Sequence," *Notes and Queries,* 5 (1958).

GRIGSON, GEOFFREY. "Correspondence," *Poetry-London* (June–July, 1948).

———. "New Poetry," *Horizon,* 1 (January, 1940).

———. "Recollections of Dylan Thomas," *London Magazine,* 9 (September, 1957).

HALPEREN, MAX. "Dylan Thomas: A Soliloquy," *Florida State University Studies,* 11 (1953).

HAMILTON, E. "Words, Words, Words; The Modern School of Verse," *Saturday Review,* 38 (November 19, 1955).

HARDING, J. "Dylan Thomas and Edward Thomas," *Contemporary Review,* 192 (September, 1957).

HARDWICK, ELIZABETH. "America and Dylan Thomas," *Partisan Review,* 23 (Spring, 1956).

HASSAN, IHAB H. "Thomas' The Tombstone Told When She Died," *Explicator,* 15 (1956).

HAUSER, MARIANNE. "Sketches of Youth," *New York Times Book Review* (December 29, 1940). (Review of *Portrait of the Artist as a Young Dog.*)

HAYS, H. R. "Surrealist Influence in Contemporary English and American Poetry," *Poetry,* 54 (July, 1939).

HECHT, ROGER. "Light and Darkness," *Bard Review,* 2 (Spring, 1947).

HEPPENSTALL, RAYNER. *Adelphi,* 9 (February, 1935). (Review of *18 Poems.*)

HESELTINE, NIGEL. "Dylan Thomas," *Wales,* 2 (August, 1937).

HEWES, HENRY. "And death shall have no dominion," *Saturday Review,* 40 (October 19, 1957).

———. "Broadway Postscript: The Backward Town of Llareggub," *Saturday Review,* 36 (June 6, 1953).

HORAN, ROBERT. "In Defense of Dylan Thomas," *Kenyon Review,* 7 (Spring, 1945).

HOWARD, D. R. "Thomas' 'In My Craft or Sullen Art'," *Explicator*, 12 (1954).

HUDDLESTONE, LINDEN. "An Approach to Dylan Thomas," *New Writing*, No. 35 (1948).

HUGHES, RICHARD. "Wales through the Looking-Glass," *Listener*, 45 (May 24, 1951).

HUMPHRIES, ROLFE. *Nation*, 174 (April 19, 1952). (Review of *In Country Sleep.*)

HYNES, S. "Dylan Thomas: Everybody's Adonais," *Commonweal*, 59 (March 26, 1954).

———. "Thomas' 'From Love's First Fever to Her Plague'," *Explicator*, 9 (1950).

JOHN, AUGUSTUS. "Dylan Thomas and Company," *Sunday Times* (London) (September 28, 1958).

JOHNSON, GEOFFREY. "The Acid Test," *Poetry Review*, 44 (April–June, 1953). (Review of *Collected Poems.*)

JOHNSON, PAMELA HANSFORD. "A Memoir," *Adam International Review*, No. 238 (1953).

JOHNSON, S. F. "Thomas' 'The force that through the green fuse'," *Explicator*, 8 (1950).

———. "Thomas' 'The Hunchback in the Park,' and 'The Marrriage of a Virgin'," *Explicator*, 10 (1952).

JONES, DANIEL. "Dylan Thomas: Memories and Appreciations," *Encounter*, 2 (January, 1954).

JONES, GLYN. "Dylan Thomas," *Welsh Review*, 2 (October, 1939).

———. "Dylan Thomas and Welsh," *Dock Leaves*, 5 (Spring, 1954).

JONES, NOEL A. "Dylan Thomas as a Pattern," *British Annual of Literature*, 6 (1949).

JOOST, NICHOLAS. "The Problem of Loving and Hating," *Commonweal*, 59 (November 6, 1953). (Review of *The Doctor and the Devils.*)

JULIAN, SISTER MARY. "Edith Sitwell and Dylan Thomas: Neo-Romantics," *Renascence*, 9 (1957).

KAZIN, ALFRED. "The Posthumous Life of Dylan Thomas," *Atlantic*, 200 (October, 1957).

KNAUBER, CHARLES F. "Imagery of Light in Dylan Thomas," *Renascence*, 6 (1954).

KNIEGER, BERNARD. "Thomas' 'Light Breaks where no Sun Shines'," *Explicator*, 15 (1957).

———. "Thomas' Sonnet I," *Explicator*, 15 (1956).

KORG, J. "Changed Dylan Thomas," *Nation*, 178 (April 24, 1954).

———. "Imagery and Universe in Dylan Thomas' '18 Poems'," *Accent*, 17 (Winter, 1957).

———. "The Short Stories of Dylan Thomas," *Perspective*, 1 (Spring, 1948).

———. "The Sound of Laughter," *Nation*, 179 (December 25, 1954).

LANDER, CLARA. "With Welsh and Reverent Rook: the Biblical Element in Dylan Thomas," *Queen's Quarterly*, 65 (1958).

LAURENTIA, SISTER M. "Thomas' 'Fern Hill'," *Explicator*, 14 (1955).

LEWIS, GLYN. "Dylan Thomas," *Welsh Review* (Winter, 1948).

———. "Some Aspects of Anglo-Welsh Literature," *Welsh Review*, (1946).

LEWIS, SAUNDERS, "Dylan Thomas," *Dock Leaves*, 5 (Spring, 1954).

LOUGEE, DAVID. "An Open Window," *Poetry*, 94 (May, 1959).

———. "Worlds of Dylan Thomas," *Poetry*, 87 (November, 1955).

MAC NEICE, LOUIS. "Sometimes the Poet Spoke in Prose," *New York Times Book Review* (December 19, 1954).

———. "The Strange, Mighty Impact of Dylan Thomas's Poetry," *New York Times Book Review* (April 5, 1953). (Review of *Collected Poems.*)

MANKOWITZ, WOLF. "Dylan Thomas," *Scrutiny*, 1 (Summer, 1946).

MATHIAS, ROLAND. "A Merry Manshape (or Dylan Thomas at a distance)," *Dock Leaves*, 5 (Spring, 1954).

MAUD, R. N. "A Note on Dylan Thomas's Serious Puns," *Audience*, 1 (April, 1955).

———. "Dylan Thomas' First Published Poem," *Modern Language Notes*, 74 (February, 1959).

———. "Dylan Thomas Manuscripts in Houghton Library," *Audience*, 1 (February, 1955).

———. "The *Over Sir John's Hill* Worksheets," *Explorations*, 6 (1956).

———. "Thomas' 'Sonnet I'," *Explicator*, 14 (1955).

MAYHEAD, ROBIN. "Dylan Thomas," *Scrutiny*, 19 (Winter, 1952). (Review of *Collected Poems.*)

MC DONALD, G. D. *Library Journal*, 77 (March 15, 1952). (Review of *In Country Sleep.*)

MC DONNELL, T. P. "The Emergence of Dylan Thomas," *America*, 91 (August 21, 1954).

———. "Who Killed Dylan?" *Catholic World*, 187 (July, 1958).

MC KENNA, ROLLIE. "Dylan Thomas," ASMP *Picture Annual*. A Ridge Press Book published by Simon and Schuster, Inc. (1957).

MERWIN, W. S. "The Religious Poet," *Adam International Review* (1953).

MEYER, G. P. "Bibliographical Sketch," *Saturday Review*, 35 (June 21, 1952). (Review of *In Country Sleep.*)

MEYERHOFF, H. "Violence of Dylan Thomas," *New Republic*, 133 (July 11, 1955).

MILLER, J. E., JR. "Four Cosmic Poets," *University of Kansas City Review*, 23 (June, 1957).

MILLS, CLARK. "Aspects of Surrealism," *Voices*, 101 (Spring, 1940).

MICHIE, JAMES. "Correspondence," *London Magazine*, 1 (February, 1954).

MIZENER, ARTHUR. "Poets," *Nation*, 163 (August 10, 1946).

MOORE, GEOFFREY. "Dylan Thomas: Significance of His Genius," *Kenyon Review*, 17 (Spring, 1955).

MOORE, NICHOLAS. "The Poetry of Dylan Thomas," *Poetry Quarterly*, 10 (Winter, 1948).

MORGAN, W. J. "Evans, Thomas and Lewis," *Twentieth Century*, 160 (October, 1956).

MORGAN, W. J. "Under Milk Wood under Milk Wood," *Twentieth Century*, 164 (September, 1958).

MOYNIHAN, W. T. "Thomas' 'Light Breaks Where No Sun Shines'," *Explicator*, 16 (1958).

MUIR, EDWIN. "The Art of Dylan Thomas," *Harper's Bazaar*, 88 (February, 1954).

———. "New Poetry," *Purpose*, 11 (October–December, 1939). (Review of *The Map of Love*.)

OLSON, ELDER. "The Poetry of Dylan Thomas," *Poetry*, 83 (January, 1954). (Review of *Collected Poems*.)

PEEL, J. H. B. "The Echoes in the Booming Voice," *New York Times Book Review* (October 20, 1957).

PHELPS, R. "In Country Dylan," *Sewanee Review*, 63 (Autumn, 1955).

PETERS, ROBERT L. "The Uneasy Faith of Dylan Thomas: A Study of the Last Poems," *Fresco* (University of Detroit), 9 (1958).

PORTEUS, HUGH GORDON. *New English Weekly*, 15 (September 7, 1939).

POTTS, PAUL. "The Poetry of Dylan Thomas," *Poetry Quarterly*, 8 (Spring, 1946). (Review of *Deaths and Entrances*.)

POWELL, CHARLES. *Manchester Guardian* (September 8, 1939). (Review of *The Map of Love*.)

PRYS-JONES. "Death Shall Have No Dominion," *Dock Leaves*, 5 (Spring, 1954).

PUDNEY, JOHN. "Wales Loses a Great Poet," *Picture Post* (November, 1953).

QUINN, KERKER. *Books* (February 25, 1940). (Review of *The World I Breathe*.)

RAINE, KATHLEEN. "Dylan Thomas," *New Statesman and Nation*, 46 (November 14, 1953).

REID, ALASTAIR. "A First Word," *Yale Literary Magazine*, 122 (1954).

RHYS, ANEURIN. "Dylan Thomas—A Further Estimate," *Poetry Review* (April–May, 1948).

———. "Dylan Thomas," *Poetry Quarterly*, 11 (Summer, 1949).

RICKEY, MARY ELLEN. "Thomas' 'The Conversation of Prayer'," *Explicator*, 16 (1957).

RIGGS, THOMAS, JR. "Recent Poetry—a Miscellany," *Nation*, 176 (May 2, 1953). (Review of *Collected Poems*.)

RITCHEY, JOHN. *Christian Science Monitor* (November 23, 1940). (Review of *Portrait of the Artist as a Young Dog.*)

RODITI, EDOUARD. *Poetry,* 63 (October, 1943). (Review of *New Poems.*)

ROETHKE, THEODORE. "Dylan Thomas: Memories and Appreciations," *Encounter,* 2 (January, 1954).

ROLO, CHARLES J. "Reader's Choice," *Atlantic,* 192 (November, 1953).

ROSENBERG, JAMES L. *Talisman,* 2 (Winter, 1952). (Review of *In Country Sleep.*)

ROSENFELD, PAUL. *Books* (November 17, 1941). (Review of *Portrait of the Artist as a Young Dog.*)

———. "Decadence and Dylan Thomas," *Nation,* 150 (March 23, 1940).

ROTHBERG, WINTERSET (pseudonym of Theodore Roethke). "One Ring-tailed Roarer to Another," *Poetry,* 81 (December, 1952). (Review of *In Country Sleep.*)

SANESI, ROBERTO. "Nell'Intricata Imagine di Dylan Thomas," *Inventario,* 8 (1957).

SAVAGE, D. S. "The Poetry of Dylan Thomas," *New Republic,* 114 (April 29, 1946).

SCARFE, FRANCIS. "The Poetry of Dylan Thomas," *Horizon,* 2 (November, 1940).

SCOTT, HARDIMAN. "From Death to Entrance," *Outposts,* 7 (1947).

SCOTT, WINFIELD TOWNLEY. "Death, and Some Dominions of It," *Yale Literary Magazine,* 122 (1954).

———. "Lyric Marvel," *Saturday Review,* 38 (January 8, 1955).

———. "Wild Man Bound," *Saturday Review,* 36 (April 11, 1953). Review of *Collected Poems.*)

SEYMOUR, WILLIAM KEAN (unsigned). "Poets and Pretenders," *Poetry Review* (April–May, 1946).

SHAPIRO, KARL. "Dylan Thomas," *Poetry,* 87 (November, 1955).

SHUTTLEWORTH, MARTIN. "Without Apologies," *New Statesman and Nation,* 40 (February 7, 1953).

SITWELL, EDITH. "The Achievement of Mr. Dylan Thomas," *Sunday Times* (London), (1936). Reprinted as "Appendix I, A New Poet," in *Dylan Thomas* by Henry Treece (London: Lindsay Drummond, Ltd., 1949).

———. "Comment on Dylan Thomas," *The Critic,* 1 (Autumn, 1947).

———. "Dylan Thomas," *Atlantic,* 193 (February, 1954).

———. "Four New Poets [William Empson, Ronald Bottrall, Dylan Thomas, Archibald MacLeish]," *London Mercury,* 33 (February, 1936).

———. "Lecture on Poetry since 1920," *Life and Letters Today,* 39 (November, 1943).

———. "The Love of Man, The Praise of God," *New York Herald Tribune Books* (May 10, 1953). (Review of *Collected Poems.*)

SMITH, WILLIAM JAY. "Life, Literature and Dylan," *Yale Literary Magazine*, 122 (1954).

SNAITH, STANLEY. "Bubble Reputation," *Library Review*, 46 (Summer, 1938).

SPENDER, STEPHEN. "Dylan Thomas," *Britain Today* (January, 1954).

———. "Movements and Influences in English Literature, 1927–1952," *Books Abroad*, 27 (Winter, 1953).

———. "Poetry for Poetry's Sake," *Horizon*, 13 (April, 1946).

———. *Spectator*, 189 (December 5, 1952).

STANFORD, DEREK. "Dylan Thomas' Animal Faith," *Southwest Review*, 62 (1957).

STEARNS, MARSHALL W. "Explication of Thomas' Poem, 'After the Funeral' ['In Memory of Ann Jones']," *Explicator*, 3 (1945).

———. "Unsex the Skeleton: Notes on the Poetry of Dylan Thomas," *Sewanee Review*, 52 (July, 1944).

STEPHENS, PETER J. "Dylan Thomas: Giant Among Moderns," *New Quarterly of Poetry*, 1 (Winter, 1946–47).

STONESIFER, R. J. "Thomas' *Adventures in the Skin Trade*," *Explicator*, 17 (1958).

SWEENEY, JOHN L. "Intimations of Mortality," *New Republic*, 126 (March 17, 1952). (Review of *In Country Sleep.*)

———. "The Round Sunday Sounds," *New Republic*, 128 (April 6, 1953). (Review of *Collected Poems.*)

SWINNERTON, FRANK. *Observer* (London) (April 7, 1940).

SYMONS, JULIAN. "Obscurity and Dylan Thomas," *Kenyon Review*, 2 (Winter, 1940).

TAMBIMUTTU. "Correspondence," *Poetry-London* (June–July, 1948).

———. "Eleventh Letter," *Poetry-London* (September–October, 1947).

———. "Fourth Letter," *Poetry-London* (January, 1941).

———. "Second Letter," *Poetry-London* (April, 1939).

TERRY, ARTHUR. "Dylan Thomas," *Rann* (March, 1953). (Review of *Collected Poems.*)

THOMAS, CAITLIN. "Dylan Thomas and Emlyn Williams," *New Statesman and Nation*, 49 (June 11, 1955).

THOMPSON, DUNSTAN. "A Time for Terror," *New Republic*, 102 (April 1, 1940). (Review of *The World I Breathe.*)

TINDALL, WILLIAM YORK. "Burning and Crested Song," *American Scholar*, 22 (Autumn, 1953). (Review of *Collected Poems.*)

———. "The Poetry of Dylan Thomas," *American Scholar*, 17 (Autumn, 1948).

TREECE, HENRY. "Chalk Sketch for a Genius," *Dock Leaves*, 5 (Spring, 1954).

———. "Corkscrew or Footrule," *Poetry-London* (May–June, 1941).
———. "Dylan Thomas and the Surrealists," *Seven*, (Winter, 1938).
TYLER, PARKER. "Then Was My Neophyte a Scriptist," *Poetry*, 87 (November, 1955).
UNTERMEYER, LOUIS. "Eight Poets," *Yale Review*, 33 (Winter, 1944). (Review of *New Poems.*)
VARNEY, H. L., and N. N. KANN. "Glamorizing Dylan Thomas," *American Mercury*, 86 (January, 1958).
VERSCHOYLE, DEREK. "Mr. Dylan Thomas," *Spectator*, 164 (April 5, 1940).
WAIN, JOHN. *Mandrake* (Summer and Autumn, 1953). (Review of *Collected Poems.*)
WANNING, ANDREWS. "Criticism and Principles: Poetry of the Quarter," *Southern Review*, 6 (Spring, 1941).
WELLS, HENRY W. "Voice and Verse in Dylan Thomas' Play," *College English*, 15 (May, 1954).
WERRY, RICHARD R. "The Poetry of Dylan Thomas," *College English*, 11 (February, 1950).
WEST, ANTHONY. "Singer and a Spectre," *New Yorker*, 30 (January 22, 1955).
———. *New Statesman and Nation*, 19 (April 20, 1940). (Review of *Portrait of the Artist as a Young Dog.*)
WHITE, WILLIAM. "Dylan Thomas and A. E. Housman," *Papers of the Bibliographical Society of America*, 52 (1958).
WILDE, MARTHA HALLER. "Dylan Thomas: The Elemental Poet," *Transactions of the Wisconsin Academy*, 44 (1956).
WILLIAMS, CHARLES. "Review of Books," *Life and Letters Today*, 23 (November, 1939). (Review of *The Map of Love.*)
WILLIAMS, MICHAEL. "Welsh Voices in the Short Story," *Welsh Review*, 6 (Winter, 1947).
WILLIAMS, WILLIAM CARLOS. "Dylan Thomas," *Yale Literary Magazine*, 122 (1954).
WOODCOCK, GEORGE. "Dylan Thomas and the Welsh Environment," *Arizona Quarterly*, 10 (1954).

Exercises

TOPICS FOR RESEARCH EXERCISES

(All of the topics below can be developed in 500–1500 words from the documents in this volume, but students should be encouraged to extend their investigation with the resources of the library.)

1. Write an introduction to Dylan Thomas that would be suitable for presentation to a student literary organization.
2. Organize a summary of various critical attitudes toward the work of Dylan Thomas and evaluate them from your own point of view.
3. Basing your inquiry upon Thomas' poems, his public statements, and the observations of his critics and associates, write a study of Dylan Thomas as a religious poet.
4. Cite differences in the respective approaches of American and British critics toward the work of Dylan Thomas and make a summary of their respective conclusions.
5. On the basis of your readings in this volume, write an account of attitudes that have led people to speak of the "legend" of Dylan Thomas.
6. Write an account of various estimates of Dylan Thomas' skill as a craftsman and poetic innovator.

LIBRARY EXERCISES

1. Make a survey of the English poetic scene at the time of Dylan Thomas' emergence and discuss the reasons why his work was considered to be something forcefully new.
2. Dylan Thomas is often regarded as being similar in character and accomplishment to the French poet Arthur Rimbaud and the American poet Hart Crane. On the basis of your own readings, discuss similarities and differences that you regard as significant.

3. Prepare an account of the English poetic movement known as "Apocalypse" and define Dylan Thomas' relation to its program and practice.

TOPICS FOR RESEARCH AND INTERPRETATION

1. Basing your inquiry upon the memoirs of his friends and upon the self-portraiture in his poems, discuss the creative character of Dylan Thomas and his attitudes toward the art of poetry.

2. Dylan Thomas' appeal to young people of the forties and early fifties was enormous. As a young reader yourself, what reasons would you give to account for this?

3. Many of Dylan Thomas' poems are based upon observations of natural phenomena. What is the nature of these observations and to what conclusions do they lead him?

4. Citing evidence from his poems and comments by his critics, discuss the role of sex in Dylan Thomas' view of life.

5. Dylan Thomas is generally regarded as a romantic poet. What are the similarities and differences between him and the English romantic poets of the early nineteenth century?

6. Assuming that significant poets are always closely attuned to the life and thought of their times, discuss the ways in which Dylan Thomas might be said to be peculiarly a product of the twentieth century.

7. The later poetry of Dylan Thomas is comparatively free of the obscurities that mark his earlier work. However, some critics have felt that his later work had lost some of the power found in his early poems. Discuss the validity of this point of view.

8. Some people believe that the tragic aspects of Dylan Thomas' life were partly the result of the difficult position of a creative artist in the modern world. In what ways do you agree, or disagree, with this belief?

9. While he did not speak the language of his country, Dylan Thomas was a Welshman and lived most of his life in Wales. On the basis of your reading, do you feel, in terms of his poetry, that this was an advantage or a disadvantage?

10. In spite of the difficulty and obscurity of much of his poetry, Dylan Thomas won a much larger audience than most poets of his time. What, in your opinion, are the reasons that might help to explain this?

11. A good number of Dylan Thomas' poems are concerned with

the effects upon civilian life of World War II, yet he has never been regarded as a "war poet." What are the qualities in his war-time poems that have prevented him from being so classified?

12. It has often been assumed that Freud, Joyce, and the Bible are important influences upon the poetry of Dylan Thomas. On the basis of your readings, make a case for or against this assumption.

Index

Index